SAP HANA SQL Script
Essentials

I0020345

Who will be benefitted from this book?

- ✓ HANA Modelers and Native HANA developers
- ✓ SAP BW on HANA Consultants
- ✓ BW-IP and Embedded BPC Professionals
- ✓ SAP S/4HANA Technical and ABAP Consultants

The contents of this book are aimed to achieve the following objectives:

- Understand the importance and *Use cases* of SQL Script programming across various applications running on SAP HANA platform

- Build expertise in SQL Script *Concepts* and their *Practical applications*

- Practice the programming techniques for effective data processing using *Table variables, Cursors and Arrays*

- *Case studies and practical solutions* to address various real-time requirements using SQL script

- Learn about the *Built-in functions* in SQL Script and implementing *User defined functions* and *Stored procedures*

- Explore *ABAP Managed Database Procedures(AMDP)* to implement optimized solutions for BW Transformations and BW-IP Planning functions

- Utilize *Debugging techniques* to analyze SQL Script stored procedures and Functions

- Tools, techniques and *Best practices* for managing HANA SQL Script based solutions

1

Context of this book

SAP HANA has been widely adopted by the enterprises as a database platform to run their ERP, Datawarehousing, Planning and other key business applications. Due to the in-memory operations on data and the columnar storage for optimized access, HANA provides various possibilities to improve the performance. Unlike traditional enterprise applications where the data need to be brought to the application server for processing, HANA based applications can be implemented to push the maximum processing logic and calculations to the database (aka *code push down*).

SQL Script is the proprietary language to implement the processing logic in HANA database. Due to the code push down capabilities, it allows most of the SAP applications to leverage SQL Script wherever the data or processing intensive logic is to be implemented. Hence, naturally there is a growing demand for the SAP Technical Consultants who can implement optimized solutions using SQL Script.

SQL Script can be used in wide range of solutions such as Enterprise Data Warehousing and Analytics, BW Integrated planning, Embedded BPC, BW transformations, ABAP Core Data Services and various other Custom applications. Based on these factors, it would be imperative for most of the SAP Technical Consultants (SAP HANA, SAP ABAP, BW, BW-IP and Embedded BPC) to build their expertise in SQL Script programming techniques.

This book explains the key features of SQL Script programming and their application to address various business requirements. It will help the readers to understand the syntax and practical application of various programming elements, along with the best practices and performance optimization guidelines. This book also covers the transitioning approach from ABAP programming to SQL script programming using AMDP (ABAP Managed Database Procedures). This knowledge will be key to implement the solutions such as BW on HANA transformations, BW Integrated Planning (Planning Functions) which can be optimized by using the ABAP Managed Database Procedures (AMDP), where the processing logic is mainly implemented using the SQL Script programming.

Disclaimer:

Although the author has made every effort to ensure that the information in this book was correct at press time, the author do not assume and hereby disclaim any liability to any party for any loss, damage, or disruption caused by errors or omissions, whether such errors or omissions result from negligence, accident, or any other cause.

The concepts, examples and screenshots of this book are mainly prepared based on SAP HANA Versions 1.0 and 2.0. Hence the readers may find some differences depending on the specific HANA Database and HANA studio versions that are being used.

Acknowledgements

I sincerely wish to thank TekLink leadership team, especially Mr. Pankaj Gupta, Mr. Manish Maheswari and Mr. Pravin Gupta for all their support and encouragement, Mr. Sandeep Khare for his valuable guidance during the HANA projects, Mr. Amol Palekar who is a well known author, for his valuable guidance. I would like to thank my friends and colleagues, for all the positive influences they have on me.

I take immense pleasure to thank all the readers of my earlier book - **SAP HANA Modeling Practical World**, whose feedback has driven me to put more energy while working on this.

I must thank my wife Manasa, my son Tejas, my parents and the rest of my family, who supported and encouraged me in spite of all the time it took me away from them. Above all, I would like to thank God for giving me all the strengh to accomplish this.

Important Notes:

Please go through the following notes and instructions to better understand and practice the examples provided in this book.

Pre-requisites to this book: The reader need to have basic exposure to SAP and Database concepts. Exposure the HANA Modeling (Calculation views) is desired

Packages and Schema names: The reader has to change the package and schema names in the code examples, as per their specific HANA system

Example: DEFAULT SCHEMA <SCHEMA NAME>

➔ *Example for Practice*

These are used to provides the references to programming examples related to the concept. Readers can jump to these examples and practice

Concept Check: At the end of the practice examples and case studies, review the concepts for better understanding of their application in real world

TABLE OF CONTENTS

1 SAP HANA and SQL Script Overview

SAP HANA platform essentially provides the services related to database, application and integration to simplify and accelerate the traditional business applications such as ERP, CRM and Data Warehousing etc. It can also be used to build advanced solutions such as Internet of Things, Predictive analytics, Machie Learning and Big Data etc. The services of HANA platform are being constantly upgraded by SAP to address more business challenges and deliver range of solutions with greater speed and flexibility.

Key Features of SAP HANA Platform:
- In-Memory Appliance: Allows larger data volumes to be processed in real time
- Columnar Storage: Optimized for analytics and data retrieval and high level of compression leading to lesser storage footprint
- Parallel Processing: Multi-core achitecture and columnar storage provides parallel processing resulting in faster response times
- Open for integration: Variety of applications and tools can be integrated with SAP HANA using various standard methods such as SQL, MDX

In this context, it is essential for us to be aware of the variety of use cases that can be addressed based on SAP HANA platform and the various approaches that cans be adopted to deliver best possible solutions.

Background of Column Store and In-Memory Database:

In a columnar database, all values of a specific column (e.g. Customer Number) are stored consecutively at one location, resulting significantly faster access than traditional row-store oriented database. Columnar database will use compression techniques such as Dictionary encoding to store data efficiently. This kind of storage and access mechanism enables much faster aggregation operations like Sum, Min, Max, Count and Average.

With SAP HANA, all data is stored in memory (RAM), which allows the processors (CPUs) to quickly access the data for processing. Typically SAP HANA can process around 1b scans/second/core and 10 m rows/second join performance. SAP HANA is basically an appliance with multi-core CPUs, multiple CPUs per board and multiple boards per server- all running in parallel provides enormous computational power.

1.1 Architecture and Building Blocks of SAP HANA Platform

The key building blocks of SAP HANA server is it's in-memory database which is closely integrated with the services related to data integration, database management, application development related to diverse set of fuctionalities such as analytics, text, graph, Big Data and other Native applications.

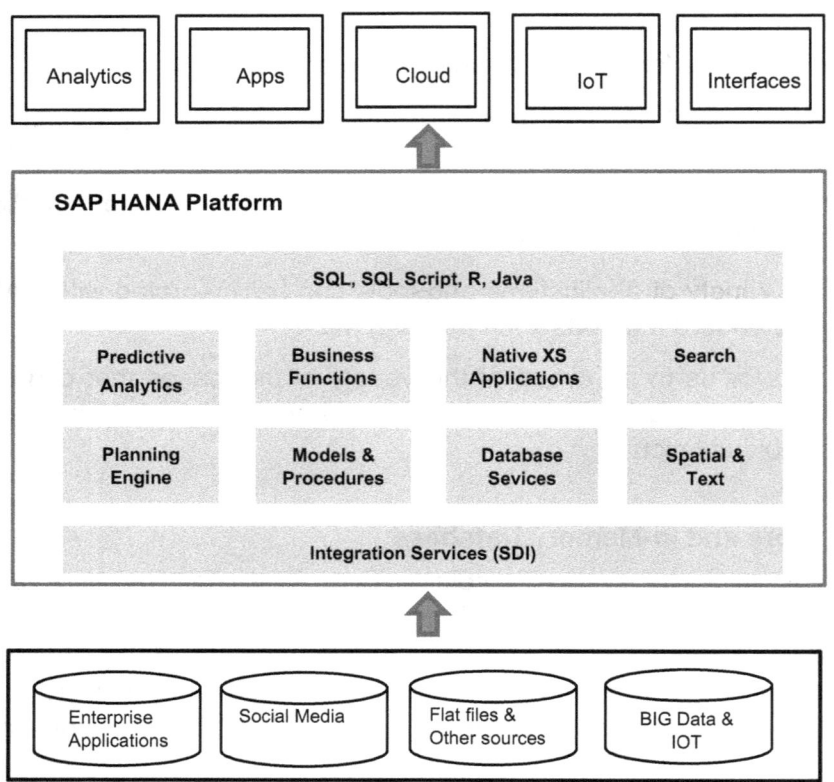

Key features of SAP HANA Database and Appliance

- Storing data in column store instead of the conventional row store
- Reducing overall data footprint due to the compression techniques
- In-memory storage of the data allowing faster query response times
- Massive parallel processing due to the multi core architecture and the column engine capabilities
- Insert only approach in adding or changing records
- Cloud and On-premise support
- Multi Tenant database support to run more than one application on single HANA database

Typical request processing flow in SAP HANA database, when we run a query against any data model:

1. Request (query) is sent to the session manager, which in turn performs the authentication and opens the session connection
2. The query will be sent to the appropriate Request Processing service such as SQL, MDX or Calculation engine – which inturn uses the optimizer to prepare the execution plan and executes the query
3. Then the query will access all the relevant data from the column store where the tables are residing in the in-memory storage
4. Once the query execution is completed, results will be returned back to the Client application such as HANA studio or the Reporting client which are connected using ODBC or MDX

Architecture and components of SAP HANA Instance:

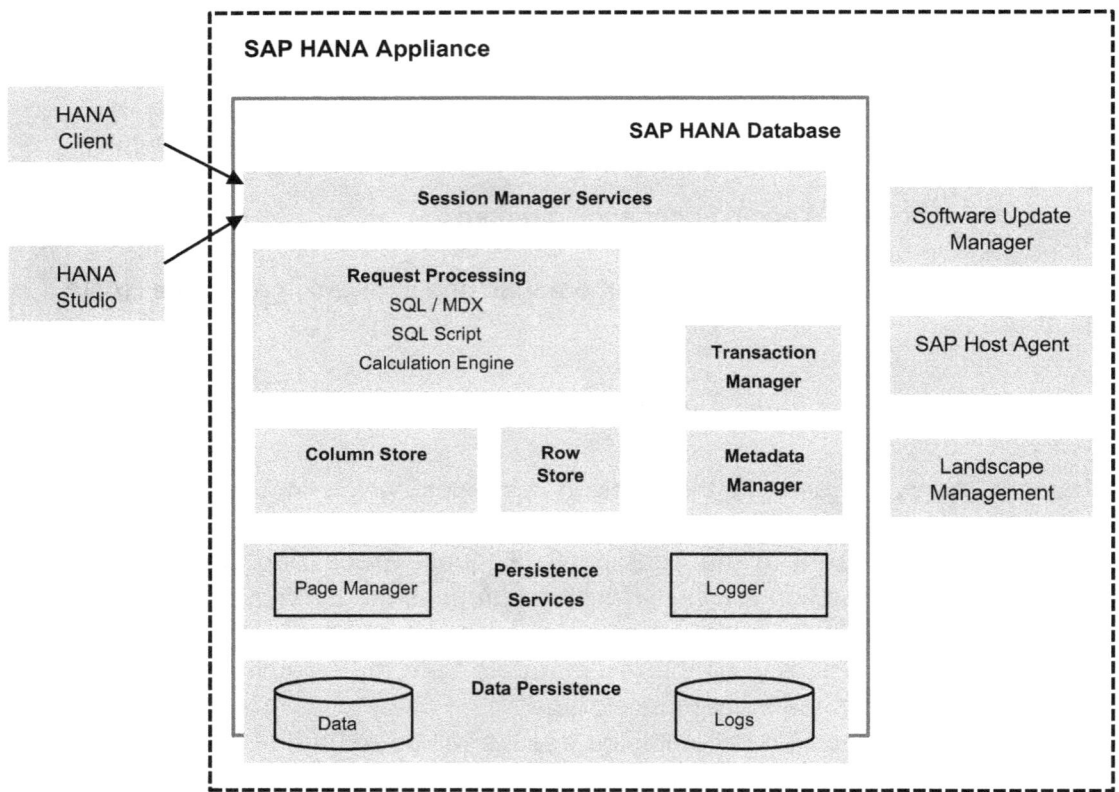

Tools for develeopers to access HANA database and build models and applications:

HANA Studio: It is an eclipse based desktop tool to perform data modeling, administration etc.

HANA Web IDE: It provides web based access to the HANA modeling, development and administration functions

1.2 Role of SQL Script in HANA Database

SAP HANA Platform will be generally chosen by the enterprises to address some of the complex requirements which involoves calculations that are highly memory and / or process intensive and to achieve optimal perfomance along with real time visibility to the key metrics. With the **Code to Data** approach of SAP HANA, we will be able to build these solutions to process the business logic using the SQL Script and other standard programming functions such as APL (Application Programming Library), PAL (Predictive Analytics Library), R (Open Source Language for Data Science).

- SQL Script is the proprietary database programming for SAP HANA, which provides procedural approach to implement the desired business logic.
- SQLScript allows us to push the data-intensive application logic into the database (Code to Data approach). This approach will help us in optimizing performance of several application areas such as:
    - Native HANA solutions
    - HANA based data mart solutions
    - BW transformations, Routines and Customer exit logic
    - Planning functions in BW-IP and Embedded BPC

Traditional DB model- "Data to Code"   HANA approach "Code to Data"

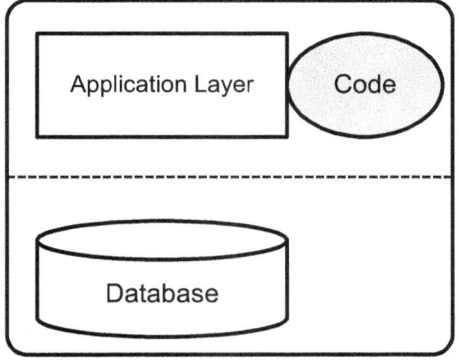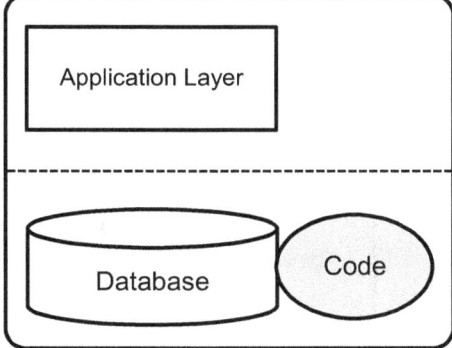

- We can implement side-effect free (Read Only) logic in SQLScript, that operate on tables using SQL queries for set processing and is therefore parallelizable over multiple processors.
- SQL Script also provides various built-in application functions and libraries like:
  - APL (Application Programming Library): Set of built-in functions related to business applications
  - PAL (Predictive Analytics Library) and AFL (Application Function Library): Programming framework to implement predictive solutions that runs on HANA
  - Graph, Spatial and Text processing functions

1.3 Use Cases of SQL Script in HANA

Since many customers are adopting SAP HANA either as a side car appliance or as a primary persistence solution, there has been an increasing rate of adoption of Code Push Down approach, where we need to implement SQL Script based solutions for several use cases.

Let us understand the some of the common use cases where we can leverage the SQL Script programming to build the optimial solutions.

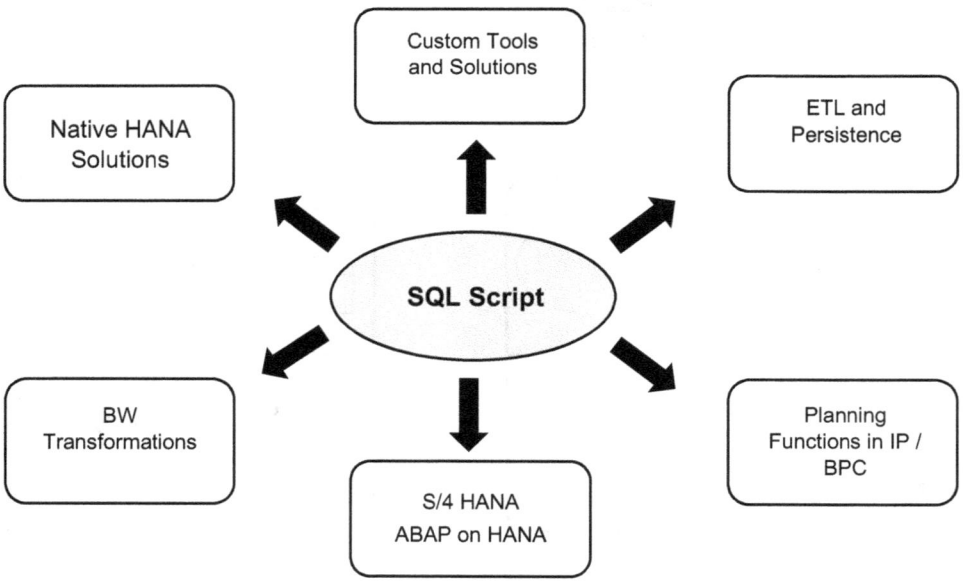

Note: It is recommeded for the readers to skim through the remaiming sections in this unit, to get a high level and understading of the SQL Script use cases. Please revisit these sections after the completion of all the units, for a clear understanding of the use cases.

1.3.1 Native HANA Modeling Solutions with Complex Logic

In HANA Native data modeling, we can implement the solutions for variety of reporting requirements using the graphical calculation views. However there are certian complex requirements, which cannot be implemented using the graphical calculation views.

We need to implement Table Funcitons or Stored Procedures in SQL Script to achieve these type of requirements.

Typical requirements where we need to consider SQL Script instead of Calculation views:

1) Recursive operations: where we need to drill down the data dynaminally to derive the results based on parent child relationships, such as flattening of hierarchies or exploding the Bill of Material compoents

2) Persistence based solutions: These are the solutions in which we prefer to store the results in a custom table within HANA, so that the reports can consume the data directly from this table.

   This is ideal for the following scenarios:
   - Storing the daily or weekly inventory snapshots etc. In this case we need to retain the periodic snapshots of the results in HANA database in order to build the reporting solution that can provide results as on specific period.
   - Data models with high level of complexity, where we may not need real-time reporting. For such kind of models, it would be ideal to persit the results in a custom table instead of running the complex logic each time during the reporting.

3) Implementing special functions: String aggregation functionality, which needs concatenation of string values from group of records into single record. Currently we cannot achieve this in graphical calculation views.

1.3.2 Implement Reusable Application Logic

To address several requirements related to business analytics and complex data processing needs, we can build reusabe modules in SQL Script in SAP HANA database platform. Following are the repository objects to implement the reusable logic in SQL Script.

- Stored Procedures
- Table functions
- Scalar Functions

Examples:

- Data Conversion functions
- Complex business rules such as Pricing Calculations, Flattening of hierarchies, Bill of Material explosion
- Generating the results and calculations which are needed for external applications – For example supply chain related snapshots etc.

Typical architecture for implementing complex calculations in SAP HANA:

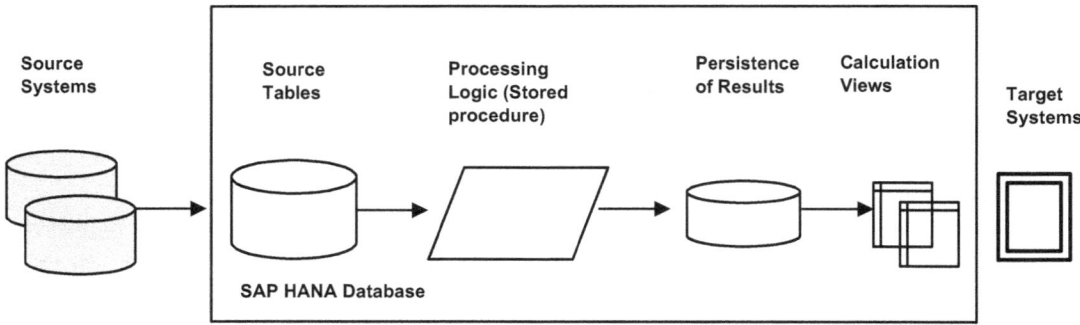

In this book, we have separate units which explains the process of implementing stored procedures, scalar functions and table functions. In additon, it will also cover the process of integrating these programming blocks into graphical calculation views (Such as – How to use a Table Function as a data source in a calculation view, How to implement input parameters based on scalar functions in calculation views..)

1.3.3 Optimized Transformations and Application Logic in BW on HANA

SAP BW transformations are usually time consuming in Non-HANA database scenarios, due to various database look up operations and looping the records. To optimize the complex and time consuming transformations and other processing logic, we can implement these using SQL Script via AMDP (ABAP Managed Database Procedures) in BW on HANA or BW4/HANA.

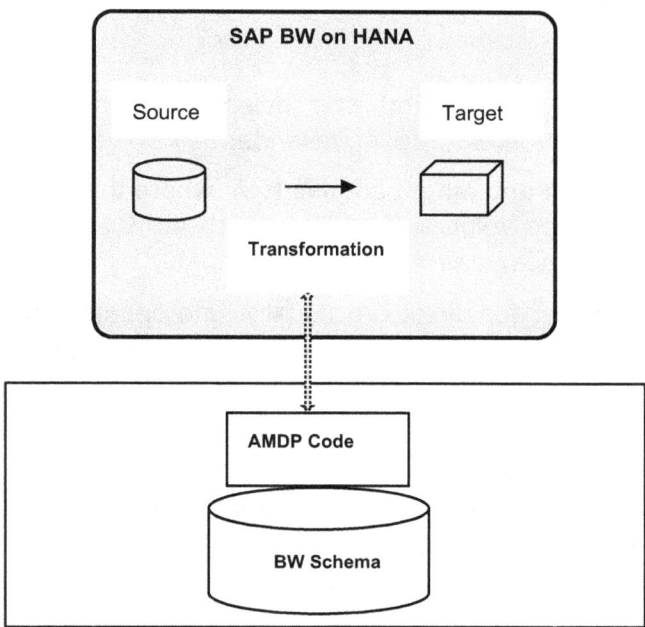

Key optimization areas related to HANA modeling in SAP BW on HANA
- Code push down for Transformations and other routines
- Optimized BW info providers based on HANA in-memory atrchitecure
- Flexibility of consuming HANA views in BW info providers

1.3.4 Accelerate Planning Functions in BW Integrated Planning and BPC

While implementing the solutions for planning applications based on SAP BW Integrated Planning or Embedded BPC (Business Planning and Consolidation), most commonly we need to process large volume of records due to more granular level planning and various calculation requirements.

Examples:

- Planning the trade spend and sales volumes as part of promotions planning at customer, product, calendar day or week level.

- Disaggregation and other complex logic where the planning functions need to process huge volume of records such as: Cost center planning results down to the employee or product level.

These type of planning functions are usually time consuming when implemented on traditional databases. In SAP BW on HANA or SAP Embedded BPC, planning functions can be implemented based on SQL Script, which helps in optimizing the performance drastically due to the code push down approach.

Prior to HANA and SQL Script, we were supposed to implement the custom planning functions either using ABAP Programming or FOX (Formula Extension) programming. Both these approaches have their own limitations. While ABAP based planning functions are more flexible, they will result in poor performance for large volume of planning records, since the logic is processed on application server.

FOX programming based planning functions are good in the performance (due to code push down mechanism), however they lack the flexibility such as performing look up on other data targets to derive the necessary values in the planning function.

By implementing the planning functions based on HANA (AMDP – ABAP Managed Database Procedures), we can achieve the advantage of code push dowm, parallel processing and we will be able to perform look up on any data models during the planning function run.

Note: Detailed examples of BW Planning functions using HANA SQL Script / AMDP is not covered in this book.

1.3.5 SQL Script for ETL logic in HANA Smart Data Integration

- Smart Data Integration (SDI) has been introduced in SAP HANA 1.0 SPS 9, as an ETL solution that runs natively in HANA. Within an SDI Data Flow (Flow Graphs) we can use SQL Script procedures to implement transformation logic.

- Prior to SDI we had to leverage the tools such Business Objects Data Service (BODS) to implement the ETL solutions to provision data into HANA from external applications with complex transformation requirements

- The main advantage of implementing ETL logic in SDI is that it can leverage the columnar storage and in-memory processing of HANA database and also we can directly conume the HANA database objects

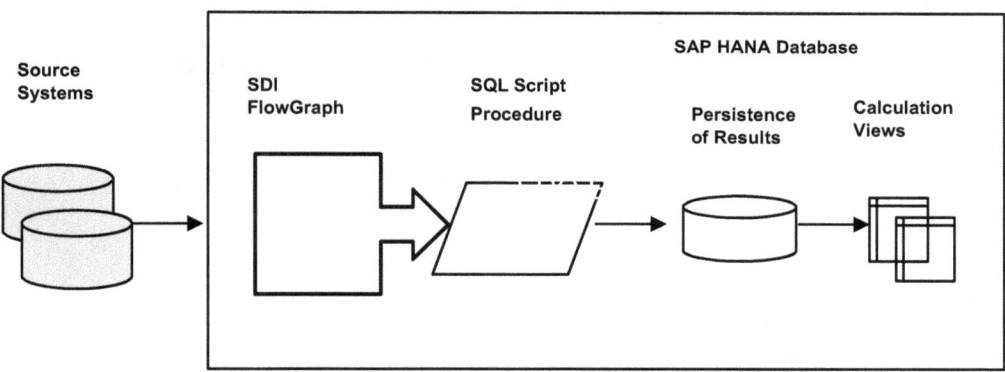

- Using SQL Script procedures in SDI Flow graph will enable us to build complex ETL trasnformation logic, which cannot be achieved using the basic set of mapping operations such as Filter, Aggregate, Pivot etc.

1.3.6 Building Custom Tools and Applications

- We can build some custom tools and applications by using SQL Script, to leverage the performance beneifts in processing large volumes of data in real time or batch processing mode.

- Customers can identify some of the applications where the business logic is complex and involves the processing of large data volumes, which is ideal to be pushed into the database and in-memory platform. SQL Script will be the preferred choice to build such applications:

  Few examples:

  1. Calculating the pricing buckets such as discounts and commissions at trasaction level to perform price waterfall analysis

  2. Shelf space planning calculations for retail stores which are based on complex algorithms

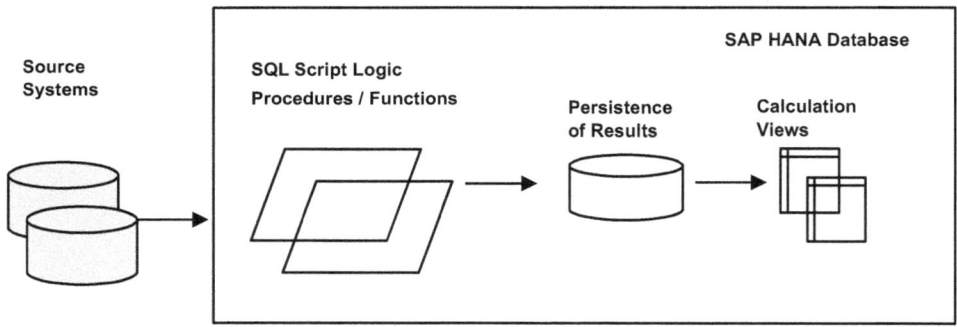

2 SAP HANA Developement Environment

In this unit, let us understand the key components related to SAP HANA data modeling and programming solutions along with the process of building these objects in a structured manner. We can use multiple tools to develop and maintain the repository objects related to the HANA database, application and integration services.

- HANA Studio: Desktop tool which is based on the eclipse framework. This book mainly covers all the screenshots based on the HANA studio.

- SAP HANA Web IDE: This provides web-based access to the HANA repository objects and supports native development with SAP HANA. We can use the URL to launch Web IDE and perform all the operations related to Development, Administration, Lifecycle management etc.

  SAP Web IDE can also be integrated with the Git Hub platform which is widely used by the developer communities.

In HANA studio, we need to use the development perspective the build all the different types of repository objects such as tables, views, procedures etc.

Menu path in HANA studio to open the HANA Development perspective:

Window → Perspective → Open Perspective → Other.. Choose SAP HANA Development.

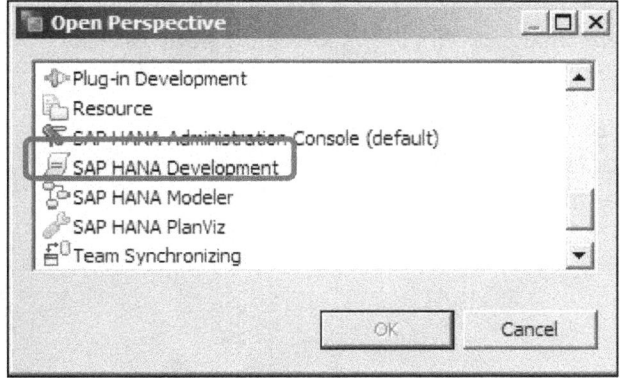

In each of the HANA instance under the System tab, the development artifacts are shown under the two main folders namely the "Catalog" and "Content".

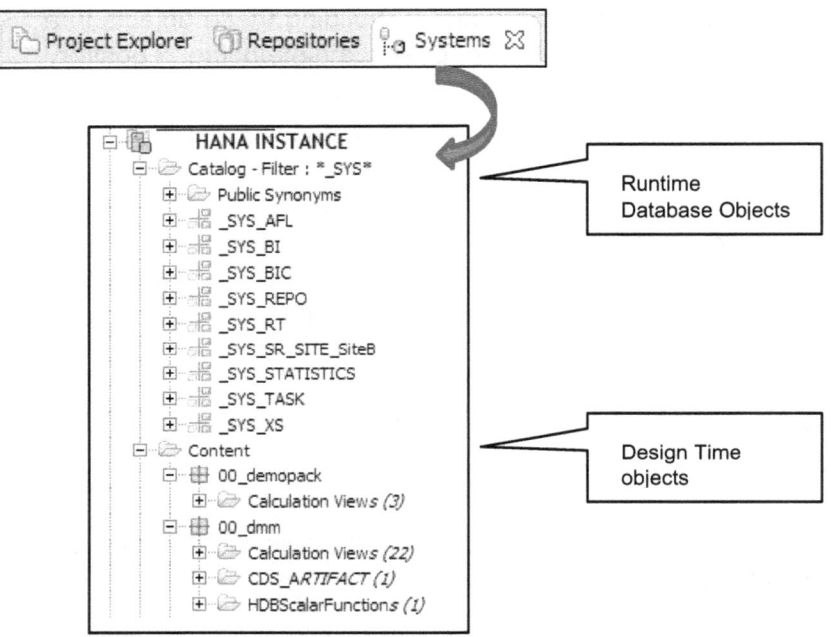

Content folder represents the HANA repository and stores the design time version of the objects. All the HANA development artifacts of the repository content are organized under the packages to enable the transport. Once we activate a HANA development artifact corresponding runtime version is generated, which is stored under the catalog.

Catalog folder represents the actual metadata stored in HANA database, which consists of the runtime versions of all objects such as database tables, information views, stored procedures etc. Catalog objects are stored under the respective schemas.

2.1 Organizing HANA Content using Schemas and Packages

Schemas: These are used to logically organize the objects in a database. Which means any database object like a table, stored procedure or a view will be uniquely identified with <Schema Name>.<Object Name>

In HANA Database instance, schemas generally represent the source systems (ECC, BW, Flat file etc.) and there will be a schema created for each database user in HANA. In addition, there are pre-defined schemas such as _SYS_BIC (consists of all the generated modeling artifacts – calculation views, stored procedures etc.), _SYS_BI and SYS which contains the important system tables and views that stores the metadata information.

Packages: These are used to classify all the development objects in HANA repository. Packages can be nested as well, which means we can create sub packages under each package. We need to define the appropriate package structure to classify the modeling content (views, tables, procedures etc.) based on the reporting application hierarchy and other criteria.

Most importantly, Packages are also used to group the HANA development objects that are to be transported together. We need to assign the package to a Delivery Unit to make the objects under the package as transportable.

As a best practice, always adopt specific naming standards to define the package hierarchy. For example: ProjectOne.Finance.AP

2.2 Building HANA Artifacts using the Developer Perspective

Understand the process of creating HANA development and modeling objects in the HANA repository:

This approach allows the developers to maintain objects in their local desktop and share with the team by updating to the repository. Apart from this, it will also provide the mechanism to transport all the development artifacts, since all the objects are created under packages in the developer perspective.

Especially the database artifacts such as column or row store tables, stored procedures are not transportable when they are created using the SQL statements such as CREATE COLUMN TABLE, CREATE PROCEDURE, since they are not maintained under packages. Hence the best approach for creating such database objects is to use the Development Perspective (hdbtable / hdbprocedure syntax), which is explained in the following sections.

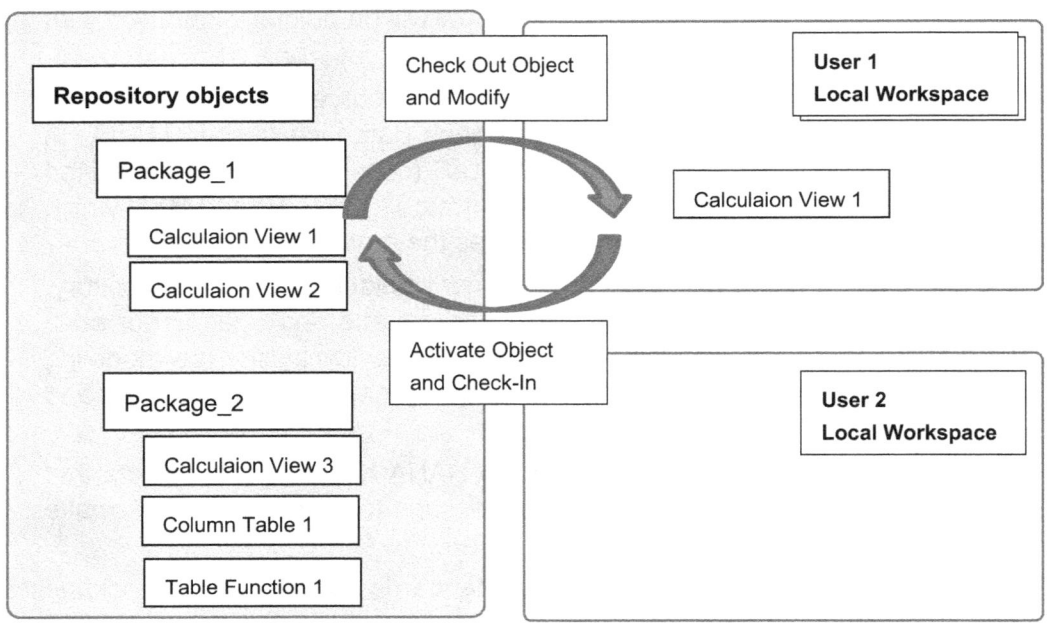

Repository: Stores all the HANA development artifacts (tables, procedures, functions, information views etc.) centrally in the HANA Database instance. Please note that there is a special user in HANA database called _SYS_REPO, who owns all the repository objects.

Workspace: Allows us to import the development artifacts into our local machine and make the necessary changes, then export them back to the repository.

Below are the detailed steps and explanations to understand the methods of utilizing the development perspective:

2.2.1 Working with the HANA Development Perspective:

Systems Tab

Step 1: Create a Package

Package: It groups all the information models and makes it easier to transport (import/export) them across difference systems in the HANA Landscape

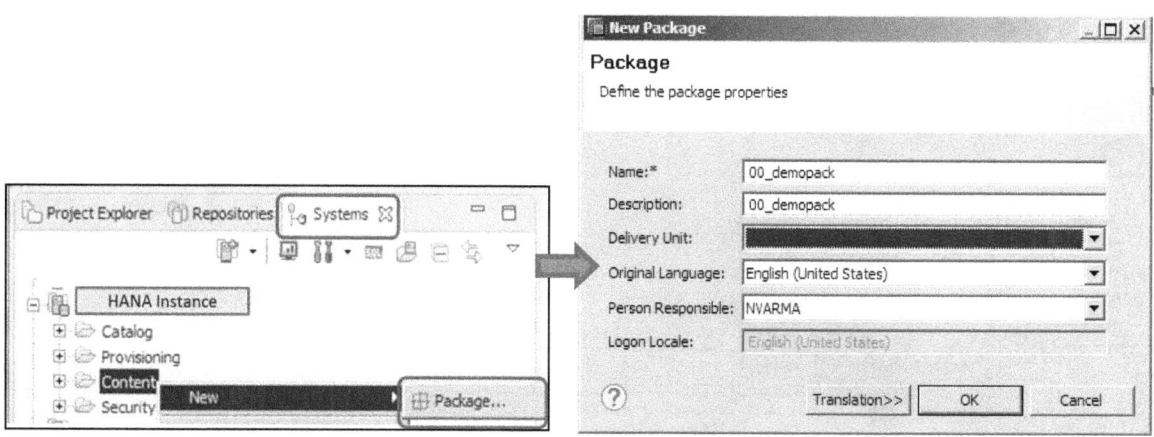

Note: We can also create new packages under the Repositories tab.

Repositories Tab:

Step 2: Create a Workspace

Repository workspace: is the location for all development files that supports version control when sharing between developers. Each repository workspace will be assigned to a folder in the User's local machine, where the development artifacts can be edited.

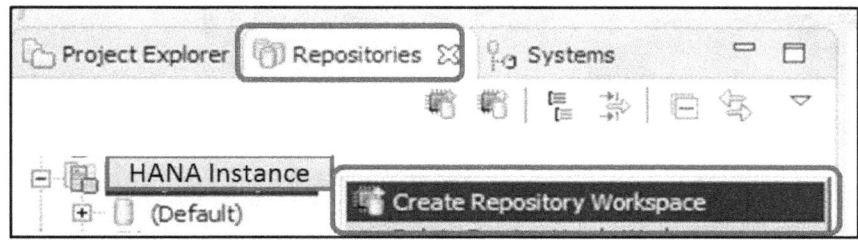

Enter the workspace properties and save

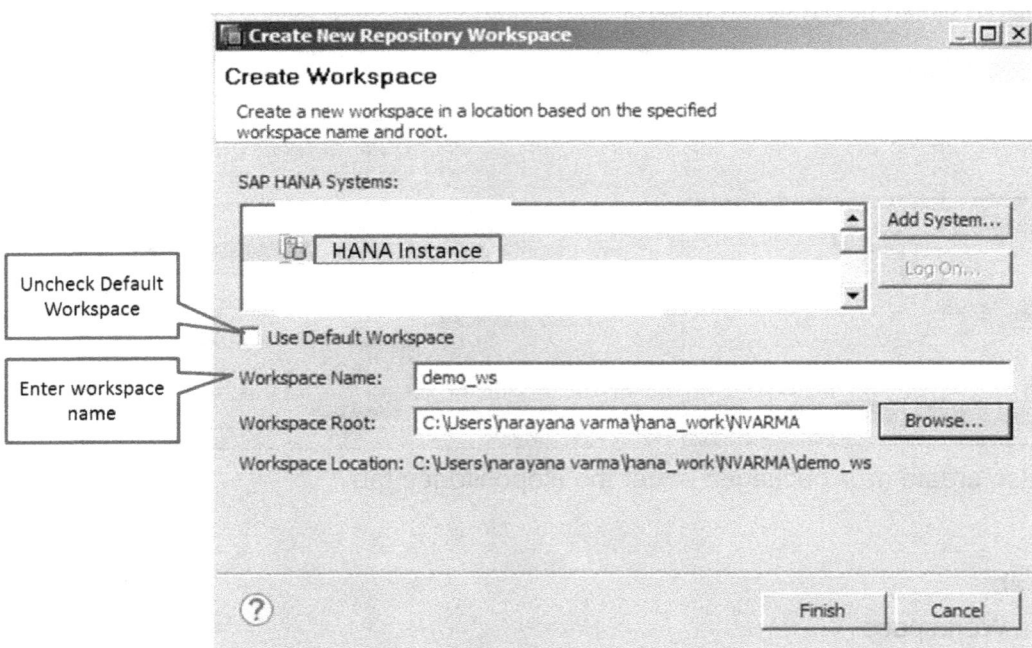

Observe the local folder generated in your system.

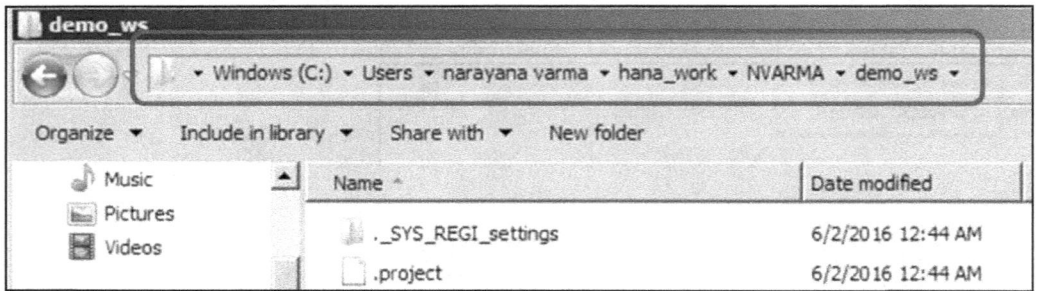

Project Explorer Tab:

Step 3: Create a Project

Projects group together all application-related artifacts, containing folders and files for the application. Multiple projects can be placed into one repository workspace.

Note: Projects are mainly essential while building native applications in SAP HANA platform. To build HANA modeling related artifacts, it is optional step to create projects.

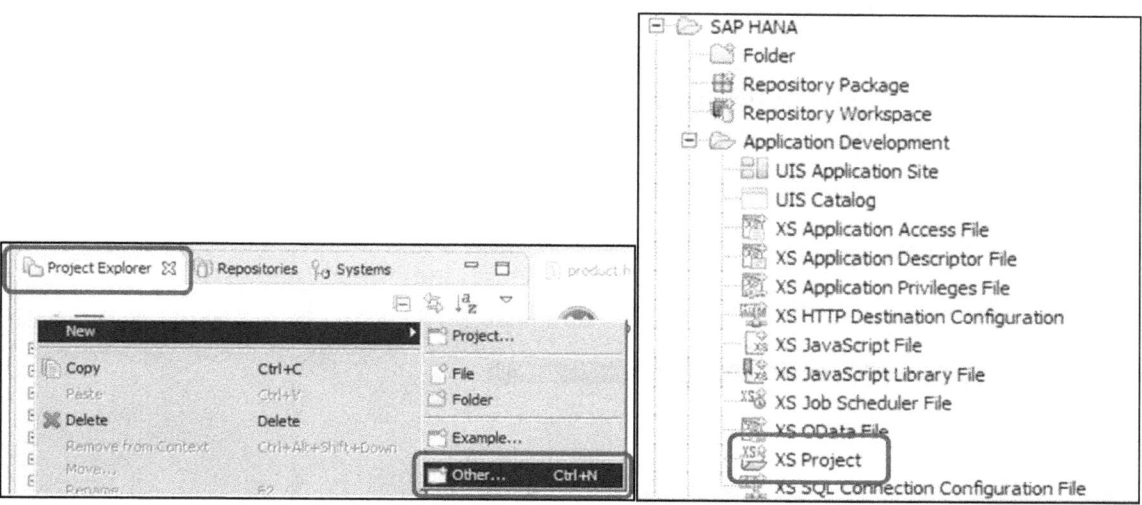

Note: Deselect the checkbox "Share project in SAP repository" if you want to maintain the development artifacts in a different folder before sharing with the repository workspace folder

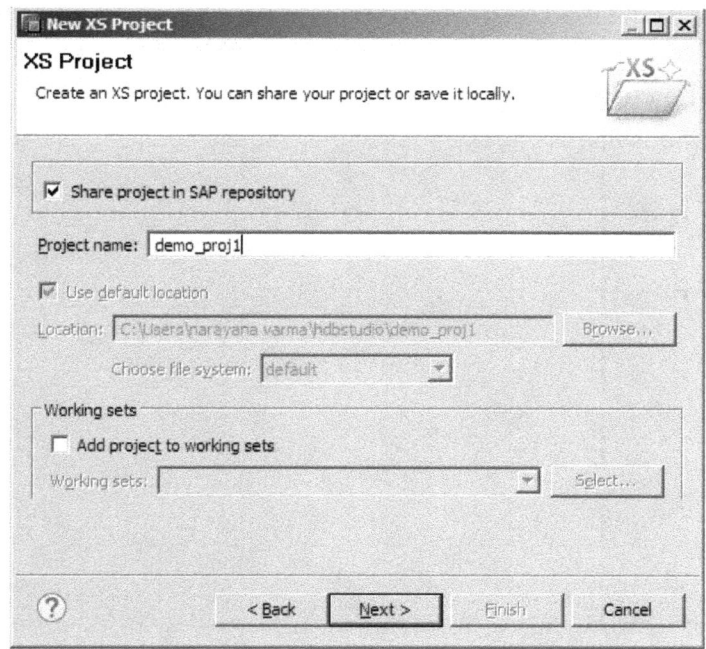

Choose the workspace, which is to be associated with the project location and the select the package, in which the development artifacts must be created or changed.

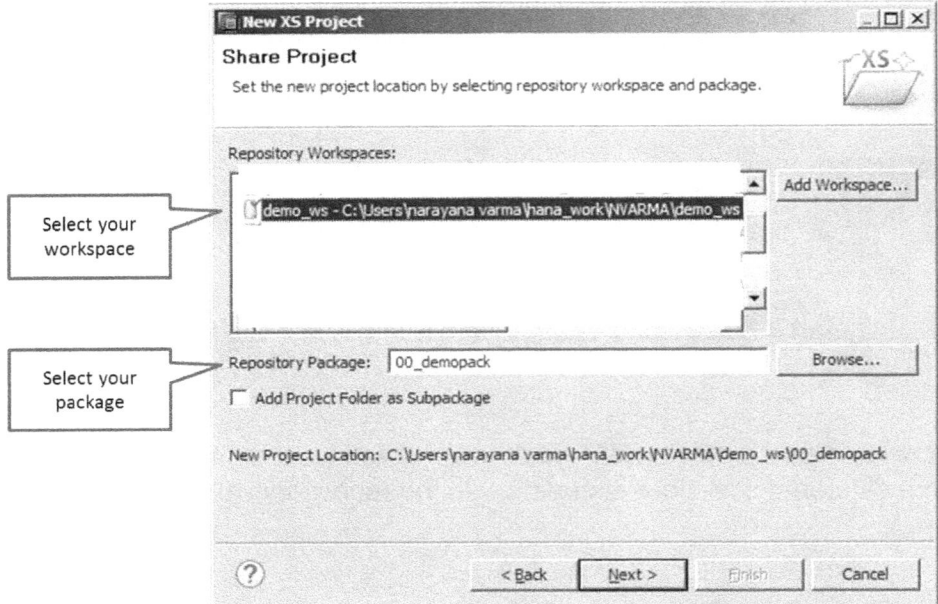

Optionally we can choose the Schema to be created.

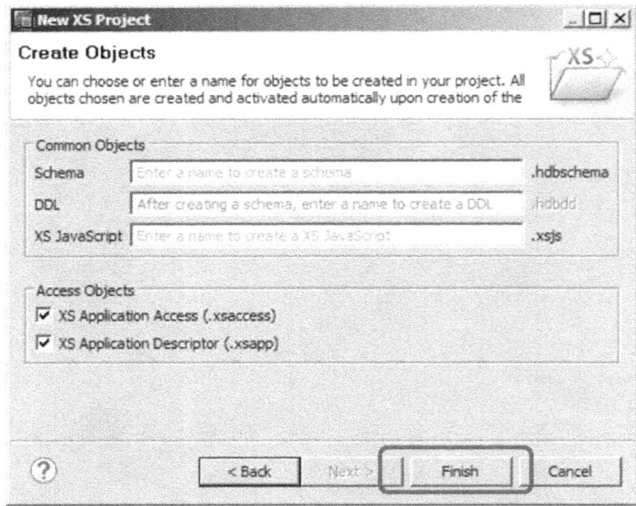

Save the Project.

2.2.2 Essential Database objects in HANA:

It is important to understand the different type of database objects that can be defined in HANA and use them appropriately while building the solutions in SQL Script. Please find the summary of the database objects below.

Database Object	Extension	Usage
Database Table	.hdbtable	Persistence of data and supports both column store and row store
DDL Source file	.hdbdd	To define data types for reusability. This can store multiple database entities such as tables, structures within a single repository object. Commonly these are used in the implementation of Core Data Services (CDS) objects in HANA
Scalar Function	.hdbscalarfunction	Reusable functions that returns single value Details are explained in the Unit: 5 (Section 5.2)
Table Function	.hdbtablefunction	Reusable functions that returns data in table structure Details are explained in the Unit: 5 (Section 5.2)
Schema	.hdbschema	Schemas are used to group database objects. Details are explained in this Unit 1.
Structure	.hdbstructure	To define reusable structure data types. One of the key application of Structure data types is to define the table variables in SQL Script programming
Stored Procedure	.hdbprocedure	To implement reusable routines Details are explained in this Unit 4.
Public Synonyms	.hdbsynonym	To provide an alias name to any database table. Currently, synonyms can be created for tables (this includes virtual tables), views, procedures, table functions, scalar functions and sequences. We can find the existing synonyms using the below query: SELECT * FROM PUBLIC.SYNONYMS;
Role	.hdbrole	A role is a collection of privileges

2.2.3 Building Repository Objects in HANA Development Perspective

Implementing Database objects using HDB Table Syntax:

Switch to the Repository tab:

Right click on the package : Choose New → Other..

Select "Database table"

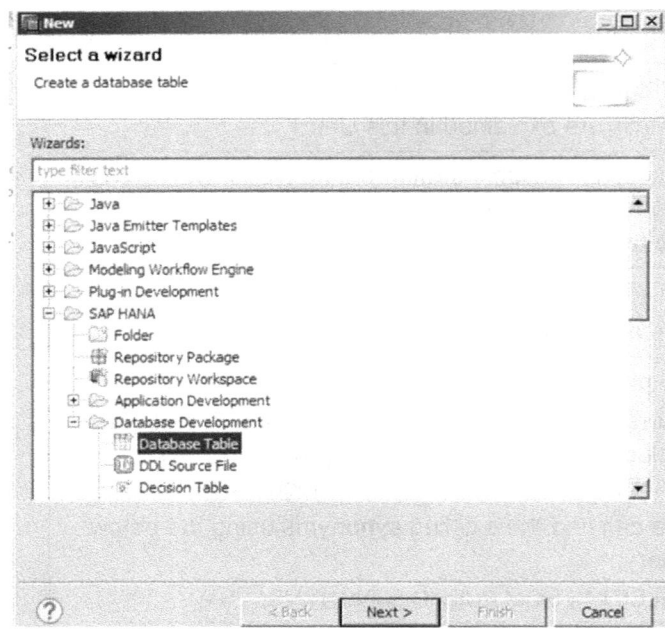

Enter the file name which represent the database table.

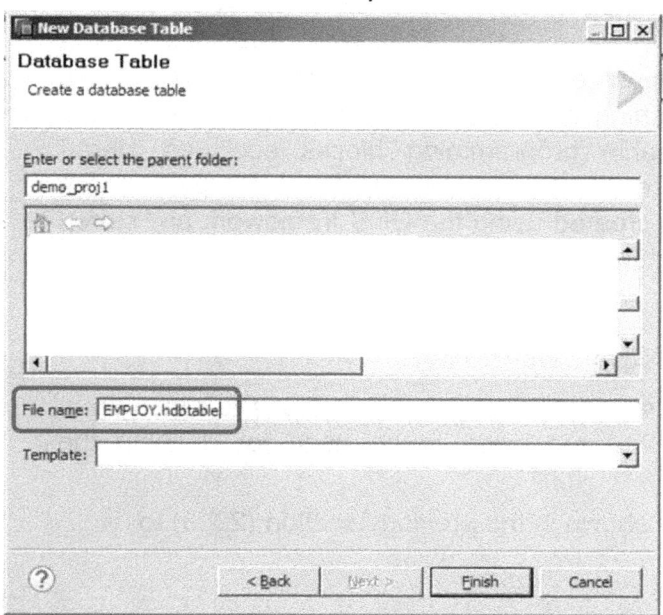

Note: We can also choose the available "Template" in the above window to get the sample definition and coding of the object.

Enter the table definition in the editor:

Note: Assign the Schema Name (table.schemaName) as per your environment.

```
product.html      prod.controller.js      *EMPLOY.hdbtable



   table.schemaName = "NVARMA";
   table.tableType = COLUMNSTORE;
   table.columns = [
   {name = "EMP_ID"; sqlType = NVARCHAR; length = 10;},
   {name = "EMP_NAME"; sqlType = NVARCHAR; length = 40;}] ;

   table.primaryKey.pkcolumns = ["EMP_ID"];
```

Save and Activate the table definition.

Observe the fully qualified name of the table, which follows the convention:

<Schema>.<package path >/<Object name>

Core Data Services (CDS) Framework in HANA

Since SAP HANA also provides the services related to application development, there is a need for comprehensive framework for defining the development artifacts such as data types, data dictionary objects and reusable programming blocks such as stored procedures and functions. Core Data Services (CDS) has been introduced in SAP HANA to address this requirement. All the objects created using the CDS framework are stored as repository objects and these are transportable.

2.2.4 Definition of a Table type using CDS

In SQL Script we can define table types or structures as global data types to reuse them across multiple functions or procedures. The extension to be used for defining the structure is .hdbstructure

Note: We need to follow the similar steps as shown in the previous section (2.2.3) to create the Core Data Services objects

namespace <Main Package>.<Sub Package>;

@Schema: '<Schema Name>'

Type <Table Type Name>
{
  Field1 : Integer;
  Field2 : String(20);
  Field3 : Date;
};

Let us go through the steps to build the following Table Type / Structure:

```
Table Type: 00_dmm:ZTT_CUMM_MONTHS.hdbstructure
table.schemaName = "NVARMA" ;
table.tableType = COLUMNSTORE;
table.columns = [
{name = "CALMONTH" ; sqlType = NVARCHAR ; length = 6;} ,
{name = "CUMM_MONTH" ; sqlType = NVARCHAR;  length = 6 ;}
];
```

In the Repository workspace, choose the appropriate package and in the popup menu choose New→ Other..

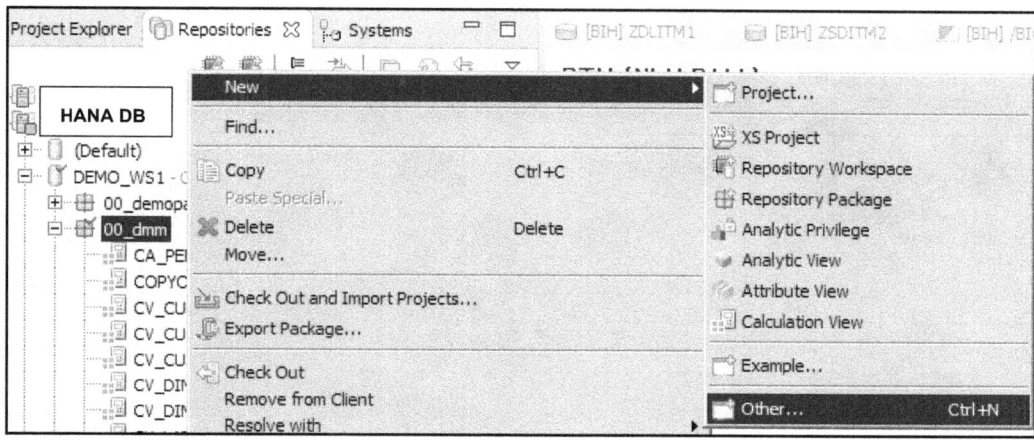

Choose the option – "General → File"

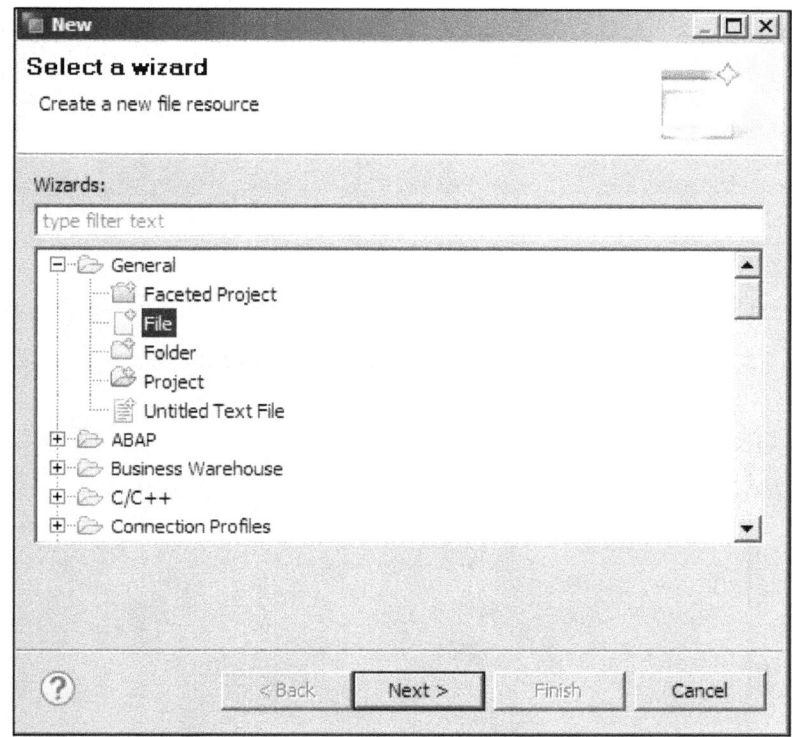

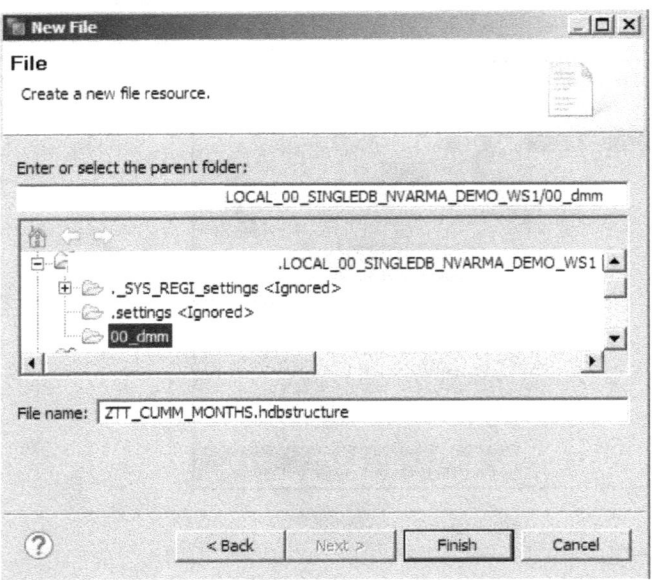

```
table.schemaName = "NVARMA" ;
table.tableType = COLUMNSTORE;
table.columns = [
{name = "CALMONTH" ; sqlType = NVARCHAR ; length = 6;} ,
{name = "CUMM_MONTH" ; sqlType = NVARCHAR;  length = 6 ;}

];
```

Save and activate the Table Type. You can find the table type under your respective schema in the Catalog folder

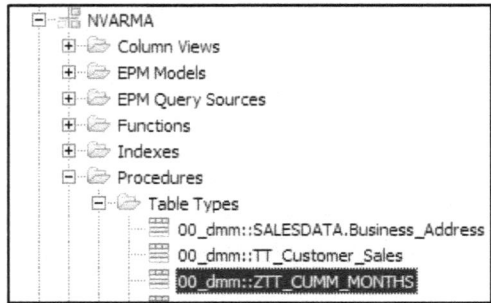

Note: We will use the above table type in the practical examples shown in the following units.

2.2.5 Definition of CDS Entities using DDL Source Files

In HANA Core Data Services framework, we can implement the repository objects called as the DDL source files, which are used to define a group of related data types and entities within one object. We need to implement the DDL Source file using the extension .hbdd. Once we activate CDS file (Core Data Services) a corresponding runtime object (a database catalog object) is created in the underlying database schema.

DDL Sources are commonly used to implement CDS Views in native HANA XS application development. However, we can also reuse them in the database development artifacts such as calculation views or SQL Script procedures and functions.

We can define the data types (both elementary and structure types) and entities (tables) in a DDL source file.

Let us go through the steps to create a new DDL Source file called SALESDATA

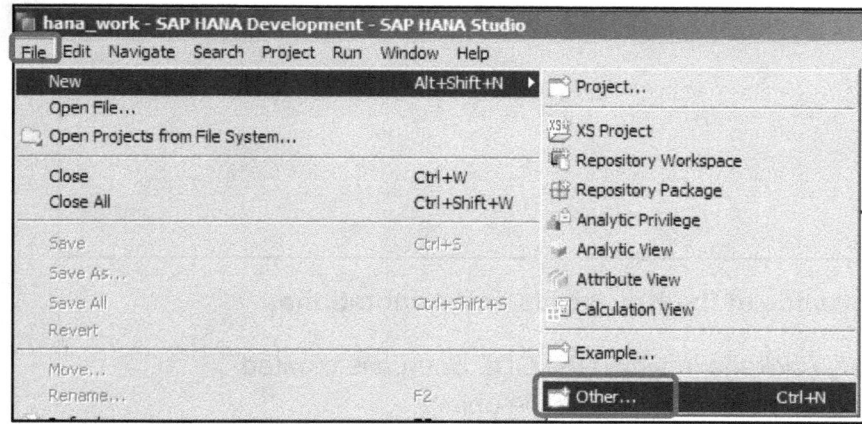

Choose the "DDL Source File" option as shown below.

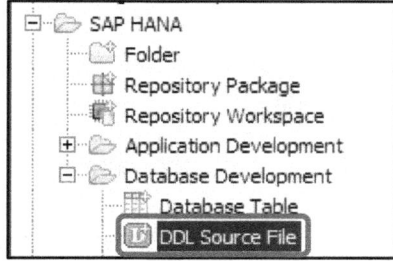

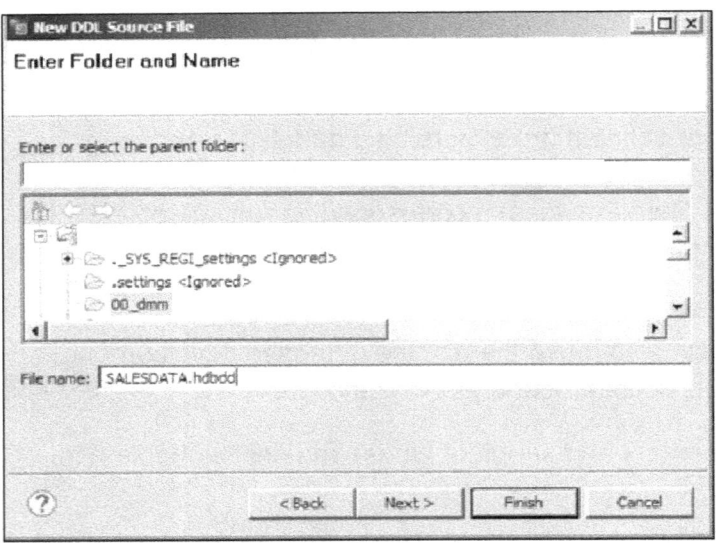

The default code looks like this.

```
namespace 00_dmm;

@Schema: 'NVARMA'
context SALESDATA {


};
```

Let us understand the importance of the Key words and Annotations:

- Namespace: Repository package in which the DDL Source is created
- Context Name: The name of the DDL Source file object
- Entity: Name of the database table to be created
- Type: Name of the data type
- View: Name of the CDS view

Annotations → These are used to assign the semantics in the data model

- @Schema: The name of the database schema where the artifacts are generated
- @Catalog – To specify the properties of a catalog object

Maintain the following code in the DDL Source file.

Here we are trying to define a structure data type called Business_Address and one Database table (Entity) called Customer in a single DDL source file. Subsequently we shall use this Entity as a database table in the data models and applications. We can also reuse the structure data type in SQL script programs.

```
namespace "00_dmm";

@Schema: 'NVARMA'
context SALESDATA {

    type Business_Address          <──── Structure type
    {
    First_Name    : String(40);
    Last_Name     : String(40);
    Country       : String(2);
    City          : String(40);
    };

@Catalog.tableType: #COLUMN
    Entity Customer                <──── Table definition
    {
    Customer_ID   : String(10);
    Cust_Address  : Business_Address;   <──── Using structure type
    Calendar_Year : String(4);
    Total_Sales   : Decimal(20,2)   ;
    };
  };
```

You can also open the above entity (Database table) in the catalog

Table Name:				Schema:		Type:		
00_dmm::SALESDATA.Customer				NVARMA	▼	Column Store		▼

Columns | Indexes | Further Properties | Runtime Information

	Name	SQL Data Type	Di...	Column Store Data Type	Key	Not Null	Default
1	Customer_ID	NVARCHAR	10	STRING			
2	Cust_Address.First_Name	NVARCHAR	40	STRING			
3	Cust_Address.Last_Name	NVARCHAR	40	STRING			
4	Cust_Address.Country	NVARCHAR	2	STRING			
5	Cust_Address.City	NVARCHAR	40	STRING			
6	Calendar_Year	NVARCHAR	4	STRING			
7	Total_Sales	DECIMAL	20,2	FIXED			

Note: We will use the above database table in the practical examples shown in the following units.

2.2.6 Developing HANA artifacts using Web IDE

SAP HANA provides the Web IDE as a web-based interface, which has a set of tools to implement end-to-end models and applications on HANA database. The biggest advantage of this tool is that we don't need to install the HANA studio.

We can use the following URL to launch the HANA editor in Web IDE.

http://<HANA Database host>:<Port>/sap/hana/ide/editor/

Sample view of a Database Table using the Editor in Web IDE.

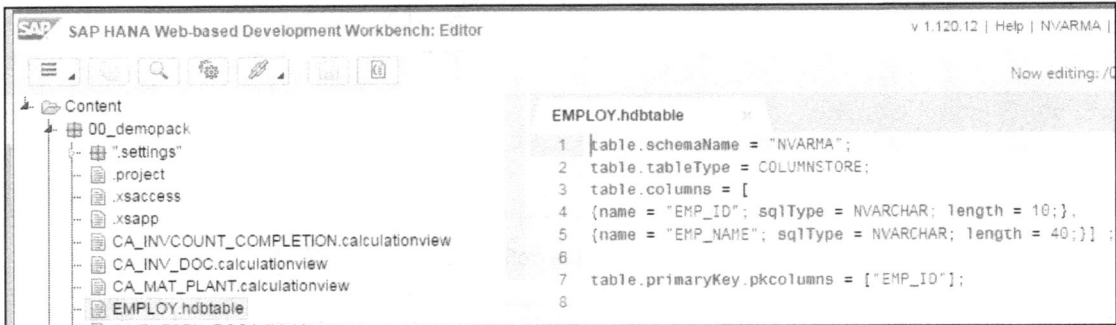

We can perform the following operations at a package level. (Right click on the package name)

Sample steps to create a database table: Choose the menu path **New → File**

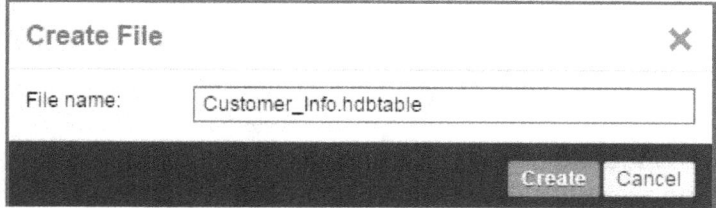

Enter the table definition

```
*Customer_Info.hdbt...    ×
1  table.schemaName = "NVARMA";
2  table.tableType = COLUMNSTORE;
3  table.columns = [
4  {name = "CUST_ID"; sqlType = NVARCHAR; length = 10;},
5  {name = "NAME"; sqlType = NVARCHAR; length = 40;} ,
6  {name = "ADDRESS"; sqlType = NVARCHAR; length = 100;}] ;
7
8  table.primaryKey.pkcolumns = ["CUST_ID"];
```

Use the menu path **File > Save** to Save and activate the development artifact

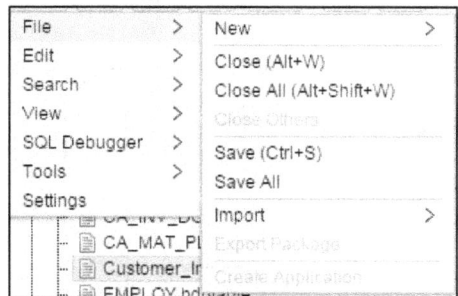

Following type of messages are shown in the SQL Console of Web IDE, to indicate whether the activation is successful or if there any errors.

[04:05:27] File /00_demopack/Customer_Info.hdbtable saved & activated successfully.

We can implement all the other HANA database artifacts such as calculation views, procedures, functions and XS applications using the Web IDE.

3 SQL Script Programming Foundations

Implementing business logic to address the analytical and transactional requirements in SAP has been traditionally based on the three-tier client server approach, where most of the logic runs in application server by the ABAP engine and only the operations related to database, such as data retrieval and manipulations are processed in the database server. However, with the introduction of SAP HANA in-memory platform, it would be ideal to process most of the business logic in the database itself to take advantage of the performance benefits.

SAP HANA has SQL Script as the proprietary language to implement procedural logic that runs natively in the in-memory platform. Hence, building the application logic based on SQL Script programming is known as the "Code push down" approach. In SQL Script, we can also leverage various built-in libraries and engines related to standard database functions, predictive analytics, text and graph processing etc. As per the future road map of most of the SAP products, it is recommended to build the solutions using the "Code push down" approach, few examples are: SAP BW Transformations, SAP BW Integrated Planning – Planning Functions etc.

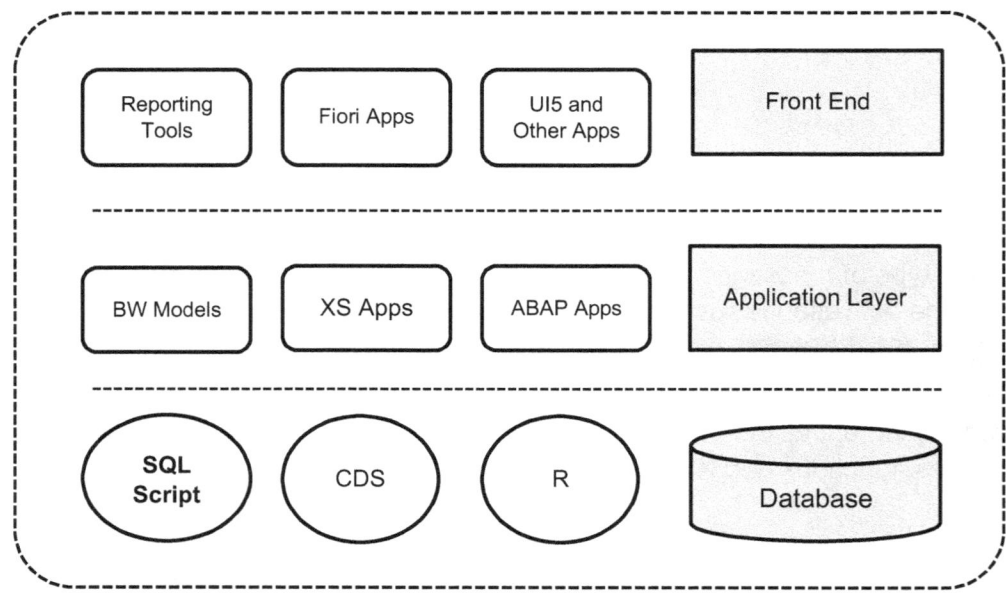

3.1 Understanding SQL Script Execution in HANA

The key motivation to build solutions in SQLScript is to push the data-intensive application logic into the database. Apart from that SQL Script allows us to implement algorithms using a set-oriented approach and exploit various performance benefits of HANA database such as parallel processing, pruning etc. Hence it is essential to understand how the SQL script programs are converted into execution plans and how these exaction plans are run by different engines.

How are the SQL Script programs converted as executable objects?

Each SQL Script program will be converted into a *Calculation Model*, which is executed by the Calculation Engine during runtime. Following diagram explains the key components which are involved in the generation of runtime objects and executing the code for SQL script.

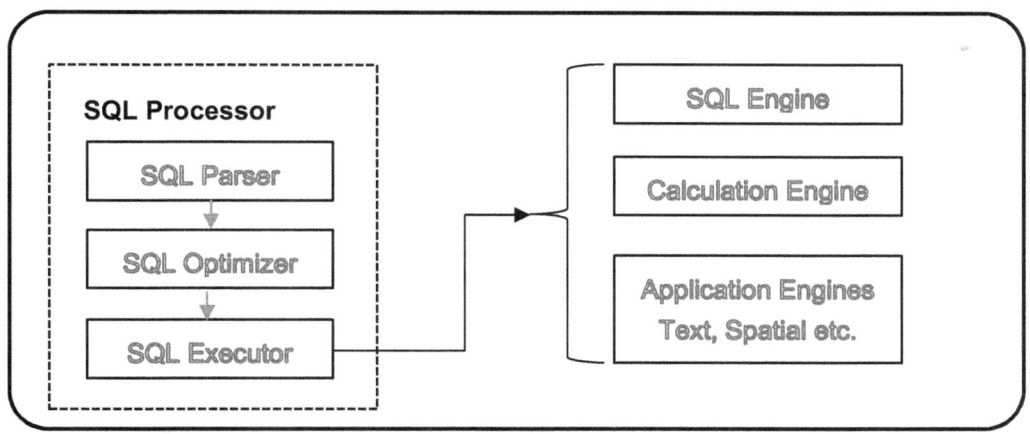

SQL Parser: Complies the SQL Script blocks such as procedures and functions after performing all the relevant syntax checks.

SQL Optimizer: Converts the complied version of the program into relational algebra - equations that include operators like selection, join, aggregations, etc. It will prepare the optimal execution plan which is in the form of a data flow graph.

SQL Executor: The SQL executor takes a query execution plan (data flow graph) generated by the SQL Optimizer and invokes the corresponding HANA engine to execute the operations.

3.2 Key elements of SQL script programming

We can use the following types of processing blocks to implement the solutions using SQL Script, natively in HANA database.

- Stored procedures – Used to perform data access or data manipulation operations

- Scalar Functions – To implement logic for deriving a single column

- Table Functions – To implement logic for deriving a set of records

Typically, the processing logic in SQL script programming involves the steps such as: data retrieval from various tables and views, performing necessary calculations and returning the results back to the calling interface (such as a procedure, function or a view etc.).

In the following sections, let us understand the key elements of SQL script programming along with their application while building different types of solutions.

Programming elements to describe the data and perform operations on the data:

- Data Types
- Variables
- Predicates
- Operators
- Expressions
- Literals
- Identifiers

Processing blocks to control the execution flow and process the data:

- Conditional statements (IF, CASE..)
- Looping operations (FOR Loop, WHILE Loop..)
- Scalar and Table Variables
- Built-in functions and User defined functions
- Cursors and Arrays
- Exception handling statements

3.2.1 Built-In Data Types

Below are the pre-defined data types in SQL Script. Each elementary field or column is defined based on these built-in data types. Depending on the nature of the values to be stored and the kind of operations to be performed, we need to specify appropriate data type of each of the variables in a program.

Classification	Data Type
Date time types	DATE, TIME, SECONDDATE, TIMESTAMP
Numeric types	TINYINT, SMALLINT, INTEGER, BIGINT, DECIMAL, REAL, DOUBLE
Character string types	VARCHAR, NVARCHAR, ALPHANUM, SHORTTEXT
Binary types	VARBINARY
Large Object types	BLOB, CLOB, NCLOB, TEXT
Multi-valued types	ARRAY

Key points about data types in SQL Script:
- The default format for the DATE data type is 'YYYY-MM-DD'
- Character string constants has to be enclosed in single quotations. (e.g.: 'Test')
- Implicit type conversion: When a given set of operand/argument types does not match what an operator/function expects, a type conversion is carried out by the HANA database.

Note: In addition to the built-in data types we can define the user defined data types using the Core Data Services (CDS) framework as explained the section: *2.3 Core Data Services(CDS) Framework in HANA*

3.2.2 Variables

Variables are used to store values during runtime of a program. Depending on the nature of data to be processed and the associated logic, we need to declare different types of variables in the SQL script programs.

In SQL Script we can define following types of Variables:

1) Scalar Variables: These are used to store values of single fields like Customer number, Order Date, Net Value etc.
2) Table Variables: They are used to store group of records in a table structure
3) Array variables: They are used to store group of elements of a specific data type
4) Cursor variables: Used to store one record at a time, while they are fetched from the underlaying database tables

---

Declaring Scalar Variables in SQL Script processing blocks:

        DECLARE V_CustID NVARCHAR(10)   ;
        DECLARE V_NetValue DECIMAL(15,2) ;
        DECLARE V_OrderDate DATE ;

Assigning Values to Variables:

        V_CustID := 'C001'   ;
        V_NetValue := 125.30 ;
        V_NetValue := :V_NetValue + 100 ;
        V_OrderDate := '2018-01-15' ;

Key Points:
- As you can observe in the above examples, we have to use := as the assignment operator
- To access the variable, sometimes we have to use :<Variable name> as shown in the example above. This is especially needed while accessing table variables.

Note: We will explore the remining types of variables such has Table variable, Arrays and Cursors in the following sections and units.

3.2.3 Using the SQL Console in HANA Studio

In HANA Studio under the modeler perspective we shall use the SQL Console as an editor for executing SQL queries. We can use the SQL console to run all the statements related to Data Definition Language (DDL), Data Manipulation Language (DML) and Data Control language (DCL). Let us understand the steps to leverage the SQL Console and execute the statements and analyze results.

How to open SQL Console in HANA Studio:

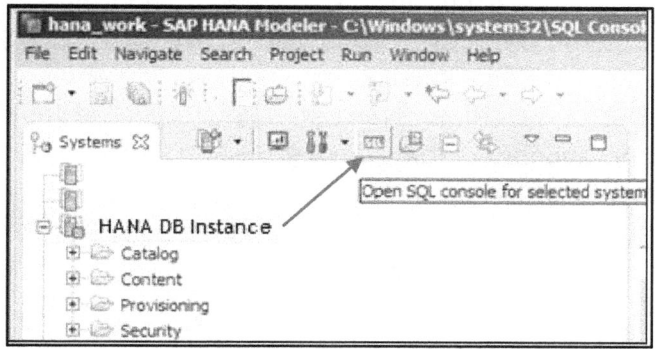

Enter SQL Statements and **Execute** as shown below and validate the query result.

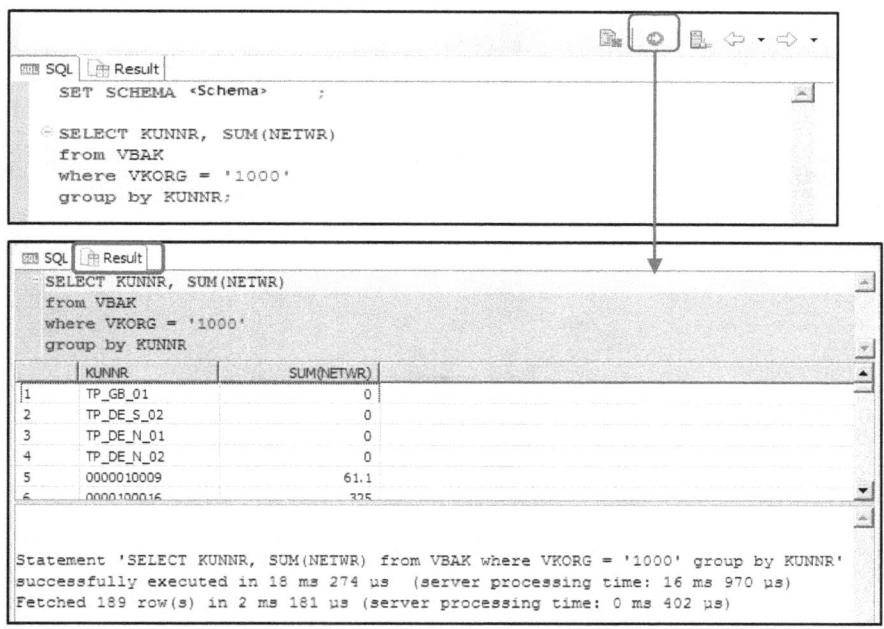

3.2.4 Anonymous Blocks in SQL Script

Even though SQL Console allows us to execute individual SQL statements, sometimes we should be able to run a group of statements (processing blocks) to analyze the results. To achieve this in the earlier versions of HANA, we had to implement a stored procedure or a function and call it in the SQL console.

Starting from SAP HANA 1.0 SPS10, we can execute the SQL Script code as "Anonymous Blocks", instead of creating any stored procedures or functions. This will be quite useful to run the code in a standalone mode in SQL Console for various testing and simulation scenarios.

Note: Parameters in anonymous blocks are only supported from HANA 1.0 SPS12

We can define these parameters in the same way we would implement while defining parameters for a stored procedure. We can define the parameters using both the simple types, table types and the data types defined via Core Data Services.

Example: Anonymous block using elementary type parameters

```
DO ( IN   i_var1 INT => 5,
     OUT o_var1 INT => ?
   )
BEGIN
     o_var1 := i_var1 + 10;
END
```

Iput and Output values as Parameters

Processing Logic

Executing Anonymous blocks in SQL Editor:

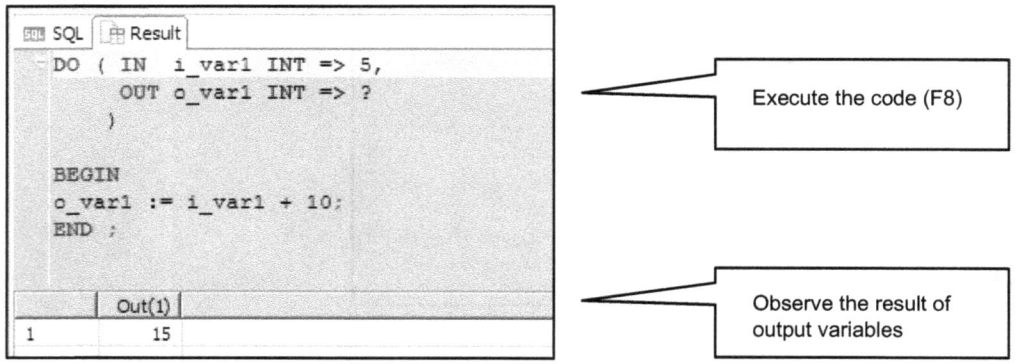

Execute the code (F8)

Observe the result of output variables

3.2.5 Program Example: Data Types and Scalar Variables

Let us try to build a program (Anonymous block) to perform the employee payroll calculations using appropriate scalar variables and operations.

```
DO (    IN   EMPID NVARCHAR(8) => '10001',
        IN   BASIC_SALARY DECIMAL => 15000,
        OUT GROSS_SALARY DECIMAL => ?,                    1
        OUT TAX DECIMAL => ?,
        OUT NET_SALARY DECIMAL => ?,
        OUT DAYS_OF_SERVICE INTEGER => ?
    )


BEGIN
        DECLARE DOJ DATE := '2018-01-01';
        DECLARE HRA DECIMAL ;                             2


        HRA = :BASIC_SALARY * 15/100;
        GROSS_SALARY = :BASIC_SALARY + :HRA;              3


        if BASIC_SALARY > 10000 Then
                TAX = :GROSS_SALARY * 20 / 100 ;          4
        else
                TAX = :GROSS_SALARY * 10 / 100 ;
        End if;


        NET_SALARY := BASIC_SALARY + HRA - TAX;


        SELECT days_between(DOJ, CURRENT_DATE) into DAYS_OF_SERVICE    5
        from dummy;


END
```

Refer to the explanations about different parts of the program given below.

1   Define the Input and Output Variables of anonymous block

2   Declare the required local variables

3   Perform the arithmetic operations

4   Implement conditional statements

5   Using a built in function called DAYS_BETWEEN

Execute the block and verify the results

```
DO ( IN  EMPID NVARCHAR(8) => '10001',
     IN   BASIC_SALARY DECIMAL => 15000,
     OUT GROSS_SALARY DECIMAL => ?,
     OUT TAX DECIMAL => ?,
     OUT NET_SALARY DECIMAL => ?,
     OUT DAYS_OF_SERVICE INTEGER => ?
   )
BEGIN

DECLARE DOJ DATE := '2018-01-01';
DECLARE HRA DECIMAL ;

HRA = :BASIC_SALARY * 15/100;

GROSS_SALARY = :BASIC_SALARY + :HRA;

if BASIC_SALARY > 10000 Then
 TAX = :GROSS_SALARY * 20 / 100 ;
else
 TAX = :GROSS_SALARY * 10 / 100 ;
End if;

NET_SALARY := BASIC_SALARY + HRA - TAX;

select days_between(DOJ, CURRENT_DATE) into DAYS_OF_SERVICE from dummy;

END
```

	Out(1)	Out(2)	Out(3)	Out(4)
1	17,250	3,450	13,800	278

3.2.6 Program Example: Queries on Database Tables

Let us try to build a program (Anonymous block) to fetch the total sales order value for a given Customer and Year.

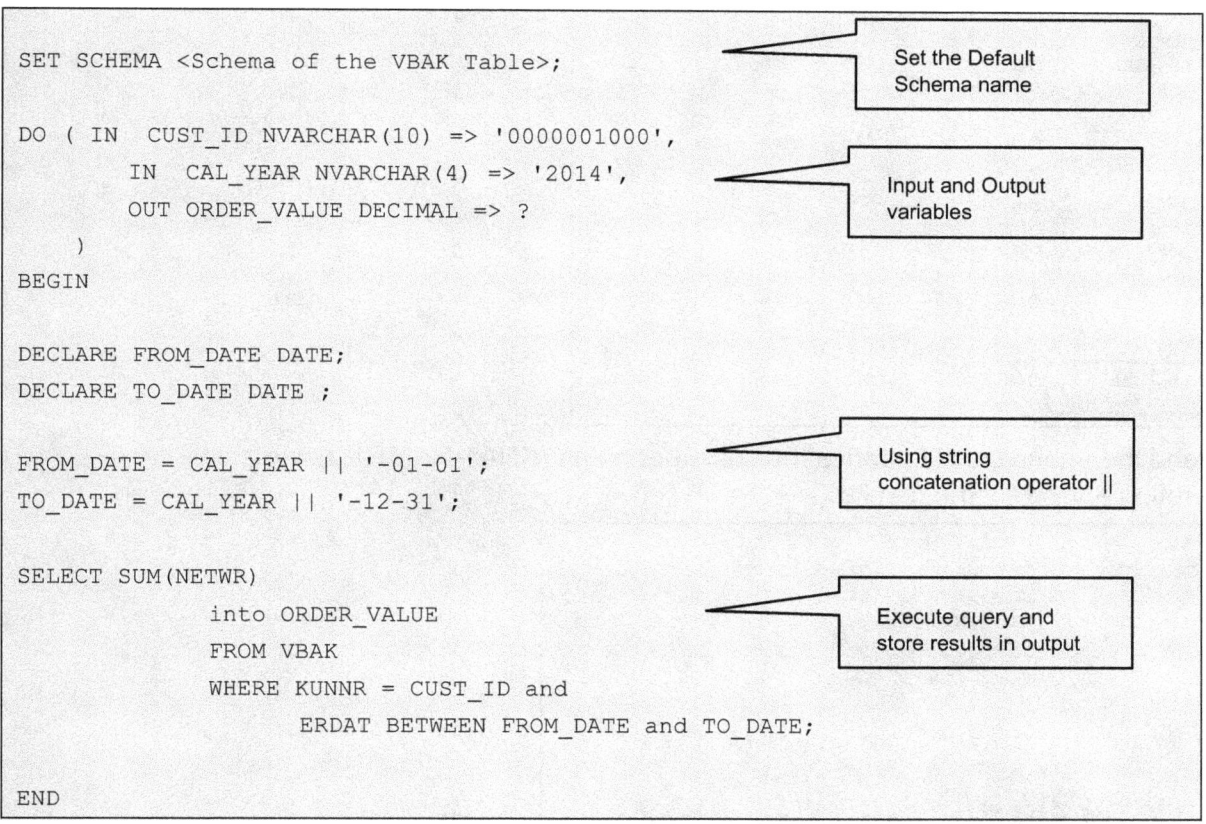

```
SET SCHEMA <Schema of the VBAK Table>;                    Set the Default
                                                          Schema name

DO ( IN  CUST_ID NVARCHAR(10) => '0000001000',
        IN  CAL_YEAR NVARCHAR(4) => '2014',              Input and Output
        OUT ORDER_VALUE DECIMAL => ?                     variables
    )
BEGIN

DECLARE FROM_DATE DATE;
DECLARE TO_DATE DATE ;

FROM_DATE = CAL_YEAR || '-01-01';                        Using string
TO_DATE = CAL_YEAR || '-12-31';                          concatenation operator ||

SELECT SUM(NETWR)
            into ORDER_VALUE                             Execute query and
            FROM VBAK                                    store results in output
            WHERE KUNNR = CUST_ID and
                ERDAT BETWEEN FROM_DATE and TO_DATE;

END
```

Note: All the objects in SAP HANA database are organized under different Schemas. Hence, we must specify the schema name for all the database tables used in the code. We can perform this in different ways:

1) Specify the table name along with the schema name
2) Using the SET SCHEMA statement as shown in the above example
3) Using the DEFAULT Schema option (In case of Stored procedures or views etc.)

Execute the block and verify results.

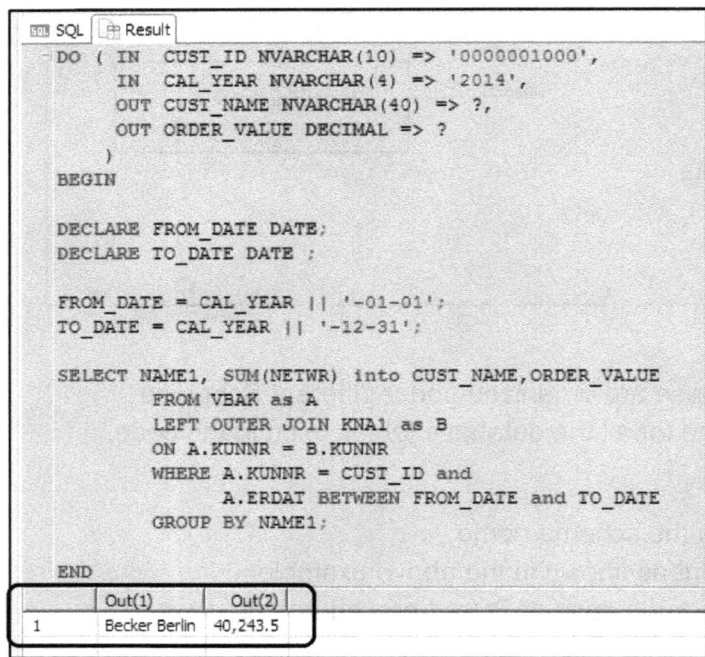

Extend the above block to derive the customer name (KNA1-NAME1) using a Join operation and verify the results.

```
DO ( IN  CUST_ID NVARCHAR(10) => '0000001000',
     IN  CAL_YEAR NVARCHAR(4) => '2014',
     OUT CUST_NAME NVARCHAR(40) => ?,
     OUT ORDER_VALUE DECIMAL => ?
   )
BEGIN

DECLARE FROM_DATE DATE;
DECLARE TO_DATE DATE ;

FROM_DATE = CAL_YEAR || '-01-01';
TO_DATE = CAL_YEAR || '-12-31';

SELECT NAME1, SUM(NETWR) into CUST_NAME, ORDER_VALUE
       FROM VBAK as A
       LEFT OUTER JOIN KNA1 as B
       ON A.KUNNR = B.KUNNR
       WHERE A.KUNNR = CUST_ID and
             A.ERDAT BETWEEN FROM_DATE and TO_DATE
       GROUP BY NAME1;

END
```

	Out(1)	Out(2)
1	Becker Berlin	40,243.5

3.2.7 Data Sources for Queries in SQL Script

Let us understand the different types of data sources, which can be queried fetch data in the SQL Script logic.

1) Database tables (Column / Row store):
   - Database tables are usually loaded into HANA using the data provisioning tools such as SLT, SDI or BODS
   - We can also populate the data into the tables using the DML operations (INSERT, UPDATE and UPSERT)
   - These tables are accessed using the notation <SCHEMA>.<TABLE_NAME>
   - For example ECP.VBAK → Here is ECP is the schema that represents the corresponding ECC system.

2) Native HANA: Calculation Views or Table Functions
   - We can leverage the existing data models (calculation views and table functions) to fetch the data records and process them further

3) BW: ADSO or Info Object tables
   - When the HANA database in the backend of a BW application instance, we can directly fetch the data from the respective BW tables (ADSO active table or Info objects Master data attributes / text tables)
   - These HANA modeling objects are always stored in the _SAP_BI schema

4) Remote database objects through Smart Data Access: Virtual Tables
   - Smart Data Access allows us to consume the data directly from the remote database without persisting in HANA.
   - These HANA modeling objects are always stored in the respective schema of the remote source

3.3 Table Variables

Table variables are used to store a group of records during the runtime of a program. These are the most widely used objects in SQL Script, since they allow us to process the data from different sources such as database tables, calculation views as per the desired logic. Essentially these are used to prepare the intermediate results and perform various SQL query operations during the program execution.

For those who are familiar with the ABAP programming, Table Variables are similar to the Internal Tables. While Internal tables in ABAP or created and processed in application server, table variables in HANA are created and processing within the in-memory storage of database. This would result in significant performance improvement, since there is no need for data transfer between the Database and Application Servers.

During the execution of an SQL Script processing bock such as stored procedure or Table Function, we can fetch the data from any database table, database view, Information views (Calculation views, Attribute and Analytic Views) into a table variable. Another interesting aspect is, we can run a query (SELECT statement) against a table variable in the same way as we run on a database table or view.

Programming approach using Table Variables

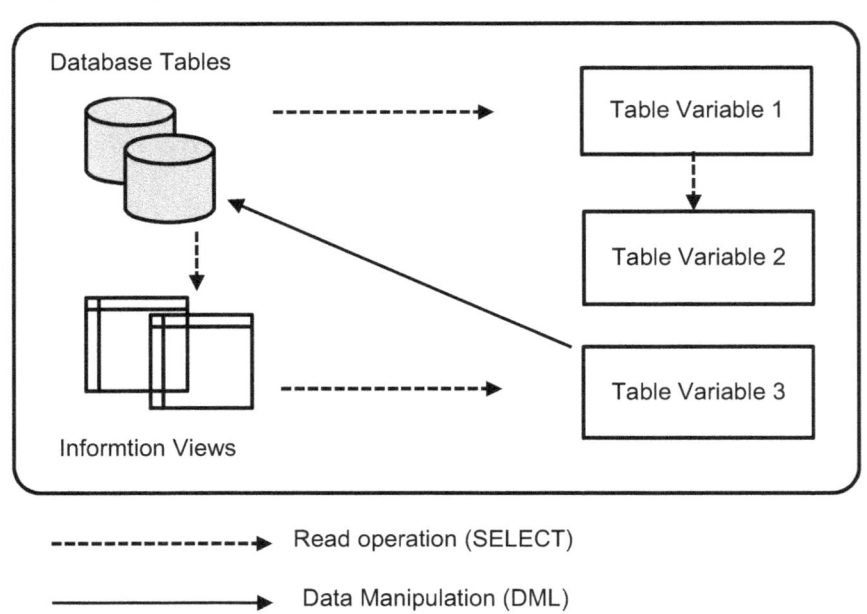

3.3.1 Declaring a Table variable:

There are different ways to define the structure for table variables as explained below. Depending on the scenario, we will use any of these approaches to define table variables in the processing blocks.

- Automatic generation of table variables based on SQL query

```
TAB_MATERIAL = SELECT MATNR, MTART, MATKL from MARA;
```

In this method the structure of table variable will be generated based on the fields of the SQL query. This provides great flexibility in SQL Script, since we don't need to declare the data type for the table variable.

- Definition of Table variable based on a pre-defined structure (Table type)

Following are the different scenarios where we can leverage a predefined structure data type to declare the table variables.
- Table variables as parameters in the stored procedure or table functions
- To declare table variables within the processing logic of stored procedures and table functions

To address these requirements, we can define the structure for a table variable using a predefined data type called **Table Type**

There are two ways to declare the table types:

1) Global table types (as Repository or Catalog object)

Table Type as Repository Object: (Core Data Services)

This is the most commonly used method to create table types, which is already explained in the previous section: 2.3.1 Definition of a Table type using CDS

Ideally, we will prefer to create table types globally when we need to reuse them across different processing blocks.

45

Example of a Repository Structure (Table Type):

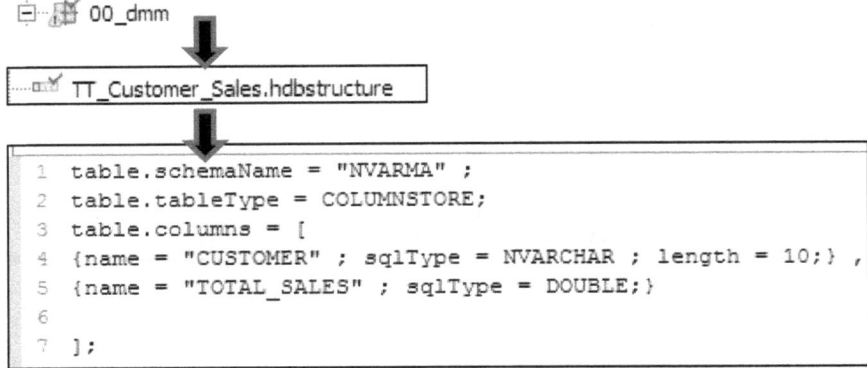

```
1   table.schemaName = "NVARMA" ;
2   table.tableType = COLUMNSTORE;
3   table.columns = [
4   {name = "CUSTOMER" ; sqlType = NVARCHAR ; length = 10;} ,
5   {name = "TOTAL_SALES" ; sqlType = DOUBLE;}
6
7   ];
```

Table types are also shown under the catalog schemas:

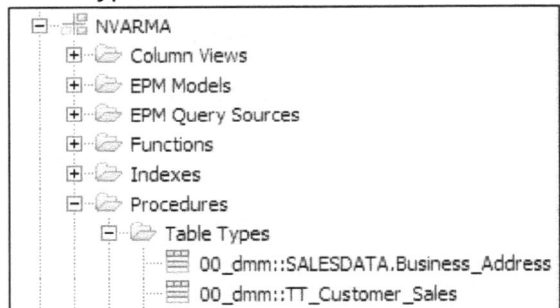

Table Type as Catalog Object:
In this type of definition, the Table type has a runtime object but there is no design time object.

CREATE TYPE [schema.]name AS TABLE
    (Column1 DataType [, Column2 DataType,...])

DROP TYPE [schema.]name [CASCADE]

Example:
CREATE TYPE NVARMA.SALES_DATA as TABLE
(KUNNR NVARCHAR(10),
 TOTAL_SALES DECIMAL(17,4)) ;

Note: The above example creates a table type as a catalog object only. Hence it cannot be transported.

2) Local Table type – Inline definition: In this approach we shall define the table type as part of the Table Variable declaration locally in the procedure or function.
   Syntax:
   DECLARE <Table Variable> TABLE (Column1 <Data Type>,
                                    Column2 <Data Type>) ;
   Example:
   DECLARE TAB_CUSTOMERS TABLE (KUNNR NVARCHAR(10),
                                        NAME1 NVARCHAR(40),
                                        LAND1 NVARCHAR(3));

- Example: Anonymous block using Table variables and Table type based parameters
  Here we are using the table type "00_dmm::TT_Customer_Sales" which is already defined in the previous unit and section: 2.3.1

```
SET SCHEMA <SCHEMA>;
DO ( IN i_VKORG NVARCHAR(4) => '1000',
     OUT ex_tab "00_dmm::TT_Customer_Sales" => ?)
BEGIN
ex_tab = select KUNNR as CUSTOMER, sum(NETWR) as TOTAL_SALES
   from VBAK where VKORG = I_VKORG
   group by KUNNR;
END
```

```
DO ( IN i_VKORG NVARCHAR(4) => '1000',
     OUT ex_tab "00_dmm::TT_Customer_Sales" => ?)

BEGIN
ex_tab = select KUNNR as CUSTOMER, sum(NETWR) as TOTAL_SALES
   from            .VBAK where VKORG = I_VKORG
   group by KUNNR;
END
```

	CUSTOMER	TOTAL_SALES
9	0000002140	25,891,931.27
10	0000002200	25,605,224.1
11	0000002004	27,011,074.62
12	0000002130	17,343,382.76
13	0000002007	17,012,587.31

Let us implement the same code using a Table Variable as parameter which is defined using local table type.

```
SET SCHEMA <SCHEMA>;
DO ( IN i_VKORG NVARCHAR(4) => '1000',
   OUT ex_tab TABLE (CUSTOMER NVARCHAR(10),
                     TOTAL_SALES DECIMAL(20,2))
                  => ?)
BEGIN
ex_tab = select KUNNR as CUSTOMER, sum(NETWR) as TOTAL_SALES
   from VBAK where VKORG = I_VKORG
   group by KUNNR;
END
```

3.3.2 Fetching records into Table Variable

We can use the SELECT query to fetch the records into a table variable from various sources (Database Tables, Views, Calculation Views, Table Functions and even from other Table Variables).

Prior the HANA version 2.0, table variables do not support any data manipulation operations such as INSERT, UPDATE, DELETE since these are only runtime objects and not persisting results in the database.

In the following example, we are fetching the records from the database tables (VBAP and VBAK) into the table variable called SALES_TAB

```
TAB_SALES = SELECT VBAP.MANDT, VBAP.VBELN, VBAP.POSNR,VBAP.VGBEL,
VBAP.VGPOS, VBAK.ERDAT, VBAK.NETWR
 FROM VBAP INNER JOIN VBAK
         ON VBAP.MANDT = VBAK.MAND and
         VBAP.VBELN = VBAK.VBELN;
```

3.3.3 Reading records from Table Variables

Table variables will store the data during runtime of a program using the columnar storage, in the similar way how the database tables store data. Hence, we can use the SELECT statement to fetch the record from Table Variables in the just like the way we execute queries on a database table or a view.

Note: We need to address the Table variables with the prefix : (Colon)

In the below example we are populating the records in the table variable DEL_TAB by reading from another table variable SALES_TAB.

```
TAB_DELIVERY =
    SELECT S.*,D.VBELN AS LIPSVBELN, D.POSNR as LIPSPOSNR
    FROM :TAB_SALES AS S
    INNER JOIN LIPS as D
        ON S.MANDT = D.MANDT and
           S.VBELN = D.VGBEL and
           S.POSNR = D.VGPOS;
```

3.3.4 Accessing records from Table Variables based on index:

We can access specific record from a table variable using the Index, which is nothing but the corresponding row number. This will provide the flexibility of accessing field values from specific records in a table variable.

To achieve the fields of a specific record, we need to reference the name of the table variable and the field which you we need to access separated by a dot(.), followed by the index of the row within the square brackets. The index of the records in a table variable begins with 1.

Note: Prior to the HANA 1.0 SPS11 version, we are supposed to use ARRAY type variables to achieve the similar functionality.

```
Example: to access specific data records based on the row index:

FIRST_DEL_NUM = :TAB_DELIVERY.LIPSVBELN[1];
```

3.3.5 Searching for records in a Table Variable

In SAP HANA 2.0 SPS03, there is a new operator called SEARCH, which enables efficient search by key-value pairs in table variables. We can use this operator to find data records that matches specific condition in a table variable.

In the below example, we are trying the perform a search on the table variable for a given material number.

```
DO ( IN i_MATNR NVARCHAR(18) => 'M3',
      OUT SEARCH_RESULT NVARCHAR(10) => ?,
     OUT PRODUCTS TABLE (MAT_NUM NVARCHAR(18),
                         QTY DOUBLE
                    ) => ?
                    )
BEGIN

PRODUCTS.MAT_NUM[1] = 'M1' ;
PRODUCTS.MAT_NUM[2] = 'M2' ;
PRODUCTS.MAT_NUM[3] = 'M3' ;
PRODUCTS.QTY[1] = 50 ;
PRODUCTS.QTY[2] = 25;
PRODUCTS.QTY[3] = 10 ;


if (:PRODUCTS.SEARCH("MAT_NUM", :i_MATNR, 1)) > 0 Then
     SEARCH_RESULT = 'FOUND' ;
Else
     SEARCH_RESULT = 'NOT FOUND' ;
End if;

END
```

3.3.6 Data Processing Techniques using Table Variables:

Please note that the table variables are only run time data objects, which are meant to store the data records based on a specific structure. Until the release HANA 2.0 SPS 01, there was no option to perform any data manipulation statements like INSERT, UPDATE or DELETE against the table variables. However, we can use the following programming techniques to achieve similar functionality whenever we need to perform some data manipulations on the table variables. Learning these techniques will be very much essential to understand the power of table variables and achieve complex processing requirements in more optimal ways.

Merging or Appending records into Table Variables

We can use the UNION operation to append new records into an existing table variable. This is helpful when we do not want to overwrite the existing records in a table variable, but we need to insert new records.

1) **To append new records to a table variable without clearing the existing records:**

   In the below example we are using the SQL Operator UNION ALL, for appending records to an existing table variable called TAB_RESULT.

```
TAB_RESULT = SELECT * FROM :TAB_RESULT
             UNION ALL
             SELECT * from :TAB_OPEN_ORDERS;
```

2) **To merge records from multiple data sets into one table variable**

   In the below example we are using the SQL Operator UNION ALL, to merge the records from two separate table variables into another table variable called TAB_RESULT.

```
-- Open & Closed order information is merged.
TAB_RESULT = SELECT * FROM :TAB_OPEN_ORDERS
             UNION ALL
             SELECT * FROM :TAB_CLOSED_ORDERS;
```

3) Updating records of Table Variables

We can use the SELECT statement in the following way to update the records within a table variable.

For example, we need to increase the Sales Revenue by 100 for all the Sales orders of a specific Customer in the existing dataset of a table variables called TAB_SALES:

```
--Update the records for specific customer in a table variable
TAB_SALES   = SELECT VBELN, KUNNR, NETWR + 100 as NETWR
              From :TAB_SALES
              Where KUNNR = '10000011';
```

4) Deleting records from Table Variables

For example, we need to delete the records from table variable where the Sales orders net value is below 1000:

```
TAB_SALES   = SELECT * From :TAB_SALES
              Where NETWR >= 1000;
```

Clearing the contents in Table Variables:

We can use the following technique to delete all the records from a table variable. Here we are enforcing a WHERE condition that will never match, hence the results will be empty, causing the table variable TAB_SALES to get initialized.

```
TAB_SALES   = SELECT * From :TAB_SALES
              Where 1 = 2;
```

Note: This technique will be quite useful to clean up the data in the table variables, which are no longer needed in the subsequent program logic.

3.3.7 Program Example: Table Variables

Let us implement a program (Anonymous block) to derive the KPIs related to sales order delivery performance. In this program we can explore the essential features of table variables, such as:

- Declaration of table variables
- Fetching data from database tables into table variables
- Updating, Deleting and merging records of table variables

```
SET SCHEMA <Schema for the Tables>;

DO ( IN i_VKORG NVARCHAR(4) => '1000',
      IN i_FROMDATE DATE => '2011-01-01',
      IN i_TODATE DATE => '2011-12-31',                    Input and Output
      OUT ORDER_SUMMARY TABLE (ORDER_NUM NVARCHAR(10),     Parameters
                      ORDER_ITEM NVARCHAR(4),
                      ORDER_TYPE NVARCHAR(4),
                      ORDER_DATE DATE,
                      PGI_DATE DATE,
                      ORDER_QTY DECIMAL(20,2),
                      PGI_QTY DECIMAL(20,2),
                      ITEM_STATUS NVARCHAR(10)
                ) => ?,
      OUT PRODUCT_SUMMARY TABLE (MAT_NUM NVARCHAR(18),
                      ORDER_QTY DECIMAL(20,2),
                      PGI_QTY DECIMAL(20,2),
                      OPEN_QTY DECIMAL(20,2),
                      ORDER_VALUE DECIMAL(20,2),
                      RETURN_QTY DECIMAL(20,2),
                      RETURN_VALUE DECIMAL(20,2)
                ) => ?
                )
```

```
BEGIN

--Fetch the sales order items based on the input parameters
tab_orders = select I.VBELN, I.POSNR , I.MATNR, I.KWMENG, I.NETWR,
                    H.AUART, H.ERDAT
                    from VBAP as I
                    inner join VBAK as H
                    on
                         I.VBELN = H.VBELN
                    where H.VKORG = :I_VKORG and
                          H.ERDAT between I_FROMDATE and I_TODATE ;

--Fetch the order lines of type Return Orders into another table variable
tab_return_orders = SELECT * from :tab_orders where AUART = 'RE';

--Delete all the order lines where the order type is 'RE' (return orders)
tab_orders = SELECT * from :tab_orders where AUART != 'RE';

--Derive the delivery qty and status for order lines
tab_orders_pgi = select o.vbeln , o.posnr, o.matnr, o.kwmeng, o.netwr,
o.auart, o.erdat ,

                                    di.lfimg, dh.wadat_ist
                                    from :tab_orders as o
                                    left outer join lips as di
                                    on
                                         o.vbeln = di.vgbel and
                                         o.posnr = di.vgpos
                                    left outer join likp as dh
                                    on di.mandt = dh.mandt and
                                         di.vbeln = dh.vbeln;
```

```
--Preparing the output table for Order Summary
Order_Summary = select vbeln as order_num,
                            posnr as order_item,
                            auart as order_type,
                            erdat as order_date,
                            wadat_ist as pgi_date,
                            kwmeng as order_qty,
                            lfimg as pgi_qty,
                            case when lfimg >= kwmeng then 'Closed'
                                    else 'Open'
                            end as item_status
                            from :tab_orders_pgi;

--Merging data from multiple table variables using UNION
Product_Summary = SELECT MATNR as MAT_NUM,
                        SUM(KWMENG) as ORDER_QTY,
                        SUM(LFIMG) as PGI_QTY,
                        SUM(KWMENG) - SUM(LFIMG) as OPEN_QTY,
                        SUM(NETWR) as ORDER_VALUE,
                        0 as RETURN_QTY,
                        0 as RETURN_VALUE
                        from :tab_orders_pgi group by MATNR
                UNION ALL
                        SELECT MATNR as MAT_NUM,
                        0 as ORDER_QTY,
                        0 as PGI_QTY,
                        0 as OPEN_QTY,
                        0 as ORDER_VALUE,
                        SUM(KWMENG) as RETURN_QTY,
                        SUM(NETWR) as RETURN_VALUE
                        from :tab_return_orders group by MATNR;

END
```

Execute the above code and observe the results generated for each of the table variables defined as output parameters

Result Table #1: Order Summary Table variable

Delivery status (ITEM_STATUS) has been derived based on Order Date and Goods Issue (PGI) date.

```
SQL | Result | Result
DO ( IN i_VKORG NVARCHAR(4) => '1000',
     IN i_FROMDATE DATE => '2011-01-01',
     IN i_TODATE DATE => '2011-12-31',
     OUT ORDER_SUMMARY TABLE (ORDER_NUM NVARCHAR(10),
```

	ORDER_NUM	ORDER_ITEM	ORDER_TYPE	ORDER_DATE	PGI_DATE	ORDER_QTY	PGI_QTY	ITEM_STATUS
8	0000014215	000010	TA	Dec 17, 2011	?	2	?	Open
9	0000014221	000001	TA	Dec 22, 2011	?	1	?	Open
10	0000013824	000010	TA	Jan 21, 2011	Jan 21, 2011	10	10	Closed
11	0000013825	000010	TA	Jan 21, 2011	Jan 21, 2011	7	7	Closed
12	0000013861	000010	TA	Feb 21, 2011	Feb 21, 2011	12	12	Closed
13	0000013862	000010	TA	Feb 21, 2011	Feb 21, 2011	9	9	Closed
14	0000013936	000010	TA	Mar 8, 2011	Mar 8, 2011	15	15	Closed
15	0000013937	000010	TA	Mar 8, 2011	Mar 8, 2011	9	9	Closed

Result Table #2: Product Summary Table Variable

Open Order Quantity (OPEN_QTY) is calculated based on Order Qty and Goods Issue Qty (PGI). Return Qty and Value are added to the table variable using the Union

```
SQL | Result | Result
DO ( IN i_VKORG NVARCHAR(4) => '1000',
     IN i_FROMDATE DATE => '2011-01-01',
     IN i_TODATE DATE => '2011-12-31',
     OUT ORDER_SUMMARY TABLE (ORDER_NUM NVARCHAR(10),
                              ORDER_ITEM NVARCHAR(4),|
```

	MAT_NUM	ORDER_QTY	PGI_QTY	OPEN_QTY	ORDER_VALUE	RETURN_QTY	RETURN_VALUE
1	GTS-RES-0001	100	100	0	100,000	0	0
2	GTS-30003	10	?	?	9,980	0	0
3	GTS-72002	10	10	0	2,500	0	0
4	GTS-14001	7	5	2	900,000	0	0
5	HT05-F10500	1	1	0	10	0	0
6	M-12	5	2	3	3,937	0	0

3.4 Predicates in HANA SQL

Predicates are typically used in the WHERE clause of a SELECT statement. A predicate is specified by combining one or more expressions or logical operators and returns one of the following logical or truth values: TRUE, FALSE, or UNKNOWN

Let us understand the essential predicates which can be used in the SQL Script queries with the help of some examples.

IN – To compare against a list of values using a sub query and fetch the matching records in the main query.

Example: Fetch all the Customers and their Total Order Value for the customers that belongs to US.

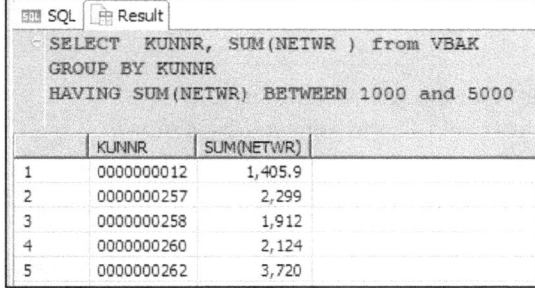

```
SQL  Result
SELECT  KUNNR, SUM(NETWR ) from VBAK
where KUNNR IN (SELECT KUNNR from KNA1 where LAND1 = 'US')
GROUP BY KUNNR
```

	KUNNR	SUM(NETWR)
1	TP-CUST30	210
2	TP_US_C_02	1,030
3	CMS0000041	73,369
4	0000000266	270,995
5	RFID_CUST	80

Note: We can use the **NOT IN** predicate to fetch the non-matching records in the above example.

BETWEEN – Use this to verify the existence of records within the given range of values

Example: Fetch all the Customers and their Total Order Value for the customers whose Total Order value is in the range of 1000 to 5000.

```
SQL  Result
SELECT  KUNNR, SUM(NETWR ) from VBAK
GROUP BY KUNNR
HAVING SUM(NETWR) BETWEEN 1000 and 5000
```

	KUNNR	SUM(NETWR)
1	0000000012	1,405.9
2	0000000257	2,299
3	0000000258	1,912
4	0000000260	2,124
5	0000000262	3,720

IS NULL – To validate the field for NULL values

Example: To identify the missing master data records (in MARA table) for the materials which has sales order items (VBAP table)

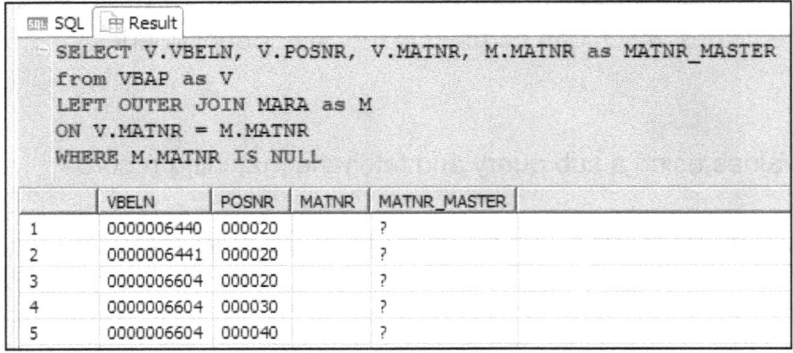

LIKE – To compare any character string field with a specific pattern

% → to refer to any set of characters

_ → to specify a placeholder for single characters

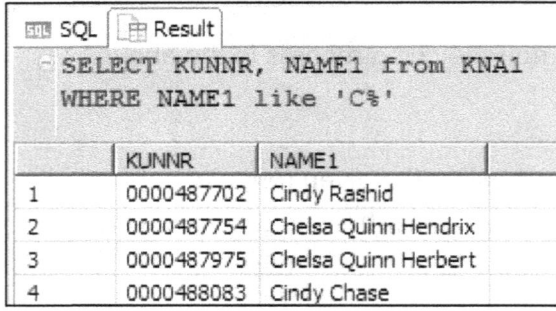

Example: Get the list of customers whose name starts with C.

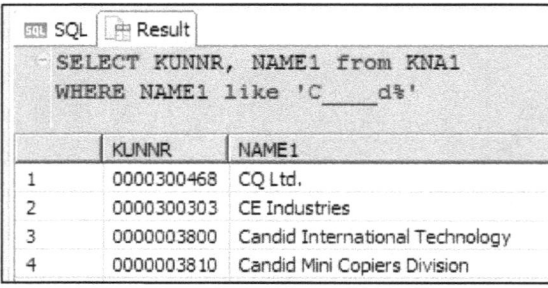

Example: Get the list of customers whose name starts with C and followed by 4 other characters and then a letter d, followed by any set of characters.

EXISTS – We can use this predicate validate the existence of matching records in a subquery. The main query returns only those records where the matching records or found in the subquery.

Example: Get the list of sales orders where the customers country is US.

SQL	Result

```
SELECT VBELN, ERDAT, KUNNR, NETWR from VBAK as A
WHERE EXISTS (SELECT KUNNR from KNA1 as B where B.KUNNR = A.KUNNR and B.LAND1 = 'US' )
```

	VBELN	ERDAT	KUNNR	NETWR
1	0000011767	20060324	TP-CUST30	10
2	0000011805	20060426	TP_US_C_02	1,000
3	0000011811	20060428	TP_US_C_02	30
4	0000013359	20090715	CMS0000...	1,999

ALL - We can use this predicate validate the existence of all the matching records in a subquery. This operator returns true only when all the subquery records meet the condition.

Example: List of customers where the total revenue is higher than the revenue of all customers of Sales Org. 1000.

SQL	Result

```
SELECT KUNNR, SUM(NETWR) from VBAK as A
GROUP BY KUNNR
HAVING SUM(NETWR) > ALL (SELECT SUM(NETWR)  from VBAK  as B where B.VKORG = '1000' GROUP BY KUNNR)
```

	KUNNR	SUM(NETWR)
1	0000003271	785,488,822.97
2	0000003279	296,726,437.9
3	0000012354	253,200,000
4	0000020001	111,625,111.2

DISTINCT- We can use this predicate to fetch the distinct set of values for a given column. This predicate is also commonly used to derive the DISTINCT COUNT as shown in the below example.

SQL	Result

```
SELECT VKORG, COUNT(DISTINCT(KUNNR)) from VBAK group by VKORG
```

	VKORG	COUNT(DISTINCT (KUNNR))
21	4110	5
22	4300	2
23	5000	4

3.5 Statements for Program Flow Control

SQL Script provides various programming constructs to control the flow of program execution. Typically, these statements are used to address the following requirements:

- Alter the processing flow conditionally
- Perform certain operations repetitively
- Terminate the processing block

3.5.1 Conditional Statements:

In several instances during the program flow, we need to apply the conditional logic to decide on the next set of statements to be executed.

IF Statement: Like most of the programming languages, we can use the IF statement to determine the set of operations to be executed based on the outcome of conditional expression.

Syntax:

```
IF <conditional_expression> THEN
        <statements>
[{ELSEIF <conditional_expression> THEN
        <statements> }...]
[ELSE
        <statements> ]
END IF
```

3.5.2 Looping Statements:

We can implement different types of looping operations to run a set of statements iteratively in SQL Script. Let us understand these operations with the use cases and examples.

WHILE Loop: Repeated execution of a set of statements based on the outcome of a conditional expression.

Syntax:

```
WHILE <Conditional expression> DO
        <statements>
END WHILE
```

FOR Loop: Perform operations iteratively by iterating a specific variable

Syntax:

FOR <Looping variable> IN [REVERSE] <Start> .. <End> DO
        <statements>
END FOR

BREAK Statement: We can use this statement to explicitly terminate the loop processing, either in WHILE loop or FOR loop.

CONTINUE Statement: We can use this statement to skip the current iteration and proceed with the next iteration, either in WHILE loop or FOR loop.

EXIT Statement: This is used to terminate the loop processing

Program Example for WHILE Loop: Populate the records in table variable in loop

```
DO
BEGIN

DECLARE V_SEQ INTEGER := 2;

TAB_PRIME = SELECT 1 as PRIME_NUM from DUMMY;

WHILE :V_SEQ <=10 DO

  TAB_PRIME = SELECT 1 as PRIME_NUM from DUMMY
                UNION ALL
                SELECT * from :TAB_PRIME;

     V_SEQ := :V_SEQ + 1;

END WHILE;

SELECT * FROM :TAB_PRIME;

END;
```

Execute the above code and verify the results as shown below.

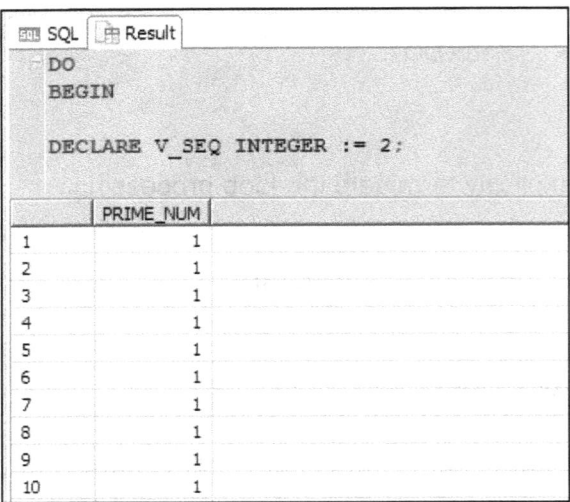

3.5.3 Program Example for WHILE Loop:

Derive the list of prime numbers between 1 to 10. In this example we can explore the usage of nested WHILE Loops and the usage of BREAK statement to terminate the loop

```
DO
BEGIN

DECLARE V_INDEX1 INTEGER := 1;
DECLARE V_INDEX2 INTEGER := 1;
DECLARE V_ROWNO INTEGER   := 2;
DECLARE V_NUM INTEGER := 1;
DECLARE V_FLAG NVARCHAR(1) := '';
DECLARE V_SEQ INTEGER := 2;

TAB_PRIME = SELECT 1 as PRIME_NUM from DUMMY;

--Initailize the Table variable values
WHILE :V_SEQ <=10 DO

  TAB_PRIME = SELECT 1 as PRIME_NUM from DUMMY
              UNION ALL
              SELECT * from :TAB_PRIME;
    V_SEQ := :V_SEQ + 1;
END WHILE;
```

```
WHILE :V_INDEX1 < 10 DO

    V_NUM := :V_NUM + 1;
    V_FLAG := 'Y';
    V_INDEX2 := 2;

    WHILE :V_INDEX2 <=  round(:V_NUM /2)    DO

        IF MOD(:V_NUM , :V_INDEX2) = 0 THEN
            V_FLAG := 'N';
            BREAK;
        END IF;
      V_INDEX2 := :V_INDEX2 + 1;
    END WHILE;
     if :V_FLAG = 'Y' THEN
      TAB_PRIME.PRIME_NUM[:V_ROWNO] = :V_NUM;
     END IF;

    V_ROWNO := :V_ROWNO + 1;
    V_INDEX1 := :V_INDEX1 + 1;

END WHILE;

SELECT DISTINCT (PRIME_NUM) from :TAB_PRIME;

END;
```

Execute the above code and verify the results (List of prime numbers between 1 to 10) as shown below.

```
SQL  Result
DO
BEGIN

DECLARE V_INDEX1 INTEGER := 1;
DECLARE V_INDEX2 INTEGER := 1;
```

	PRIME_NUM
1	1
2	2
3	3
4	5
5	7

3.5.4 Program Example: Process data in Table Variable using FOR Loop

Requirement: Generate a report on the sales orders for each of the customers and to show the difference of days between different sales orders (i.e. from previous order to the next order). This report will help in identifying the frequency of orders from the customers.

Solution approach:

- Implement an anonymous block to derive the results of sales orders
- Use FOR LOOP and process the records of a table variable sequentially to compare the customer number between the current record and previous record
- Evaluate the conditions using IF statement to implement the branching operations
- Make use of index-based access of table variable columns to perform calculations
- Perform the calculation to find the difference between current order date and previous order data using a standard function called DAYS_BETWEEN (Refer to the Unit 5 Functions SQL Script for more details about functions)

```
DO
BEGIN

DECLARE v_days_order integer;
DECLARE v_loop_counter integer;
DECLARE v_order_count integer;
DECLARE v_loop_prev integer;
DECLARE v_date1 date;
DECLARE v_date2 date;

--Populate the sales orders into a table variable
TAB_SALES = SELECT VBELN,
                   KUNNR,
                   ERDAT,
                   0 as DAYS_BETWEEN_ORDERS from VBAK
            where ERDAT between '20150101' and '20151231'
            order by KUNNR ASC, ERDAT ASC;

--Get the count of records in table variable
SELECT count(*) into v_order_count from :TAB_SALES;
    v_loop_prev = 1;
```

```
--Process each record of table variable to calculate the days
--between orders for each of the customers
FOR v_loop_counter in 1..:v_order_count DO

if :v_loop_counter > 1 then
      v_loop_prev = :v_loop_counter - 1;
end if;
--Compare if the Customer number is same as the previous record
if :TAB_SALES.KUNNR[:v_loop_counter] =
:TAB_SALES.KUNNR[:v_loop_prev] then

  v_date1 = :TAB_SALES.ERDAT[v_loop_prev] ;
  v_date2 = :TAB_SALES.ERDAT[v_loop_counter] ;

--Calculate the days since last sales order
  SELECT days_between(:v_date1, :v_date2)
                     into v_days_order  from DUMMY;
--Update value in the respective column & row of table variable
  TAB_SALES.DAYS_BETWEEN_ORDERS[:V_LOOP_COUNTER] = :v_days_order;

end if;
END FOR;

--Return the list of output records from table variable
      SELECT * FROM :TAB_SALES;
End;
```

Output: Execute the anonymous block in SQL console and observe the results. Verify if the "DAYS_BETWEEN_ORDERS" is derived correctly.

SQL | Result

```
DO
BEGIN

DECLARE v_days_order integer;
DECLARE v_loop_counter integer;
```

	VBELN	KUNNR	ERDAT	DAYS_BETWEEN_ORDERS
4	0000016698	0000001000	20150320	0
5	0000016751	0000001000	20150408	19
6	0000020157	0000001390	20151218	0
7	0000020158	0000001390	20151220	2
8	0010000063	0000001600	20150106	0
9	0000016527	0000001600	20150107	1

4 Stored Procedures

In the previous units, we have gone through the essential building blocks of SQL script programming. However, to build a standalone solution using SQL Script with all the desired processing logic, we need to implement the repository objects that can be called explicitly from different parts of the overall solution. Stored procedures and Functions are the key repository objects to implement such processing blocks in SQL Script. Depending on the use case and the desired functionality, we shall decide whether to implement a stored procedure or a function.

Stored procedures are the reusable processing blocks of SQL Script statements, which can be used to implement the logic for both reading and updating data in HANA database. In this unit, we will explore the various features, use cases and the approaches to implement and call the stored procedures.

4.1 Role of Stored procedures in HANA

We need to implement stored procedures to build the solutions for the scenarios like:

1) Reusable logic – To implement complex logic that cannot be achieved using graphical calculation views and to perform data conversions, calculations etc.

- Procedures can be defined as Read only OR Read / Write Procedures
- These are the typical ways of calling procedures:
    - Calling stored procedures from another procedure or function
    - Scheduling the procedure call from XS Job engine which is in-build in HANA
    - Scheduling the procedure call from Smart Data Integration (SDI) jobs internally in HANA OR using external ETL tools such as Business Objects Data Services

2) Persisting results in HANA database – example to store the Snapshots of results. These are typically the reusable results of HANA views, to avoid frequent execution of complex views. We also need to implement snapshot-based solutions to store the values such as inventory snapshots for specific weeks or periods, open orders, demand and forecast snapshots of specific periods etc.

4.2 Types of Stored procedures

Stored Procedures can be created in the following ways:

1. Catalog Procedures: These are not transportable, since they are created using the CREATE PROCEDURE statement and they are not created under a package. Catalog procedures are defined under a database schema.

2. Repository Procedures: These are the procedures created using the HANA development perspective (Extension .hdbprocedure). These procedures are always created under a specific package.

   Note: This is the recommended approach for creating stored procedures since they can be transported, and version management is also possible

Definition of procedure:

```
PROCEDURE <Name> (Parameters)
      LANGUAGE SQLSCRIPT
      SQL SECURITY INVOKER / DEFINER
      DEFAULT SCHEMA <SCHEMA>
      READ ONLY
       AS
BEGIN
      --- Processing Block----

END;
```

Calling Procedure:

```
CALL <Procedure Name> (<Actual Parameters>);
```

Parameter types:

IN: These are passed as input values to the procedure

OUT: They will act as return values from the procedure

INOUT: Combination of both the above – acts both as and input and return values

We can use both Scalar variables and Table Variables as the parameters for stored procedures.

DEFAULT SCHEMA: This option will help us to specify the Database Schema of the database objects such as tables and views which are being accessed the body of the procedure.

READ ONLY: This option will restrict procedure to perform any data manipulations on the data base tables. Please note that the parallel processing is only supported by READ ONLY procedures. Remove this option, whenever you implement a procedure that performs some data manipulations on tables.

Key Features of Catalog based Stored Procedures

As already described in the previous section, a database procedure comprises input parameters, output parameters, and the processing logic.

Major differences between stored procedures and information views in HANA:

1) Stored procedure can return multiple result sets (called Output parameters), where as a HANA view (calculation views) can return only one result set
2) Stored procedures can READ and UPDATE the database, while the information views can only read data

Technically we can use SQL to Create, Call, Change or Delete database procedures.

- CREATE PROCEDURE statement to create a new database procedure.
- CREATE TYPE command to create a table type for use in the database procedure interface.
- ALTER PROCEDURE statement to recompile the calculation model for a database procedure.
- CALL statement to call a database procedure.
- DROP PROCEDURE statement to delete a database procedure

Even though we can execute these commands directly via the SQL console, it is not the recommended approach (except for simple tests), because procedures created via the SQL console are not stored in the SAP HANA Repository.

Essential features like version management and transport management are only supported by repository-based objects. Hence, it is recommended to use the SAP HANA Development perspective or Web IDE to create database procedures in the SAP HANA Repository.

4.3 Using Parameters to exchange data with stored procedures

In Stored Procedures we can use the Input (IN), Output (OUT) and Input/Output (INOUT) parameters, to get data into and results out of procedures. The OUT parameters can either be bound to other SQLScript variables (when we call the procedure from another procedure), or a HANA client can read the result sets that get created for each OUT parameter of type TABLE). For example, a Business Objects Data Services client would find multiple result sets after the procedure execution and would fetch those.

Let us understand the process of defining and calling stored procedures through some examples.

Example #1: In the following example, we will create a stored procedure (Catalog based) with an output parameter which is a table variable

```
CREATE PROCEDURE NVARMA.PR_GET_SALES
        (OUT SALES_TAB TABLE(KUNNR NVARCHAR(10),
                             TOTAL_VALUE DECIMAL(18,2)))
LANGUAGE SQLSCRIPT
DEFAULT SCHEMA <Schema for ECC Data>
READS SQL DATA AS

BEGIN
     SALES_TAB = Select KUNNR,
                        SUM(NETWR) as TOTAL_VALUE
                 from VBAK
                 GROUP BY KUNNR;
END;
```

We can call the procedure using the statement below and observe the results. To display the values of output variables using ? symbol.

```
CALL NVARMA.PR_GET_SALES(?);
```

	KUNNR	TOTAL_VALUE
1		0
2	0000000001	0
3	0000000011	796.5
4	0000000012	1,405.9
5	0000000255	6,971

Example #2: In the following example, we are calling a stored procedure from another procedure and exchanging the values through parameters.

```
CREATE PROCEDURE NVARMA.PR_GET_SALES_ABOVE_LIMIT
(   IN V_LIMIT DECIMAL(18,2),
    OUT SALES_TAB_NEW TABLE(KUNNR NVARCHAR(10),
                            TOTAL_VALUE DECIMAL(18,2)))
LANGUAGE SQLSCRIPT
DEFAULT SCHEMA <Schema for ECC Data>
READS SQL DATA AS
BEGIN
DECLARE TAB_SALES TABLE(KUNNR NVARCHAR(10),
                        TOTAL_VALUE DECIMAL(18,2));
CALL NVARMA.PR_GET_SALES(TAB_SALES);
    SALES_TAB_NEW = Select  KUNNR, TOTAL_VALUE
                    from :TAB_SALES
                    WHERE TOTAL_VALUE > V_LIMIT;
END;
```

When we can call the procedure `PR_GET_SALES_ABOVE_LIMIT` using the statement as shown below, it will in turn call the procedure `PR_GET_SALES` which returns a table variable.

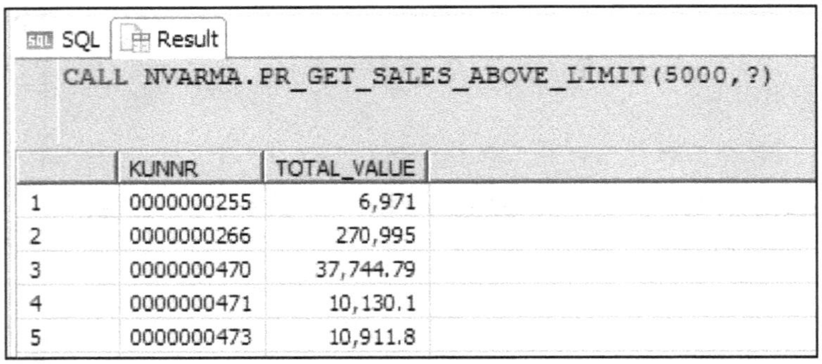

	KUNNR	TOTAL_VALUE	
	CALL NVARMA.PR_GET_SALES_ABOVE_LIMIT(5000,?)		
1	0000000255	6,971	
2	0000000266	270,995	
3	0000000470	37,744.79	
4	0000000471	10,130.1	
5	0000000473	10,911.8	

Statement for Creating a Table Type

In the previous example we have defined the table variables as output parameter using inline definition of the structure. Using Table types, we can implement reusable structures in HANA database, which can be used to declare table variables in all the processing blocks of HANA. Table Types are an enhancement to the SQL standard and are part of the data types supported by the HANA database.

We can define the table types in two ways:

1) Catalog based – These are not transportable objects
2) Repository object – These are created under specific package and support transport and version control

Catalog based table types can be defined using the statement CREATE TYPE:

CREATE TYPE <type_name> AS TABLE (<column_definition>

[{,<column_definition>}...])

Creating a Stored Procedure using catalog based Table Type:

In the following example, we will create the database tables, table type and stored procedures as catalog objects. We need to execute the statements directly in SQL console to create the catalog-based objects in the respective database schema.

Step #1: Create the database tables for Products, Market and Sales data

```
SET SCHEMA NVARMA;
---- Create Product table

DROP TABLE "NVARMA"."PRODUCT" ;
create column table "NVARMA"."PRODUCT"(
     "PRODUCT_ID" NVARCHAR(10),
     "PRODUCT_NAME" VARCHAR (100),
     primary key ("PRODUCT_ID")
);

insert into "PRODUCT" values('P01', 'Chocolate');
insert into "PRODUCT" values('P02','Cake');
insert into "PRODUCT" values('P03','Biscuit');
insert into "PRODUCT" values('P04','Candy');
insert into "PRODUCT" values('P05' ,'Chips');
```

```
SET SCHEMA NVARMA;
DROP TABLE MARKET;
-- Create Market table
create column table NVARMA."MARKET"(
     "MARKET_ID" NVARCHAR(2),
     "REGION_NAME" VARCHAR (100),
     "MARKET_NAME" VARCHAR (100),
     PRIMARY KEY ("MARKET_ID")
);

insert into "MARKET" values('M1','Americas','North-America');
insert into "MARKET" values('M2','Americas','South-America');
insert into "MARKET" values('M3','Asia','India');
insert into "MARKET" values('M4','Asia','Japan');
insert into "MARKET" values('M5','Europe','Germany');
```

```
-- Create Sales table
Drop Table "NVARMA"."SALES_DATA";
create column table "NVARMA"."SALES_DATA"(
     "MARKET_ID" NVARCHAR(2),
     "PRODUCT_ID" NVARCHAR(10) ,
     "SALES_AMOUNT" DOUBLE, PRIMARY KEY ("MARKET_ID",
"PRODUCT_ID") );

insert into "SALES_DATA" values('M1','P01',10000);
insert into "SALES_DATA" values('M2','P01',9900);
insert into "SALES_DATA" values('M5','P01',8005);
insert into "SALES_DATA" values('M2','P02',8800);
insert into "SALES_DATA" values('M1','P02',7500);
insert into "SALES_DATA" values('M3','P03',1250);
insert into "SALES_DATA" values('M4','P04',4500);
insert into "SALES_DATA" values('M1','P04',6500);
insert into "SALES_DATA" values('M2','P05',5000);
```

Step #2: Create a Table Type which is used define a Table Variable as parameter in the stored procedure

```
DROP TYPE NVARMA.TT_SALES ;
CREATE TYPE NVARMA.TT_SALES AS TABLE (
         PRODUCT_NAME NVARCHAR(20),
         REGION_NAME NVARCHAR(100),
         MARKET_NAME NVARCHAR(100),
         SALES_AMOUNT DECIMAL,
         NET_AMOUNT DECIMAL
         ) ;
```

Step #3: Create a stored procedure to calculate the discount on the sales revenue and to add the Tax to calculate Net Sales amount

```
DROP PROCEDURE NVARMA."PR_SALES_REPORT";

CREATE PROCEDURE NVARMA."PR_SALES_REPORT"(
         IN DISCOUNT INTEGER,
         OUT SALES_TABLE NVARMA."TT_SALES" )
LANGUAGE SQLSCRIPT
DEFAULT SCHEMA NVARMA
AS
/*********BEGIN PROCEDURE SCRIPT ************/
BEGIN

Declare V_NUM INTEGER := 10;

T_SALES = SELECT T2.REGION_NAME, T2.MARKET_NAME, T1.PRODUCT_ID,
T1.SALES_AMOUNT
         FROM SALES_DATA AS T1
         INNER JOIN MARKET AS T2
         ON T1.MARKET_ID = T2.MARKET_ID;

T_PROD =  SELECT T1.REGION_NAME, T1.MARKET_NAME, T1.PRODUCT_ID,
T1.SALES_AMOUNT, T2.PRODUCT_NAME
         FROM :T_SALES AS T1
         INNER JOIN PRODUCT AS T2
         ON T1.PRODUCT_ID = T2.PRODUCT_ID;
```

```
SALES_BASE = SELECT
                    SUM(SALES_AMOUNT) AS SALES_AMOUNT,
              SUM( SALES_AMOUNT - (SALES_AMOUNT * :DISCOUNT/
100)) AS SALES_AFTER_DISCOUNT,
              CASE when "REGION_NAME" = 'Americas' then 30
                   when "REGION_NAME" = 'Europe' then 20
                   else 10 end as TAX_PERCENT,
         PRODUCT_NAME,
         REGION_NAME,
         MARKET_NAME
         FROM :T_PROD
         GROUP BY PRODUCT_NAME, REGION_NAME, MARKET_NAME;

SALES_TABLE = SELECT PRODUCT_NAME, REGION_NAME, MARKET_NAME,
                    SALES_AMOUNT,
                     (SALES_AFTER_DISCOUNT +
SALES_AFTER_DISCOUNT * TAX_PERCENT /100) as NET_AMOUNT
              FROM :SALES_BASE;

END;
```

Step #4: Execute the procedure in SQL Console using the CALL statement and observe the results:

SQL	Result				
CALL NVARMA."PR_SALES_REPORT"(15, ?)					
	PRODUCT_NAME	REGION_NAME	MARKET_NAME	SALES_AMOUNT	NET_AMOUNT
1	Chocolate	Americas	North-America	10,000	11,050
2	Chocolate	Americas	South-America	9,900	10,939.5
3	Chocolate	Europe	Germany	8,005	8,165.1000000000003...
4	Cake	Americas	South-America	8,800	9,724
5	Cake	Americas	North-America	7,500	8,287.5
6	Biscuit	Asia	India	1,250	1,168.75
7	Candy	Asia	Japan	4,500	4,207.5
8	Candy	Americas	North-America	6,500	7,182.5
9	Chips	Americas	South-America	5,000	5,525

4.4 Examples for Stored procedures (Repository Based)

We would like to implement a stored procedure to derive the delivery status of each sales order item (Tables: VBAK, VBAP and LIPS). Let us build this procedure in the HANA studio under Development Perspective. Same approach need to be used while working with HANA Web IDE also.

Step #1: Create the following table type as repository object (Extension .hdbstructure)

Choose the respective package within the repository workspace.

Menu path: New → Other → General → File

Name: SALES_ORDER_STATUS.hdbstructure

```
table.schemaName = "NVARMA";
table.columns =
  [
    {name = "ORDER_NO";  sqlType = VARCHAR;  length = 10; },
    {name = "ORDER_ITEM";  sqlType = VARCHAR;  length = 6; },
    {name = "ORDER_QTY";  sqlType = DOUBLE;  },
    {name = "DEL_QTY";  sqlType = DOUBLE;  },
    {name = "OPEN_QTY";  sqlType = DOUBLE;  },
    {name = "ORDER_STATUS";  sqlType = VARCHAR;  length = 20; }
];
```

Save and Activate the structure.

Step #2: Create the following stored procedure (Extension .hdbprocedure)

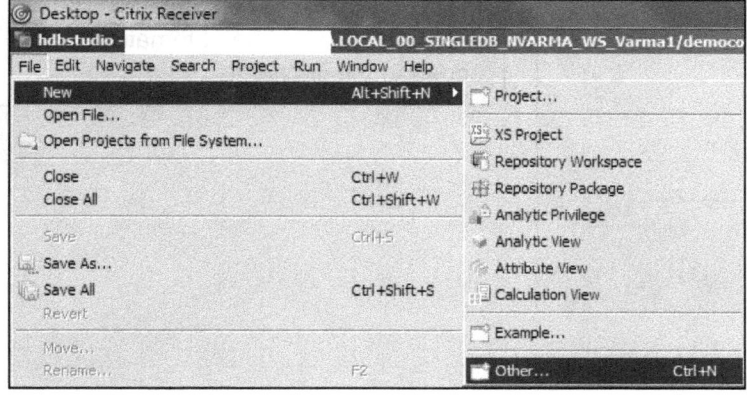

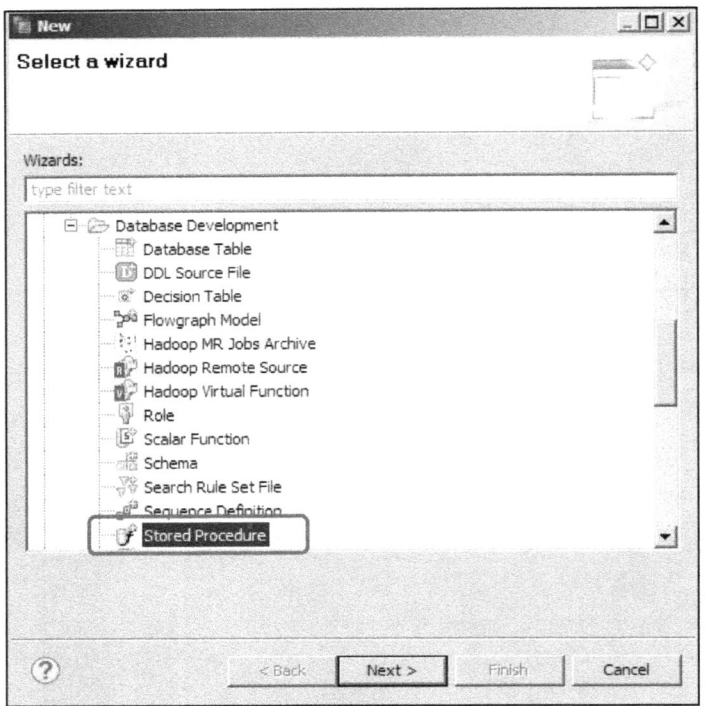

Choose the "Stored Procedure" option under the Database Development folder

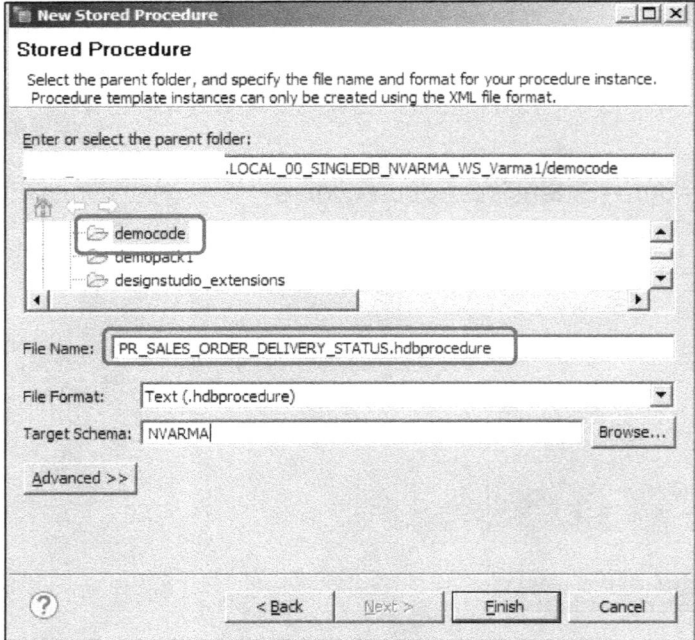

Choose the Package and enter the Procedure name. The extension .hdbprocedure will be automatically added to the file name.

Enter the source code of the procedure as shown below.

```
PROCEDURE "NVARMA"."democode::PR_SALES_ORDER_DELIVERY_STATUS"
      ( IN DATEFROM DATE,
        IN DATETO DATE,
        OUT ORDER_STATUS "NVARMA"."democode::SALES_ORDER_STATUS")
      LANGUAGE SQLSCRIPT
      SQL SECURITY INVOKER
      DEFAULT SCHEMA <SCHEMA NAME>
      READS SQL DATA AS
BEGIN
/****************************
      Write your procedure logic
****************************/

DECLARE V_FLAG NVARCHAR(1);

--Fetch Sales order Header records for the given Date Range

T_ORDERS = SELECT MANDT, VBELN, ERDAT, KUNNR, VKORG from VBAK
              where ERDAT BETWEEN :DATEFROM and :DATETO;

--Fetch Sales order Items of the corresponding orders

T_ORDER_ITEMS = SELECT ITEM.MANDT, ITEM.VBELN , ITEM.POSNR,
MATNR, KWMENG, MEINS from VBAP as ITEM
              INNER JOIN :T_ORDERS as HDR
              on ITEM.MANDT = HDR.MANDT and
                 ITEM.VBELN = HDR.VBELN;

--Fetch Delivery items for the respective Sales order Items

T_DEL_ITEMS = SELECT ITEM.VBELN , ITEM.POSNR, ITEM.MATNR,
ITEM.KWMENG, ITEM.MEINS, DLV.LFIMG  from :T_ORDER_ITEMS as ITEM
              LEFT OUTER JOIN LIPS as DLV
              on ITEM.MANDT = DLV.MANDT and
                 ITEM.VBELN = DLV.VGBEL and
                 ITEM.POSNR = DLV.VGPOS;
```

Table Type used to define table variable as the Output parameter.

```
--Derive Open Order Qty and status for each Sales order item
ORDER_STATUS = SELECT VBELN as ORDER_NO,
                      POSNR as ORDER_ITEM,
                      KWMENG as ORDER_QTY,
                      LFIMG as DEL_QTY,
                      KWMENG - LFIMG as OPEN_QTY,
                      CASE
                      when LFIMG >= KWMENG then 'Completed'
                      else 'Open' end as ORDER_STATUS
                      from :T_DEL_ITEMS;

END;
```

Step #3: Save and Activate the repository stored procedure using the popup menu (Team → Activate). Activation will be successful only when there are no syntax errors.

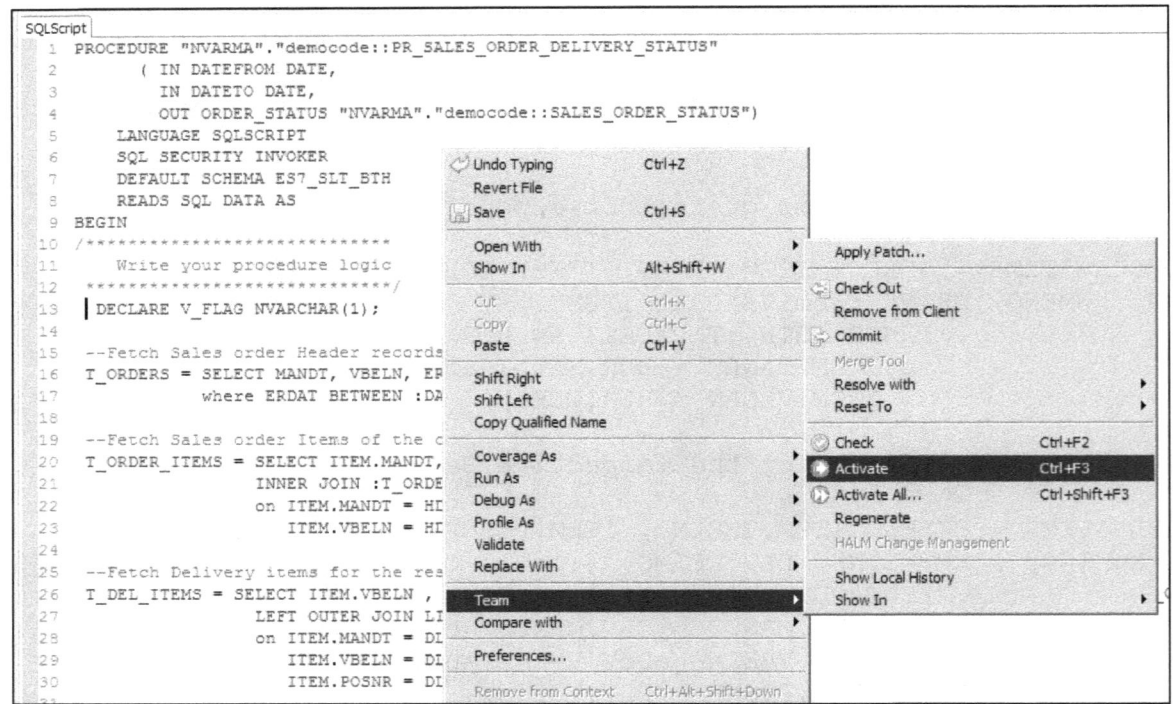

Step #4: Execute the stored procedure using CALL statement in SQL Console

```
CALL "NVARMA"."democode::PR_SALES_ORDER_DELIVERY_STATUS"
('2012-01-01', '2012-12-31', ?);
```

```
SQL   Result

CALL "NVARMA"."democode::PR_SALES_ORDER_DELIVERY_STATUS" ('2012-01-01', '2012-12-31', ?)
```

	ORDER_NO	ORDER_ITEM	ORDER_QTY	DEL_QTY	OPEN_QTY	ORDER_STATUS
148	0000014441	000010	100	?	?	Open
149	0000014442	000010	10	?	?	Open
150	0000014444	000010	300	300	0	Completed
151	0000014445	000010	500	350	150	Open
152	0000014445	000010	500	150	350	Open
153	0000014446	000010	10	?	?	Open
154	0000014446	000020	10	?	?	Open
155	0000014447	000010	10	10	0	Completed
156	0000014447	000020	10	10	0	Completed

```
Statement 'CALL "NVARMA"."democode::PR_SALES_ORDER_DELIVERY_STATUS" ('2012-01-01', '2012-12-31', ?)'
successfully prepared
```

Note: We can also create the stored procedures using the Web IDE with the same approach. Login to HANA database using Web IDE URL and follow the below path to create a stored procedure.

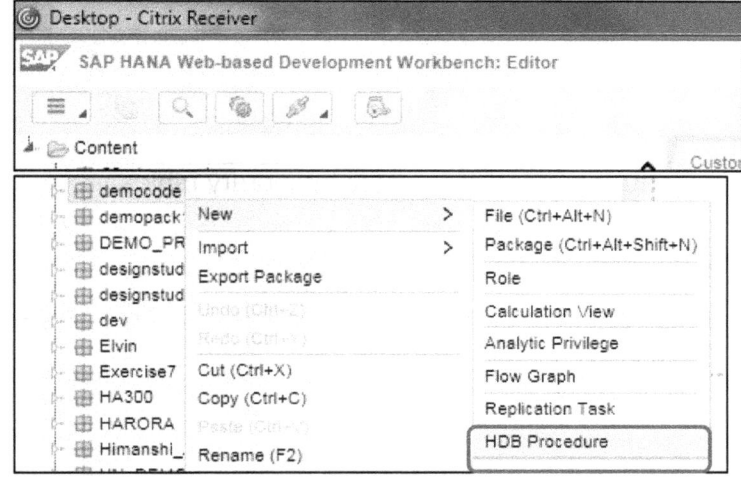

4.4.1 Local Temporary Table Variables

One of the challenges we encounter with the table variables is that we cannot perform any data manipulations on these, using the standard SQL operations such as INSERT or UPDATE. We can address this limitation using the local temporary tables, which are created with the same structure as the table variable. However, all the data manipulations can be performed on the temporary table variables.

After we perform all the necessary data manipulations using temporary table, it can be assigned to the table variable using a SELECT statement. At the end of the processing block we need to clear the temporary tables. Otherwise we may get a run-time error in the next execution of the block, which states that the table already exists. Local temporary table name should always start with a '#'.

```
CREATE PROCEDURE NVARMA.PR_SALES_DATA_TEMP
AS
BEGIN

CREATE local temporary table #tmp_sales
    (MATNR NVARCHAR(18),
    SALES_QTY DECIMAL(18,2),
    SALES_UOM NVARCHAR(3));

INSERT into #tmp_sales (SELECT MATNR, SUM(KWMENG), VRKME
                        from VBAP GROUP BY MATNR, VRKME);
SELECT * from #tmp_sales;
DROP Table #tmp_sales;

END;
```

Call the stored procedure and observe the results generated by local temporary tables.

SQL | Result

CALL NVARMA.PR_SALES_DATA_TEMP

	MATNR	SALES_QTY	SALES_UOM
1	M-17	9,061	ST
2	M-15	7,384	ST
3	M-07	11,121	ST
4	M-16	7,366	ST
5	M-08	10,214	ST
6	M-04	8,549	ST

4.5 Global Session Variables

For certain requirements we should be able to preserve the values of some variables during the entire user session and process them within multiple stored procedures and functions. Global session variables (introduced in HANA 1.0 SPS12) are the solution for this. These variables can be used to share scalar values between procedures and functions which runs in the same user session.

- We can use the SET statement to define global session variables and assign values.
  Syntax: SET '<Global Variable>' = <Value>;
- We can read the values of global session variables by using the built-in function called SESSION_CONTEXT in a nested procedure or function call.

In the following example, we will be creating two stored procedure to understand the process of defining and accessing the Global Session variables

```
--Procedure that creates the Global Session Variable
CREATE PROCEDURE NVARMA.DEMO_SESSION_VAR (
          OUT RESULT_VALUE integer)
AS
BEGIN
SET 'GV_VALUE' = 100;

     CALL GET_GLOBAL_VAR(RESULT_VALUE );
END;

--Procedure that reads the value from Global Session Variable
CREATE PROCEDURE NVARMA.GET_GLOBAL_VAR ( OUT V_RESULT integer  )
AS
BEGIN
   V_RESULT = SESSION_CONTEXT('GV_VALUE');
END;
```

Observe the value of Global session variable

SQL	Result	
CALL NVARMA.DEMO_SESSION_VAR(?)		
	Out(1)	
1	100	

4.6 Real time reporting vs Persistence Based Solutions

One of the key decision criteria that we often encounter in the HANA modeling solutions is whether to implement the calculations views to enable real time reporting or to implement it based on the persisted results, which are stored in a custom table in HANA. These custom tables shall be updated using stored procedures or flow graphs (SDI)

Which are the ideal scenarios to implement Persistence based solutions?
- Some of the highly processing intensive calculations where the real time reporting is not desired (For example: Flatting of hierarchies)
- The scenarios like calculating and storing snapshots of results (such as weekly inventory snapshots)

Solution Approach: Implement the core logic using Procedures in HANA to persist the results in a database table. Subsequently a calculation view can be built on this table to enable reporting.

Persistence Based Solutions: Solution Approach Diagram:

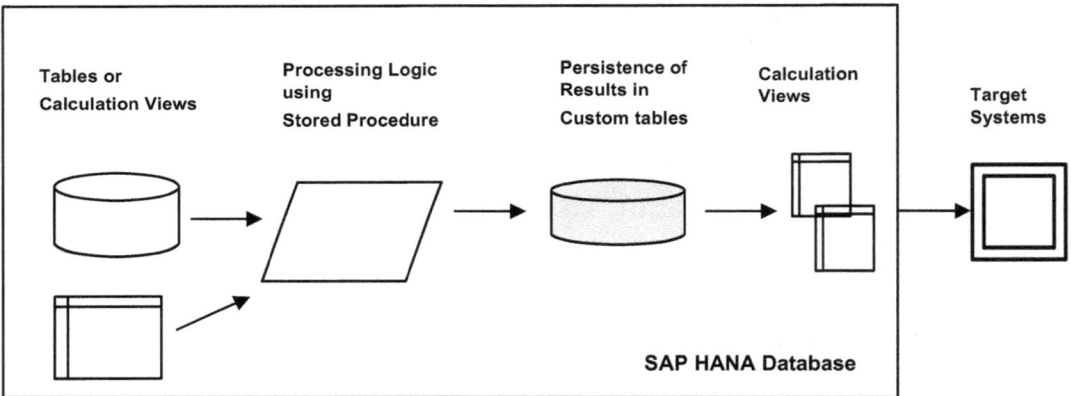

Advantages:
- Allows us build historical truth-based reporting solutions in HANA such as Snapshots
- Optimal system performance by avoiding repeated execution of complex logic

Disadvantages:
- Does not provide real time reporting
- Needs additional storage in HANA database to persist the results

→ *Example for Practice*
    Refer to the following for "Persistence based solutions using stored procedures"
    7.4 Business Case: Implementing Sales Order Delivery Status Snapshots

5 Functions in SQL Script

Modularization and code reusability are essential features of any programming language, since they are quite essential to implement complex solutions in a structured and more easily manageable approach. Procedures and Functions are the two common techniques to achieve modularization in HANA SQL Script programming.

Quite often we will come across the requirements, for which we can implement reusable functions that can be called from different parts of the HANA data models and other applications running on HANA database. Apart from that, we need to know how to leverage the wide range of built-in functions of the HANA database to address several requirements.

In this unit, we will explore the usage of various built-in functions as well as the techniques to implement the user defined functions in SQL Script. We will also learn about the Table Functions and Scalar Functions, which are needed in achieving complex business logic that cannot be implementing using the graphical calculation views in HANA.

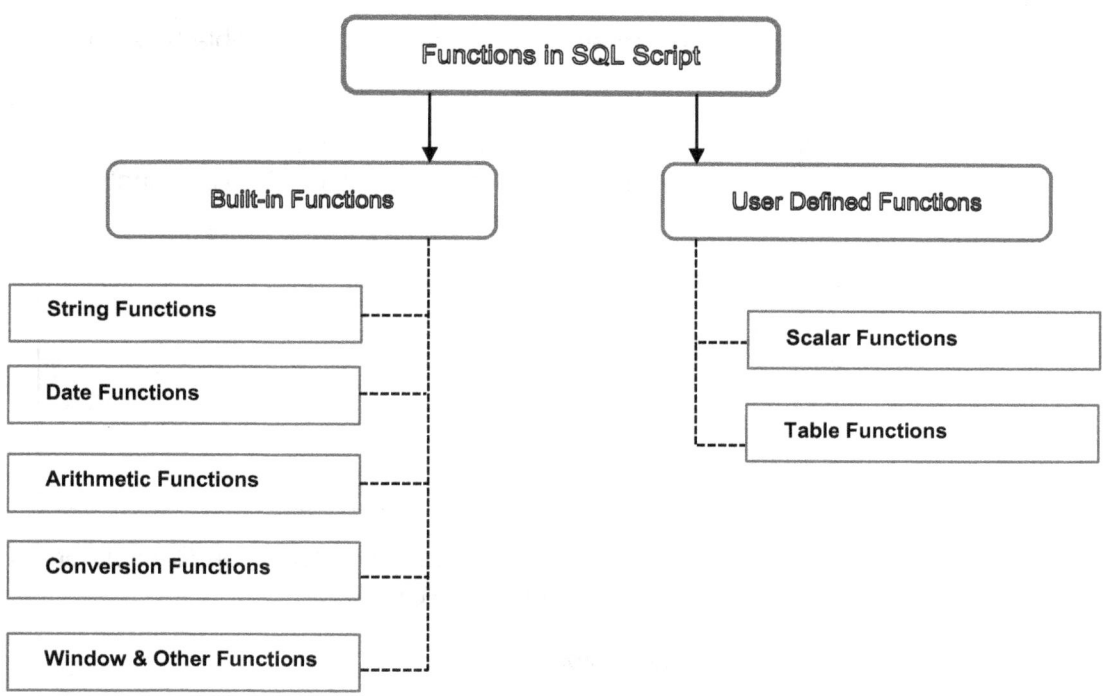

5.1 Built-in Functions in SQL Script

In this section we are going to explore the built-in functions in SQL Script, which can be used to perform common operations. These standard functions will help us greatly while implementing the logic in SQL script.

Note: DUMMY is a pseudo table in SAP HANA database, which does not have any structure. Hence it can be used to run a query to derive one of more columns with the required functionality. We will be using the DUMMY table to run the queries in various examples.

5.1.1 Data Type Conversion Functions

In different scenarios, we will find the requirement to move the data of one data type to another. This can be achieved using the Conversion Functions.

TO_DATE: This function will allow us to convert a field of another compatible type and value into a DATE field.

Example: In the below example, the field AEDAT in table EKKO is maintained as NVARCHAR(8). We shall use the TO_DATE function to convert it into DATE format.

```
SELECT EBELN, AEDAT, to_date(AEDAT), to_date('2018-01-01') as REPORT_DATE from EKKO
where EKORG = '1000'
```

	EBELN	AEDAT	TO_DATE(AEDAT)	REPORT_DATE
1	4500017109	20060508	May 8, 2006	Jan 1, 2018
2	4500017343	20100329	Mar 29, 2010	Jan 1, 2018
3	4500017377	20110518	May 18, 2011	Jan 1, 2018
4	4500017793	20131205	Dec 5, 2013	Jan 1, 2018
5	3005000581	20111111	Nov 11, 2011	Jan 1, 2018

Note: Similar to the TO_DATE function, we can also use the other data type Conversion functions such as TO_DECIMAL, TO_STRING, TO_NVARCHAR etc.

CAST: To convert a field to the desired data type.

Syntax: CAST (<expression> AS <data_type>)

Example: We can use the CAST function to convert a Decimal field such as EKKO.WKURS to VARCHAR data type, since we want to use it in the Character string function like CONCAT.

```
SQL | Result
  SELECT lfa1.lifnr,
                 lfa1.name1,
                 ekko.ebeln,
                 ekko.bukrs,
                 concat( 'Exch Rate: ',cast(ekko.wkurs as varchar(15))) as EXCH_RATE
         FROM lfa1 AS lfa1 LEFT OUTER JOIN ekko AS ekko
         ON lfa1.lifnr = ekko.lifnr
```

	LIFNR	NAME1	EBELN	BUKRS	EXCH_RATE	
1	0000000002	Electronic Components Distributor	4600000018	1000	Exch Rate: 0.51129	
2	0000000002	Electronic Components Distributor	5500000043	1000	Exch Rate: 1.00000	
3	0000000002	Electronic Components Distributor	5500000016	1000	Exch Rate: 0.51129	
4	0000000002	Electronic Components Distributor	5500000003	1000	Exch Rate: 0.51129	
5	0000000008	Jose Fernandez	4500017149	3000	Exch Rate: 0.09000	

COLEASCE: Returns the first non-NULL argument from a given list. At least two arguments are needed in the list, and all these must be comparable. It will return the result as NULL only when all the arguments are NULL.

Example: We need to derive the STREET_ADDRESS based on the lookup on multiple tables such as ADRC and KNA1 and return the STREET value which based on an order of precedence (i.e to return the first non-NULL value).

```
SQL | Result
  SELECT KUNNR, C.NAME1,C.STRAS, A.STREET, COALESCE( A.STREET, C.STRAS) as STREET_ADDRESS
  from KNA1 AS C
  left outer join ADRC as A
  on C.ADRNR = A.ADDRNUMBER
  where C.LAND1 = 'IN'
```

	KUNNR	NAME1	STRAS	STREET	STREET_ADDRESS	
104	0000090062	Paragon	#123	?	#123	
105	0000090064	dell	jublee	?	jublee	
106	CUSTWS_01	WholeSaler 1 -Bangalore				
107	CUSTWS_...	Wholesaler 1 Bangalore-No...				
108	CUSTWS_...	Wholesaler 1 Bangalore-So...				
109	0000301435	3000	123 abc	abc	abc	

5.1.2 Arithmetic Functions

We can leverage these functions to perform some of the commonly needed arithmetic operations.

ABS – To return absolute (Non-negative) value of a given number

SQRT – Square root of a given number

CEIL – Returns the nearest whole number greater than the given number

FLOOR – Returns the nearest whole number lesser than the given number

ROUND – To perform the rounding of number to the nearest decimal

Example:

```
SQL   Result
    SELECT ABS(15.5) , SQRT(25), CEIL(25.6), FLOOR(25.6), ROUND(25.6789, 2) from dummy
```

	ABS(15.5)	SQRT(25)	CEIL(25.6)	FLOOR(25.6)	ROUND(25.6789,2)
1	15.5	5	26	25	25.68

NDIV0 – Useful to perform Division operation without the possibility of "Divide by Zero" exception. It returns 0 when the denominator is 0; else, it returns the result of the division.

Example:

```
SELECT NDIV0(100,0) as RESULT from dummy;
```

Note: NDIV0 function is available from HANA 2.0 (SP2)

5.1.3 Date Time based Functions

Date and Time related calculation are quite commonly needed while implementing business logic. SQL Script has rich set of built in Date / Time functions. Let us explore the usage of these date functions with various examples.

CURRENT_DATE: Returns the current date

NOW: Returns the Current Date and Timestamp

	CURRENT_DATE	CURRENT_TIMESTAMP
1	Nov 9, 2018	Nov 9, 2018 11:12:32.731 PM

```
SELECT CURRENT_DATE, NOW() FROM DUMMY
```

DAYS_BETWEEN: To return the number of days difference between two date variables. For example, we can use this to derive the number of days difference between the Sales order creation date and current date.

Syntax: DAYS_BETWEEN(<Date Field1>, <Date Field2>)

```
SELECT VBELN, ERDAT, CURRENT_DATE, DAYS_BETWEEN(ERDAT, CURRENT_DATE) from VBAK
where VKORG = '1000'
```

	VBELN	ERDAT	CURRENT_DATE	DAYS_BETWEEN(ERDAT,CURRENT_DATE)
1	0000011782	20060418	Nov 9, 2018	4,588
2	0000011784	20060418	Nov 9, 2018	4,588
3	0000011801	20060425	Nov 9, 2018	4,581
4	0000011802	20060425	Nov 9, 2018	4,581
5	0000011808	20060427	Nov 9, 2018	4,579

LAST_DAY: Returns the last day of the month for the given date value.

```
SELECT LAST_DAY (TO_DATE ('2010-01-04', 'YYYY-MM-DD')) "last day" FROM DUMMY
```

	last day	
1	Jan 31, 2010	

ADD_MONTHS: To add or subtract specific number of months from a given date field

Syntax: ADD_MONTHS(<Date Field>, <Number of months>)

🔲 SQL	🔢 Result	

```
SELECT ADD_MONTHS (TO_DATE ('2009-12-05', 'YYYY-MM-DD'), 1) "add months" FROM DUMMY
```

	add months
1	Jan 5, 2010

EXTRACT: To fetch specific part such as Month, Year or Day of a date field

Syntax: EXTRACT(<YEAR/MONTH/DAY..> from <Date Field>)

```
SELECT VBELN , ERDAT , EXTRACT(YEAR from ERDAT) as YEAR_CREATED from VBAK
```

	VBELN	ERDAT	YEAR_CREATED
1	0000016858	20150428	2,015
2	0000016859	20150428	2,015
3	0000016860	20150428	2,015
4	0000016861	20150428	2,015

5.1.4 Character String Functions

Quite often we need to handle different operations on character string-based variables or columns. Some examples related to character string operations: checking the length of string, removing leading 0s from a column, replace specific characters in a string column etc. Let us understand some of the commonly used Character String functions and their application in various scenarios.

LENGTH: To derive the length of a string variable. In the below example we are calculating the length of description for each of the material

🔲 SQL	🔢 Result	

```
SELECT MATNR, MAKTX, LENGTH(MAKTX) from MAKT
```

	MATNR	MAKTX	LENGTH(MAKTX)
1	000000000050065095	Screw	5
2	100-110	Slug for spiral casing	22
3	100-300	Hollow shaft	12

CONCAT: To return a concatenated result of two strings into single string variable. If we need to concatenate more than two strings, we need to use this function in a nested approach – as shown in the example below.

	SQL	Result		
SELECT LIFNR, NAME1, NAME2, CONCAT(CONCAT(NAME1,'-'), NAME2) as SUPPLIER_NAME from LFA1 where NAME2 != ''				

	LIFNR	NAME1	NAME2	SUPPLIER_NAME
1	0000001059	Express Ship Carrier	Parcel Service	Express Ship Carrier-Parcel Service
2	0000001150	P + S Technik	SRM	P + S Technik-SRM
3	0000001152	Camelot	SRM	Camelot-SRM
4	0000003102	Christian Barth	Garten- und Landschaf...	Christian Barth-Garten- und Landschaftsbau GmbH
5	0000003103	Werner GmbH & Co.	Straßenreinigung KG	Werner GmbH & Co.-Straßenreinigung KG

LEFT and RIGHT: Used to return a substring which either the left part or the right part of a string

In the below example we are deriving the column called Business_Unit from the first 5 characters of Material Product Hierarchy column (MARA-PRDHA)

	SQL	Result		
SELECT MATNR, PRDHA, Left(PRDHA,5) as BUSINESS_UNIT from MARA where PRDHA != ''				

	MATNR	PRDHA	BUSINESS_UNIT	
7	ADJUSTABLE_CAMS	0017000 12500000 110	00170	
8	BRAKE_AND_RESOLVER	0017000 12500000 110	00170	
9	CONNECTOR_CABLES	0017000 12500000 110	00170	
10	CONTROLLERS	0017000 12500000 110	00170	

Note: In the below example, we are using both the LEFT and LENGTH function to remove the last character in a string

	SQL	Result		
Select KUNNR, NAME1, LEFT(NAME1 , LENGTH(NAME1)-1) from KNA1				

	KUNNR	NAME1	LEFT(NAME1,LENGTH(NAME1)-1)	
1	0000487286	Sarah Yang	Sarah Yan	
2	0000487299	Kate Shriver	Kate Shrive	
3	0000487312	Lynn Harley	Lynn Harle	
4	0000487325	Daniel Kipling	Daniel Kiplin	
5	0000487338	Margaret Telep	Margaret Tele	

SUBSTR_AFTER and SUBSTR_BEFORE: Used to return a substring which either the left part or the right part of a string, based on a search on specific character of group of characters.

In the below example, we want to derive the word that follows a blank space as the Greeting Name of customer

SQL | Result

```
Select KUNNR, NAME1,SUBSTR_AFTER(NAME1 , ' ') as GREETING_NAME from KNA1
```

	KUNNR	NAME1	GREETING_NAME	
1	0000487286	Sarah Yang	Yang	
2	0000487299	Kate Shriver	Shriver	
3	0000487312	Lynn Harley	Harley	
4	0000487325	Daniel Kipling	Kipling	
5	0000487338	Margaret Telep	Telep	

TRIM: To remove all the blank spaces from both the beginning and ending of a string

SQL | Result

```
Select TRIM( '   SAP HANA   ') from DUMMY
```

	TRIM(' SAP HANA ')
1	SAP HANA

Note: We can use the LTRIM and RTRIM function to remove specific characters from left part of the right of part of a string respectively. For example, to remove the leading zeroes in Material number column, we can use LTRIM function as shown below.

SQL | Result

```
SELECT MATNR, LTRIM(MATNR,'0') from MARA
```

	MATNR	LTRIM(MATNR,'0')
1	000000000000001409	1409
2	000000000000001410	1410
3	000000000000001957	1957
4	000000000000001958	1958
5	000000000000001960	1960

We can use the TRIM function with the additional options such as LEADING and TRAILING to achieve the same functionality as LTRIM and RTRIM, as shown in the below example.

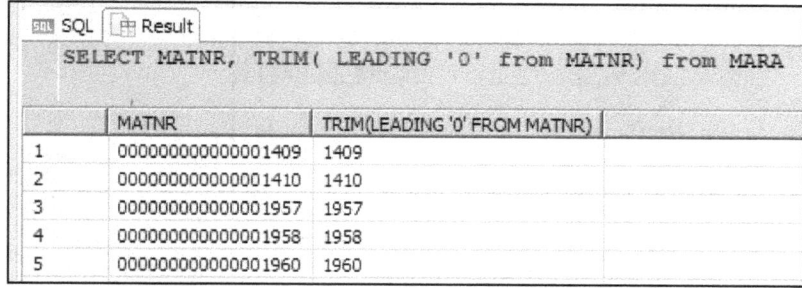

	MATNR	TRIM(LEADING '0' FROM MATNR)	
1	000000000000001409	1409	
2	000000000000001410	1410	
3	000000000000001957	1957	
4	000000000000001958	1958	
5	000000000000001960	1960	

LPAD: Used to prefix a character field with specific set of characters. In the below example, we would like to derive the Material Description as a 40 character length field, by prefixing it with the *

```
SELECT MATNR, MAKTX, LPAD( MAKTX, 40, '*') from MAKT
```

	MATNR	MAKTX	LPAD(MAKTX,40,'*')
1	000000000050065095	Screw	************************************Screw
2	100-110	Slug for spiral casing	*****************Slug for spiral casing
3	100-300	Hollow shaft	****************************Hollow shaft

We can use the RPAD function in the same way, to append specific set of characters to the end of a string.

LOCATE: Used to search for a substring within a character string column. This function returns the exact position of the substring when it is found.

In the below example we are trying to get all the material numbers, where their description has a word "Screw".

```
SQL | Result
SELECT MATNR, MAKTX, LOCATE(MAKTX,'Screw') from MAKT
where LOCATE(MAKTX,'Screw')>0
```

	MATNR	MAKTX	LOCATE(MAKTX,'Screw')
199	000000000000000642	Clamp Screw.ipt	7
200	H2114124	3.6v Lithium-Ion Auto Select Screwdriver	30
201	H3536546	3.6v Lithium-Ion Pivot Driver Screwdrive	31
202	H3794560	3.6v Lithium-Ion Compact Screwdriver wit	26
203	000000000000000641	Adjusting Screw.ipt	11

UPPER / LOWER: To return the string values in Upper case or Lower Case

```
SQL | Result
SELECT KUNNR, NAME1, UPPER(NAME1) from KNA1
```

	KUNNR	NAME1	UPPER(NAME1)
1	0000487286	Sarah Yang	SARAH YANG
2	0000487299	Kate Shriver	KATE SHRIVER
3	0000487312	Lynn Harley	LYNN HARLEY

STRING_AGG: We can use this function to perform the concatenation of column values across multiple rows based on specific grouping criteria. Consider a scenario where we need to concatenate the values of different statuses (such as Released, In-Process and Completed) of each task which are maintained in multiple rows into one row (Released*In-Process*Completed), we shall use the STRING_AGG function.

Example:
SELECT PROJECT_ID, TASK_ID, STRING_AGG(TASK_STATUS, '*')
FROM <TABLE> GROUP BY PROJECT_ID;

→ *Example for Practice*
Please find the detailed example and practical application of STRING_AGG function in the following business case

7.5 Business Case: Persistence of Marketing Promotion Status

Example for String functions: Logic to decode a multi-value string into a Table Variable

In the below example, we will pass a single input parameter of type String, which as multiple material numbers separated by commas. The procedure will return these list of material numbers in a table variable. We will use the string functions to achieve this.

```
CREATE PROCEDURE NVARMA.GET_MAT_NUMBERS (IN IP_MATNR NVARCHAR(200) ,
        OUT V_MATLIST NVARMA.TT_MATNR)
        READS SQL DATA AS
 BEGIN
 DECLARE V_MATSTR NVARCHAR(200);
 DECLARE V1, V2, V_LEN, V_POS INT;

 V_MATSTR = :IP_MATNR;
 V_MATSTR = CONCAT(:v_matstr , ',');
 V2 = 10;
 V_MAT = SELECT '000000000000000000' as MATNR from dummy;
 V_MATLIST = SELECT '000000000000000000' as MATNR from dummy;

--To remove the single quotes from the string variable value
 SELECT REPLACE (:V_MATSTR, '''' ,'') into V_MATSTR from DUMMY;

 For V1 in 1..V2 DO

  SELECT LOCATE(:V_MATSTR, ',') into v_pos from dummy;
    V_LEN = LENGTH(:V_MATSTR) - ( V_POS + 1 );

  V_MAT = SELECT SUBSTRING(:V_MATSTR,0, V_POS - 1) as MATNR from DUMMY;
  V_MATSTR = RIGHT(:V_MATSTR, V_LEN + 1 );
      V_MATLIST = SELECT MATNR from :V_MATLIST
                      UNION ALL
                      SELECT MATNR from :V_MAT;
 End for;

V_MATLIST = SELECT * From :V_MATLIST where MATNR != '000000000000000000'
and MATNR != '';
END;
```

Call the procedure using the parameters shown below and observe the output table variable.

SQL	Result
CALL NVARMA.GET_MAT_NUMBERS ('M-01,M-02,DCP1010', ?)	

	MATNR	
1	M-01	
2	M-02	
3	DCP1010	

5.1.5 Miscellaneous Functions

SQL Script provides few additional functions to address specific requirements.

SESSION_USER: Returns the current database user ID.

CURRENT_SCHEMA: Returns the current database schema name.

Example:

```
SQL    Result
   SELECT SESSION_USER, CURRENT_SCHEMA from dummy
```

	SESSION_USER	CURRENT_SCHEMA
1	NVARMA	ES7_SLT_BTH

CONVERT_CURRENCY: We can use this function to display a currency field values in a desired currency

Syntax: COVERT_CURRENCY(<pass all the mandatory parameters>)

Example:

```
SQL    Result
  select VBELN, NETWR, WAERK,
              convert_currency (amount=>NETWR,
                              source_unit_column=>WAERK,
                              schema=>'ES7_SLT_BTH',
                              target_unit_column=>'USD',
                              reference_date=>current_Date,
                              error_handling=>'set to null',
                              client=>MANDT) as NETWR_USD
              from VBAK
```

	VBELN	NETWR	WAERK	NETWR_USD
1	0000016858	900	EUR	1,003.905
2	0000016859	900	EUR	1,003.905
3	0000016860	900	EUR	1,003.905
4	0000016861	900	EUR	1,003.905
5	0000016862	900	EUR	1,003.905

5.1.6 Window Functions

To divide the result sets of a query, or a logical partition of a query, into groups of rows called window partitions.

Note: Window Functions are executed in Row Engine. Hence these functions can cause performance issues especially when we use them on larger volume of data

Few commonly used Window Functions:

RANK: To derive the Ranking Values based on the values of specific measure column

For example: To rank the customers based on total sales revenue for each Sales organization.

```
SELECT VKORG, KUNNR, NETWR,
RANK() OVER ( PARTITION BY VKORG ORDER BY NETWR DESC ) AS Rank
FROM ( SELECT VKORG, KUNNR, SUM(NETWR) as NETWR from VBAK GROUP BY VKORG, KUNNR)
WHERE VKORG = '1000'
```

	VKORG	KUNNR	NETWR	RANK	
1	1000	0000001175	45,564,039.63	1	
2	1000	0000001900	42,542,950.2	2	
3	1000	0000001390	39,557,000	3	
4	1000	0000001174	39,519,956.4	4	
5	1000	0000001321	33,524,006.3	5	

SUM (Cumulative Sum for Running Totals)

Example: Running totals (Cumulative Sum) using window function

```
SELECT VKORG, SALES_MONTH, NETWR,
SUM(NETWR) OVER ( PARTITION BY VKORG ORDER BY SALES_MONTH ) AS RUNNING_TOTAL
FROM ( SELECT VKORG, MONTH(ERDAT) as SALES_MONTH, SUM(NETWR) as NETWR from VBAK
WHERE YEAR(ERDAT)  = '2011' and VKORG = '1000'
  GROUP BY VKORG, MONTH(ERDAT))
```

	VKORG	SALES_MONTH	NETWR	RUNNING_TOTAL
1	1000	1	266,495.5	266,495.5
2	1000	2	297,310	563,805.5
3	1000	3	386,824.9	950,630.4
4	1000	4	287,141.6	1,237,772
5	1000	5	774,957.7	2,012,729.7
6	1000	6	677,498.9	2,690,228.6
7	1000	7	282,499	2,972,727.6
8	1000	8	294,248.1	3,266,975.7
9	1000	9	304,514	3,571,489.7
10	1000	10	310,537.6	3,882,027.3
11	1000	11	301,897	4,183,924.3
12	1000	12	289,544.4	4,473,468.7

5.2 Implementing Custom Functions in SQL Script

Let us go through the process of implementing custom functions in SQL Script which are also known as User Defined Functions (UDF). There are two types of UDFs in SQL Script, Scalar Functions and Table Functions. In the following sections, we will understand their key features and usage scenarios.

5.2.1 Scalar Functions

Scalar Functions allow us to implement reusable logic in those scenarios, where we need to perform some calculations and return a single value. Since Scalar functions return a single value, we can also use them to derive specific columns within a SELECT query.

For example, we can build a scalar function (named IS_NUMERIC) that can check if the given value is a numeric and return the values 0 (False) or 1 (True).

Key features of Scalar Functions:
- They can have any number of input parameters
- They are meant to return a single value
- Expression statements are allowed within the body of a scalar function
- Table operations such as CURSOR, CE functions or Array operations are not allowed
- Input parameters used in the signature of scalar function cannot be of "Table Type"

Steps to implement Scalar Functions:
- We can create scalar functions in the HANA Development perspective.
- These are created using the extension *.hdbscalarfunction*

Following are the different options to consume Scalar Functions:
- Scalar functions can be consumed in the Field List OR the WHERE clause of a SELECT statement. Basically, a scalar function represents a single field in SQL Query.
  Example: SELECT KUNNR, **IS_NUMERIC(KUNNR)** as NUM_FLAG from KNA1;
- We can also use them to derive the values of Input Parameters in Calculation Views
- They can be also used for direct assignment into variables:
  Example Var1 := scalar_function()

5.2.2 Scalar Function – Steps to create using HANA Studio and Web IDE

In the HANA Studio Development perspective, choose the menu path File → New → Other: Choose "Scalar Function" under the Database Development

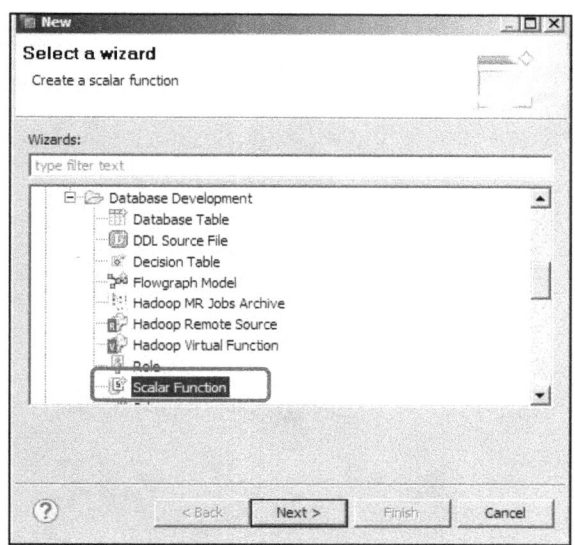 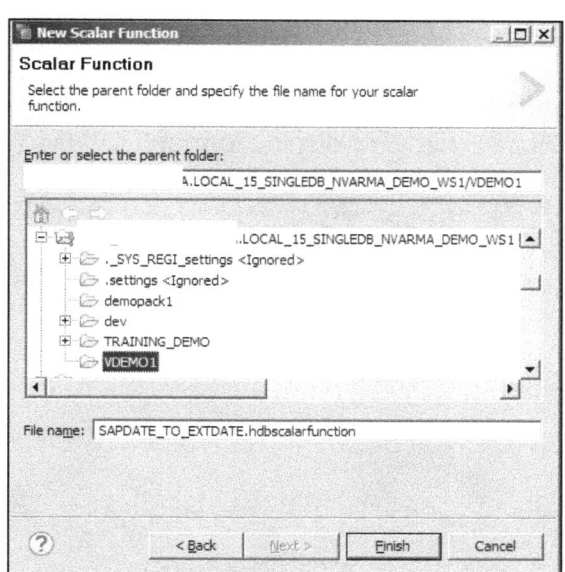

Login to HANA using WebIDE

Use the following patch to create scalar function, under your respective package.

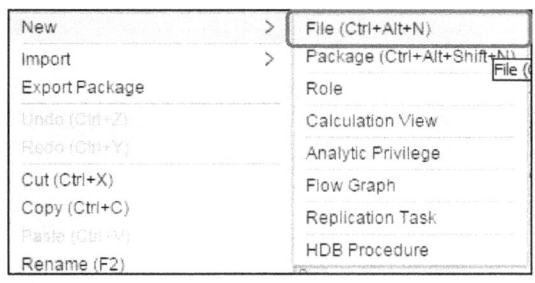 

The source code of the scalar function is provided below. Once you enter the source code in the editor, use the menu options to Save and Activate the scalar function.

5.2.3 Scalar Function Example – Converting Date to Display Format

In the following example we will create a Scalar Function that returns the given date variable in external or display format (DD-MM-YYYY):

```
FUNCTION "NVARMA"."VDEMO1::SAPDATE_TO_EXTDATE" ( I_DATE
VARCHAR(8))
    RETURNS O_DATE nvarchar(10)
    LANGUAGE SQLSCRIPT
    SQL SECURITY INVOKER AS
BEGIN

--Convert date from YYYYMMDD to DD-MM-YYYY

DECLARE lv_datemonth VARCHAR(6);

SELECT CONCAT(CONCAT(substr(i_date,7,2),'-') ,
    CONCAT(SUBSTR(i_date,5,2),'-'))
    INTO lv_datemonth from dummy;

SELECT CONCAT(lv_datemonth , SUBSTR (i_date,1,4)) into O_DATE from
dummy;
END;
```

This is how we can consume a scalar function from a SQL statement: Here we are deriving a field using the scalar function.

```
select "NVARMA"."VDEMO1::SAPDATE_TO_EXTDATE"('20180210') from dummy
```

	NVARMA.VDEMO1::SAPDATE_TO_EXTDATE('20180210')	
1	10-02-2018	

Note: We can also use Scalar function to derive the values of Input Parameters in Calculation Views.

5.2.4 Scalar Function Example: Derive Previous Fiscal Period for given date

Implement the following reporting logic to build a reusable scalar function which returns the "Previous Fiscal Period" for a given date. We can call this function to derive the required period values in a query or as a source for Input Parameters in Calculation views.

```
FUNCTION "NVARMA"."democode::SF_GET_PREVIOUS_FISCPER"
     (IP_FISCPER NVARCHAR(7), IP_NUM_PER INTEGER )
     RETURNS PREV_FISCPER NVARCHAR(7)
     LANGUAGE SQLSCRIPT
     SQL SECURITY INVOKER AS
BEGIN
 DECLARE V_YEAR NVARCHAR(4);
 DECLARE V_MONTH NVARCHAR(3);
 DECLARE V_PREV_YEAR NVARCHAR(4);
 DECLARE V_PREV_MONTH NVARCHAR(3);
 SELECT SUBSTRING(IP_FISCPER,1,4) into V_YEAR from dummy;
 SELECT SUBSTRING(IP_FISCPER,5,3) into V_MONTH from dummy;

IF to_int(:V_MONTH) <= :IP_NUM_PER  then
    V_PREV_MONTH := :V_MONTH - :IP_NUM_PER + 12;
    V_PREV_YEAR := :V_YEAR - 1;
ELSE
    V_PREV_MONTH := to_int(:V_MONTH) - :IP_NUM_PER;
    V_PREV_YEAR := V_YEAR;
END IF;
SELECT CONCAT(V_PREV_YEAR, lpad(V_PREV_MONTH,3,'0')) into PREV_FISCPER
from dummy;
END;
```

Test #1: Get the value of one period prior to 2018/002

```
SQL | Result
SELECT  "NVARMA"."democode::SF_GET_PREVIOUS_FISCPER" ('2018002', 1) from DUMMY
```

	NVARMA.democode::SF_GET_PREVIOUS_FISCPER('2018002',1)
1	2018001

Test #2: Get the value of two periods prior to 2018/002

```
SQL | Result
SELECT  "NVARMA"."democode::SF_GET_PREVIOUS_FISCPER" ('2018002', 2) from DUMMY
```

	NVARMA.democode::SF_GET_PREVIOUS_FISCPER('2018002',2)
1	2017012

5.3 Table Functions

Table Functions are used to implement potentially reusable solutions, where we need to return the results represented in a table. We can implement table functions to address some of the data modeling requirements, which cannot be achieved using graphical calculation views. Apart from that, table functions can be used as reusable blocks and can be called from different processing areas as explained the following sections.

Key features of Table Functions:

- Repository object with an extension .hdbtablefunction
- They have replaced the Script based Calculation views in the HANA modeling space
- Can be used as data sources in graphical calculation views
- Read-only – we cannot implement any logic that updates the data in tables
- Can accept multiple input parameters and returns exactly one result table
- We need to use the RETURN statement to return the output table variable at the end of the table function processing

Points to be noted:

- We can pass the values from Calculation views to Table functions using Input Parameters mapping technique. (Manage Mappings option)
- Table functions do not support the input parameters with multiple values. We need to address this limitation using some work around solution to decode the input parameter to multiple values. This has been explained in the examples.
- We should always watch out for the performance while consuming the Table functions in Calculation views, since certain optimizations like filter push down and column pruning may not be enforced.

Syntax: Table Function definition

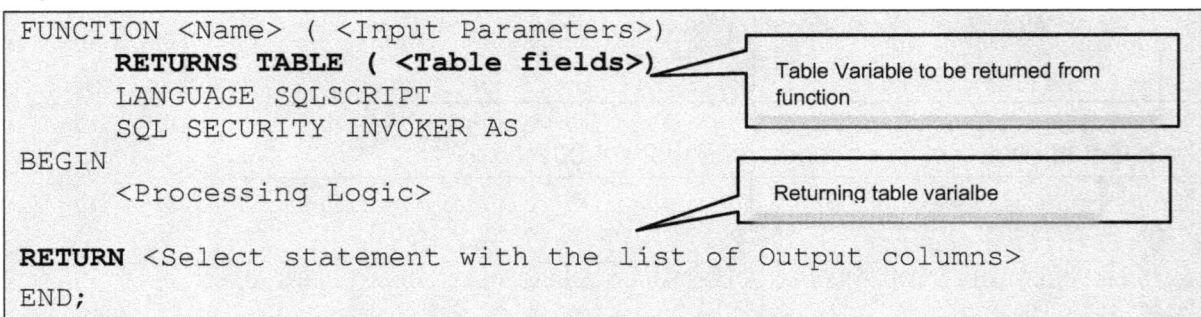

```
FUNCTION <Name> ( <Input Parameters>)
    RETURNS TABLE ( <Table fields>)          Table Variable to be returned from
    LANGUAGE SQLSCRIPT                         function
    SQL SECURITY INVOKER AS
BEGIN
    <Processing Logic>                        Returning table varialbe

RETURN <Select statement with the list of Output columns>
END;
```

Table functions are commonly used in the SQL Script solutions to encapsulate business logic and return the desired result data set. We can leverage them to address various use cases, since they enable modularization and reusability of code. Let us understand the key options to consume Table Functions:

- We can use the table functions as data sources in calculation views in the same way as we use other data sources such tables and calculation views etc. This will help us to achieve complex requirements in HANA modeling, which cannot be implemented using the graphical calculation views

- We can call the table functions from stored procedures and other table functions as well. To call a table function, we need to use the SELECT statement as shown below. We need to pass the necessary input parameters to the table function.

  SELECT <fields> from <Table Function> [Where <conditions>];

- We can call the table functions from various ETL tools like BODS and from HANA Smart Data Integration (SDI) Flow graphs. This will help us to implement the logic that runs on HANA database, which can be called from external tools.

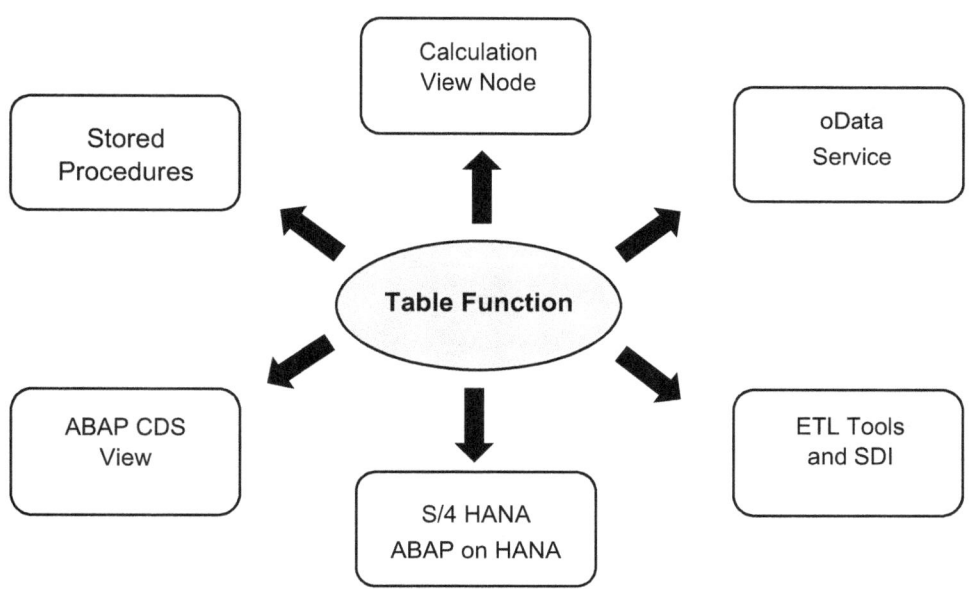

5.3.1   Steps to implement Table Functions in HANA

We can create Table Functions from the HANA Studio Development perspective or using HANA Web IDE. Let us create a table function that returns list of customers along with the total sales order value for a given year.

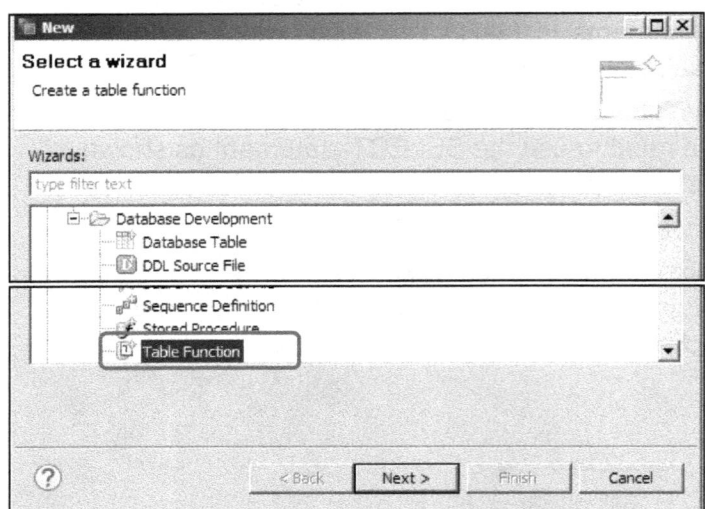

Choose the menu path: File →
New → Other → Database
Development → Table Function

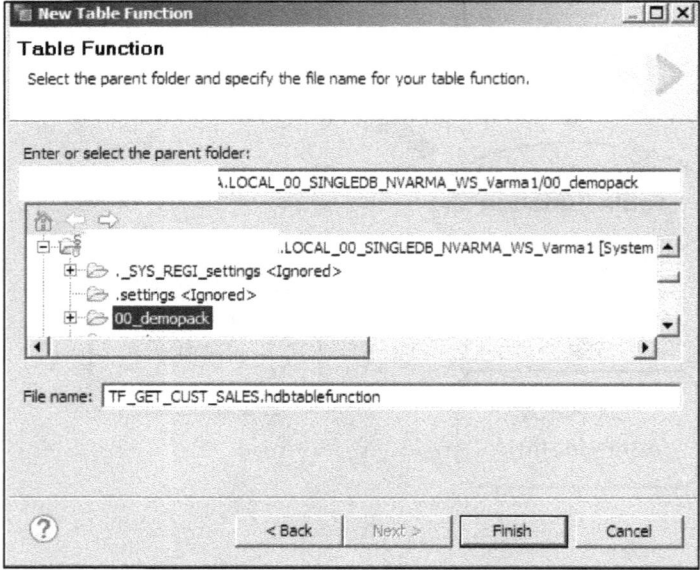

Choose the Package and enter
the Table function name

Enter the source code of the Table function:

```
FUNCTION "NVARMA"."00_demopack::TF_GET_CUST_SALES" (IN_YEAR NVARCHAR(4) )
        RETURNS TABLE ( KUNNR NVARCHAR(10), ORDER_AMT DECIMAL(18,2) )
        LANGUAGE SQLSCRIPT
        SQL SECURITY INVOKER
        DEFAULT SCHEMA <SCHEMA NAME>
        AS
BEGIN
/*****************************
      Write your function logic
*****************************/
DECLARE V_FROMDATE DATE;
DECLARE V_TODATE DATE;

SELECT CONCAT( :IN_YEAR , '0101') INTO V_FROMDATE FROM DUMMY;
SELECT CONCAT( :IN_YEAR , '1231') INTO V_TODATE FROM DUMMY;

RETURN SELECT KUNNR, SUM(NETWR) AS ORDER_AMT
        FROM VBAK
        WHERE ERDAT BETWEEN :V_FROMDATE AND :V_TODATE
        GROUP BY KUNNR;

END;
```

Note: We need to ensure that the Output columns generated by the RETURN statement should match with the structure of the Result Table Variable mentioned in the signature

Save and **Activate** the Table function.

Table Functions can be treated like virtual data models in HANA database. Hence, we can call the Table function using the SELECT query as shown below:

```
SQL  Result
SELECT * FROM "NVARMA"."00_demopack::TF_GET_CUST_SALES"('2015')
```

	KUNNR	ORDER_AMT
1	FIO-CUST01	997,150
2	FIO-CUST02	484,330
3	FIO-CUST04	586,850
4	FIO-CUST03	742,280
5	0000003000	15

5.3.2   Consuming Table Functions in Calculation Views

HANA Modeling is largely driven by the implementation of calculation views, that provides graphical framework to build data models as per the reporting KPI requirements. However, for some of the complex requirements that needs recursive logic using looping operations or complex calculations and look-up operations, we may not be able to build the solution using calculation views. Table functions are meant to overcome these limitations, since we can implement most of the logic that is supported by SQL Script inside a table function.

We can use the Table Function as a data source in the calculation view nodes such as projection, aggregation, union and join. Accordingly, we can encapsulate the complex logic using Table Functions and consume them within the calculation views. You may have an obvious question: How can we pass certain values between the Calculation view and Table Function? This is where we can leverage the "Input Parameters" and "Manage mappings" functionality of Calculation views. Let us implement a solution to consume Table Function within a calculation view.

Step #1: Create a calculation view as shown below.

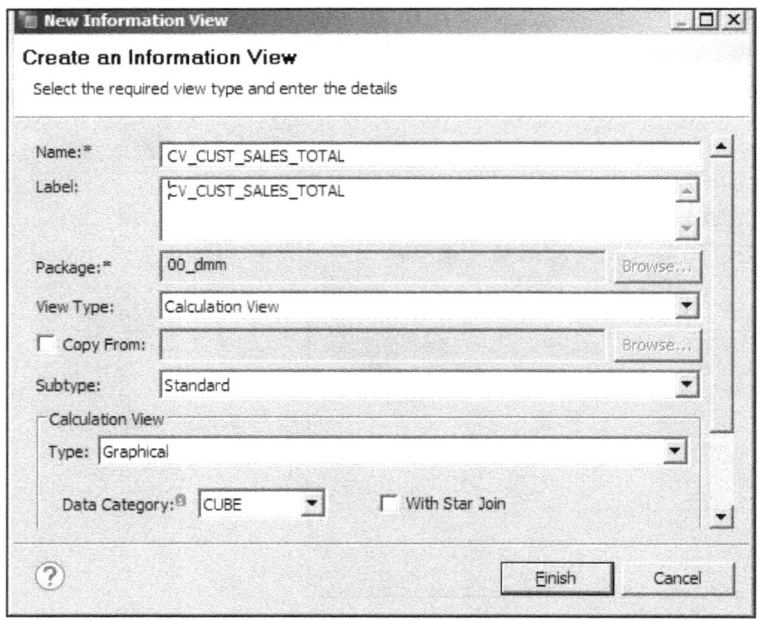

Add a Projection node and select the table function as its data source

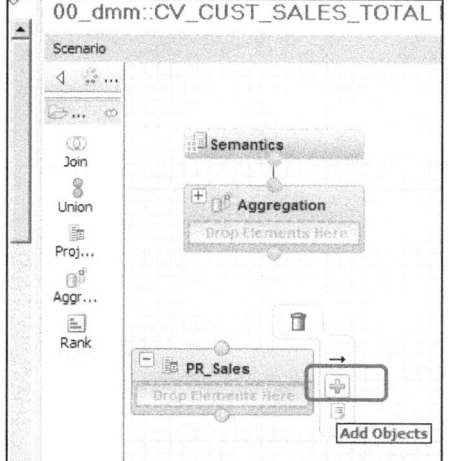
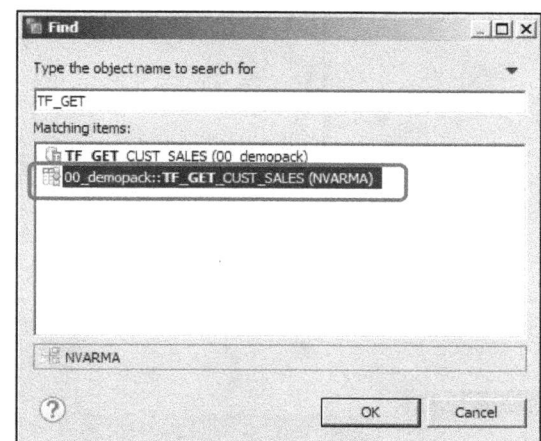

Add the columns of Table function to the Output of projection node

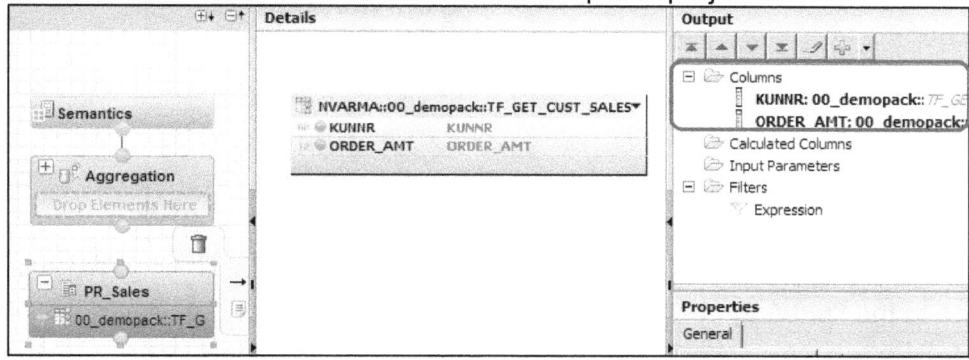

Add another projection node for Customer attributes using KNA1 table as the source and add the columns to the output as shown here.

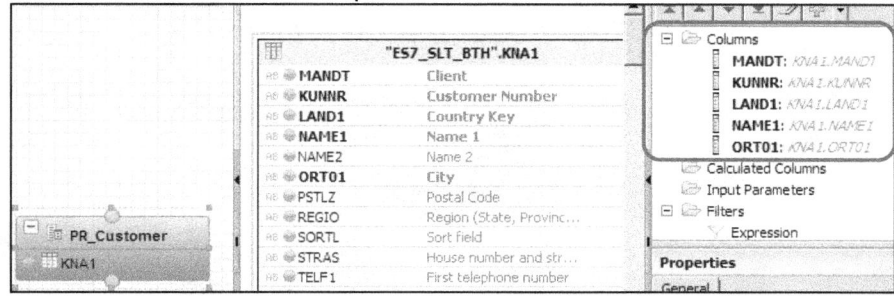

Add a Join node to perform join of both the projection nodes and maintain join relationship based on Customer Number (KUNNR)

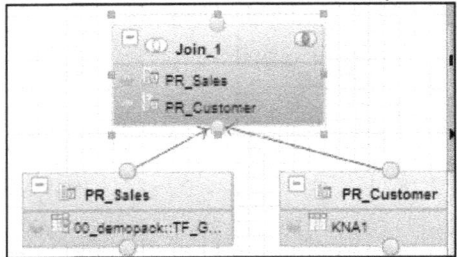

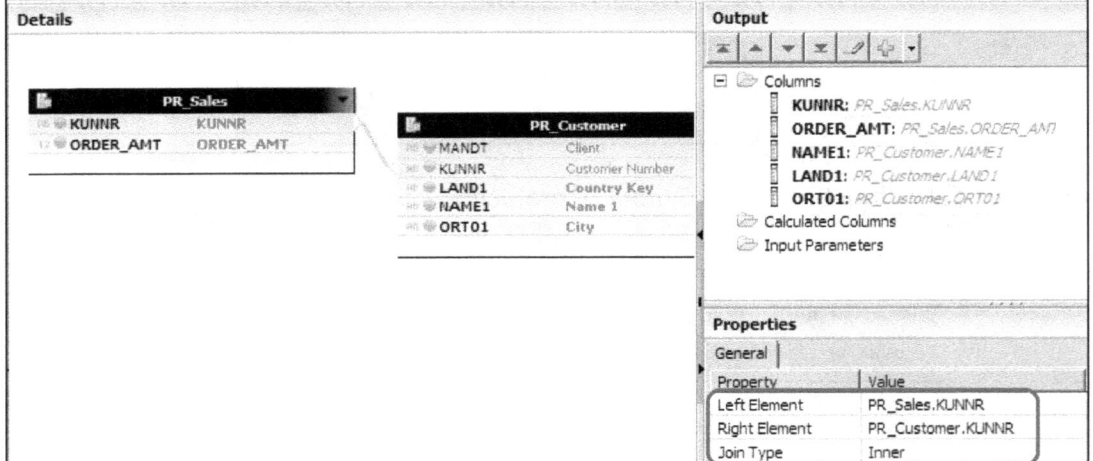

Connect the Join node to the final Aggregation node and add the fields to Output

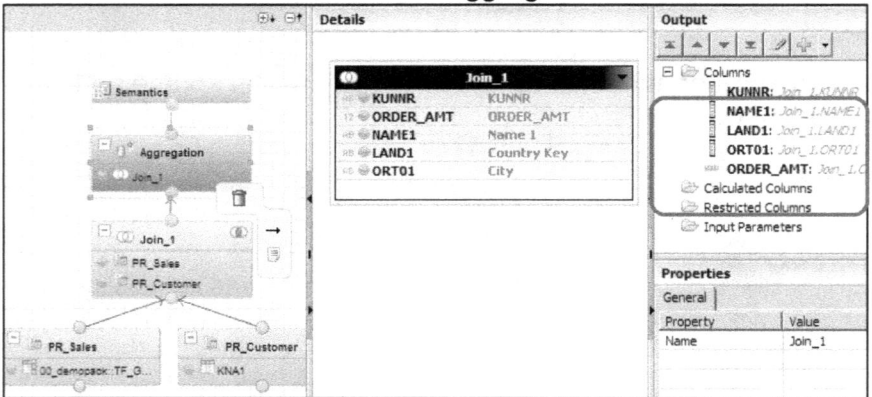

We need to create an Input Parameter to pass the YEAR from the calculation view to the Table Function (Since this Table Function expects an input parameter called IN_YEAR)

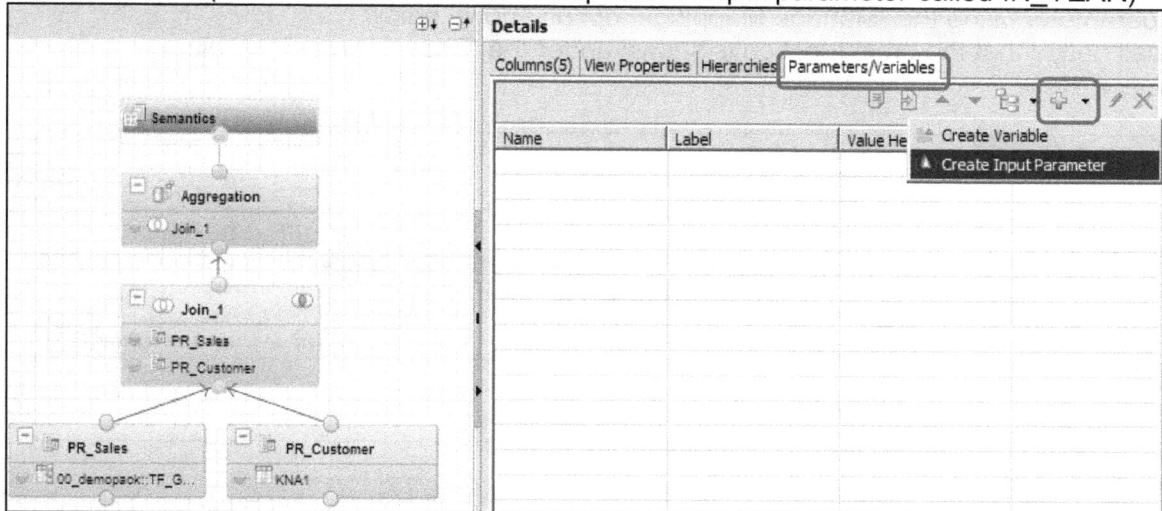

Following are the properties of Input Parameter

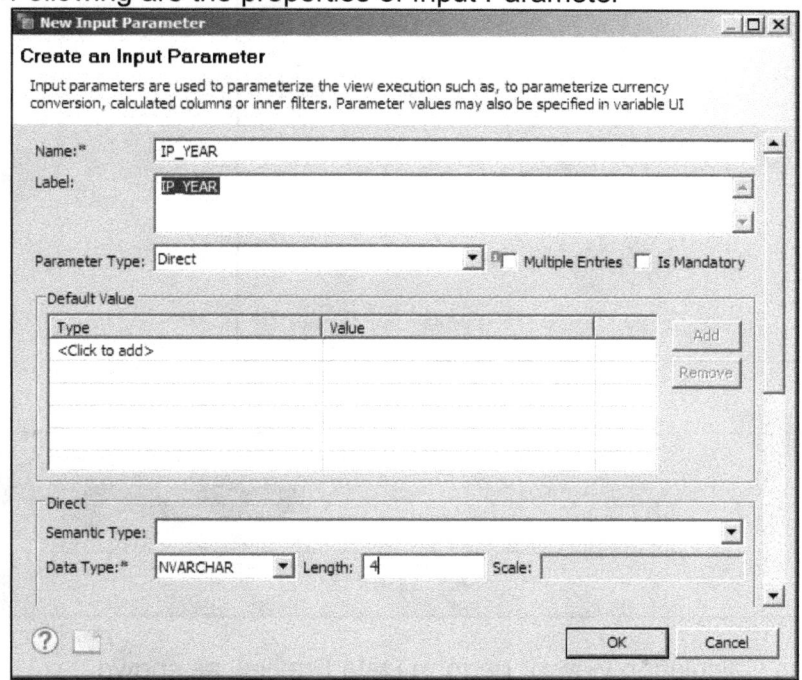

Map the input parameters of the data source (Table Function) from the calculation view input parameter using the "Manage Mappings" option shown below.
We shall notice that the table function is shown under the "Data Sources" for this calculation view.

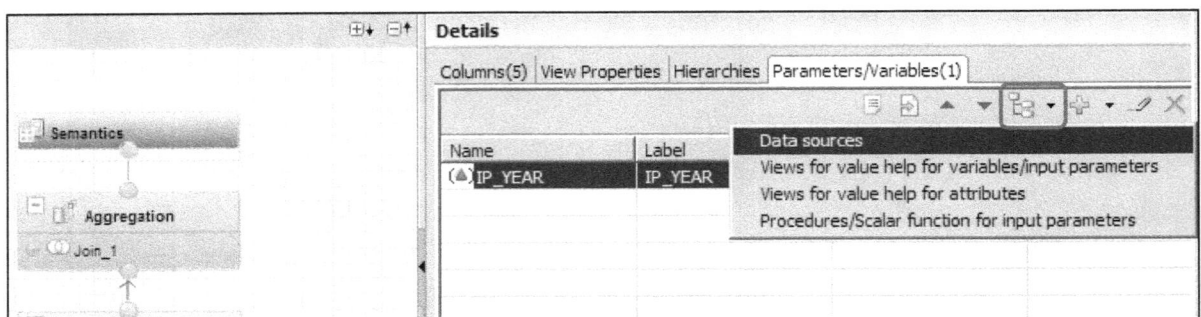

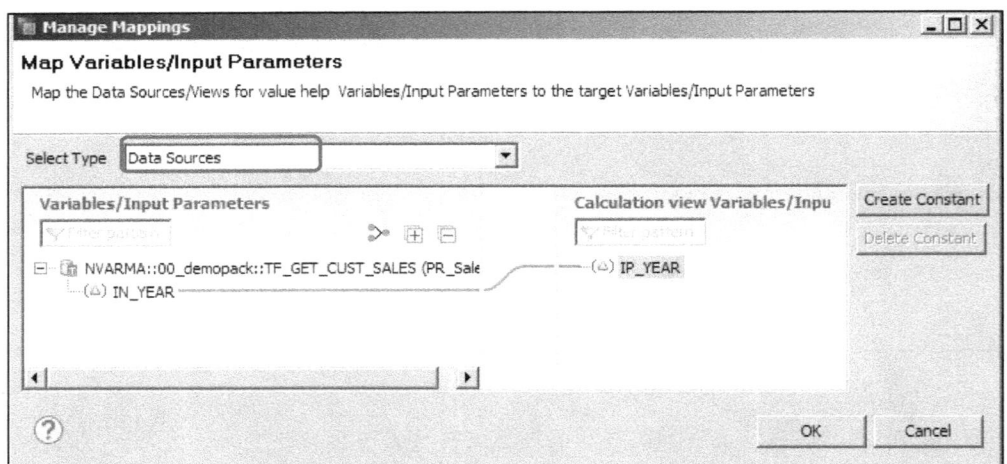

Save and Activate the calculation view.

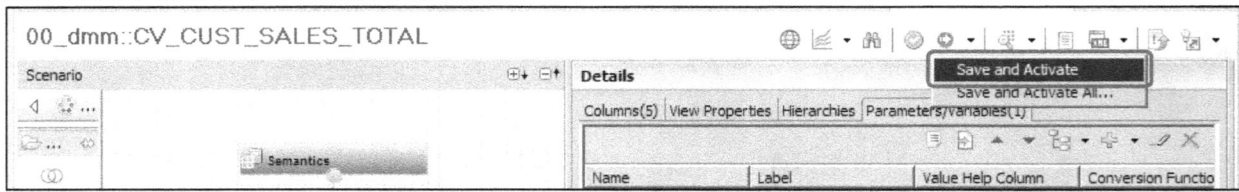

Now we can run any queries on the Calculation view or perform Data Preview as shown below.

Data Preview on Calculation view:

Pass the value to input parameter

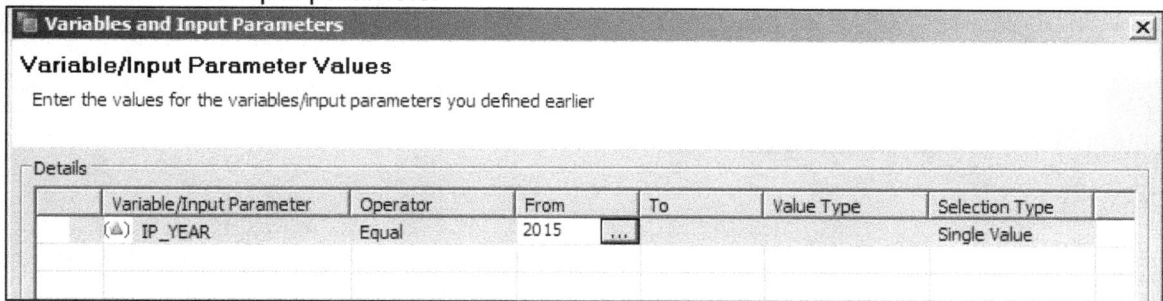

Check the results as shown below and compare the same with the result of the table function. We shall observe that the results are matching at each customer level, when we compare with the results of the query on table function.

KUNNR	NAME1	LAND1	ORT01	ORDER_AMT
FIO-CUST02	Berlin Shoppi...	DE	Berlin	484,330
FIO-CUST04	Electronics O...	DE	Berlin	586,850
0000500100	Kim Possible ...	US	Cambridge	10,319.7
0000499775	Nora Setlur	US	Cheyenne	3,270

Analysis | **Distinct values** | **Raw Data**

56 rows retrieved - 59 ms

Verify the Filter Push down functionality of Table Functions:
Run the following query on the calculation view using "Plan Visualizer" tool and observe the generated execution plan.

```
SELECT "KUNNR", "NAME1", "LAND1", "ORT01", sum("ORDER_AMT") AS "ORDER_AMT"
FROM "_SYS_BIC"."00_dmm/CV_CUST_SALES_TOTAL"
('PLACEHOLDER' = ('$$IP_YEAR$$', '2015'))
WHERE KUNNR = 'FIO-CUST02'
  GROUP BY "KUNNR", "NAME1", "LAND1", "ORT01"
```

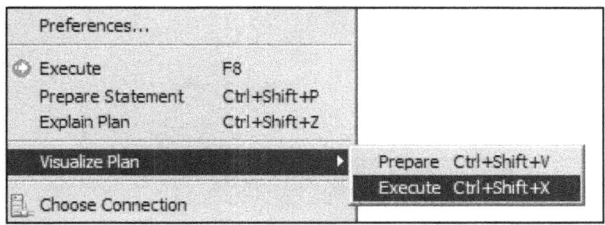

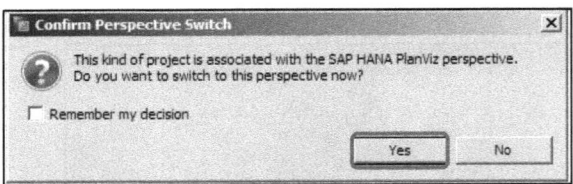

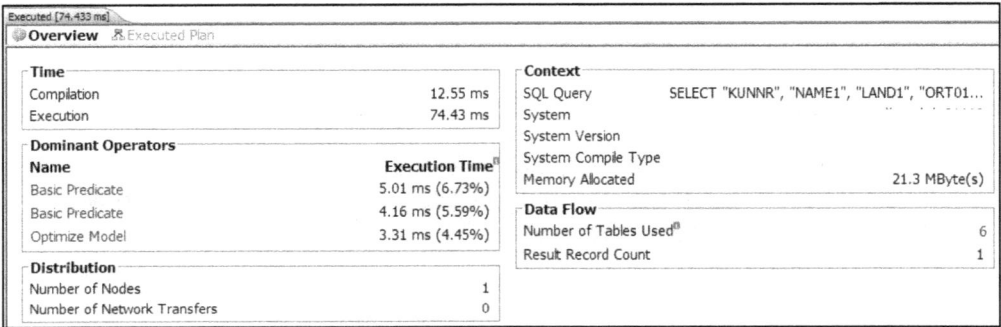

Switch to the "Executed Plan" tab from the above Overview Screen and drilldown in the Execute Model.

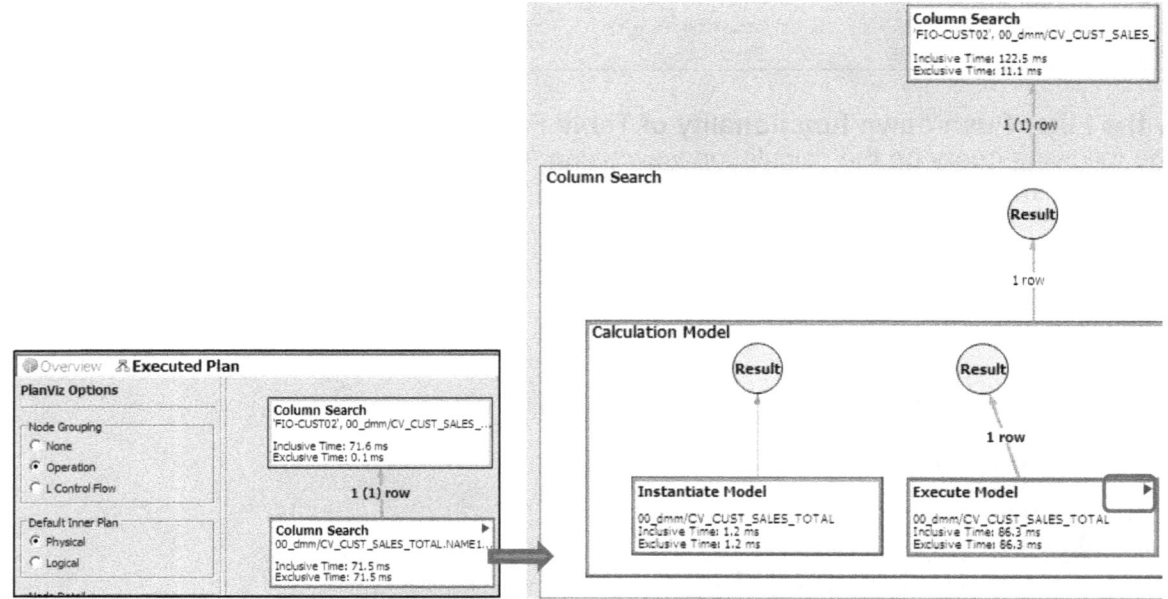

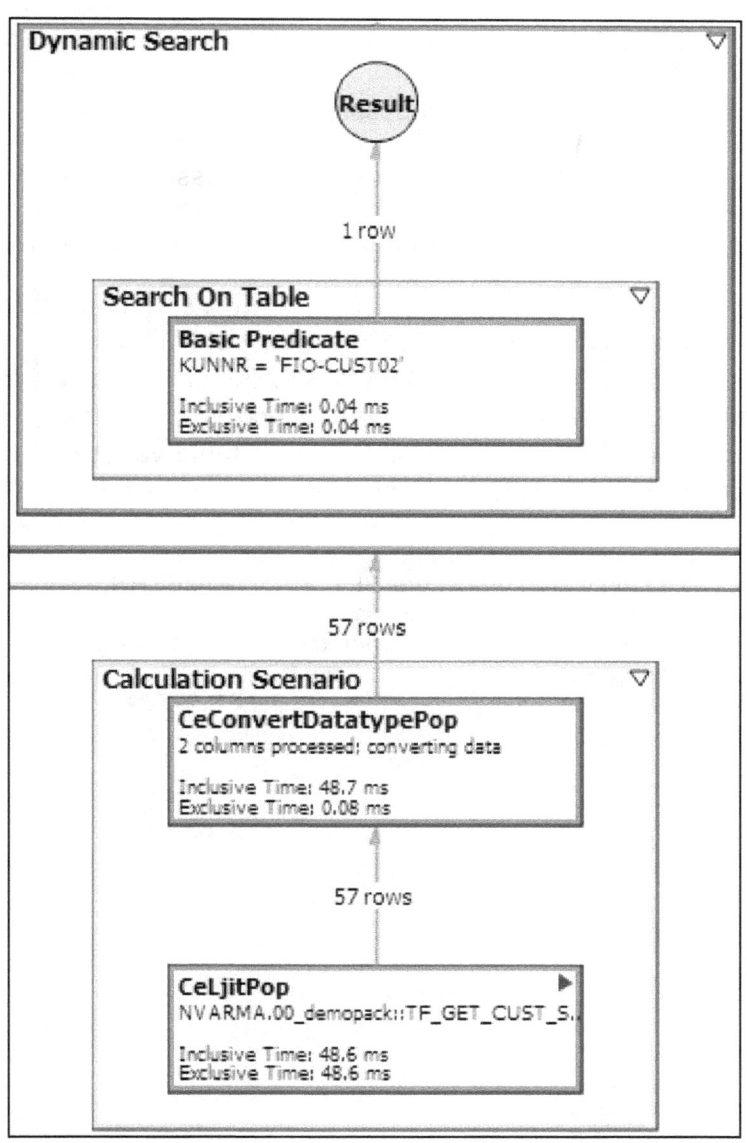

From this plan, we shall observe that the results of Table Function are filtered with the Customer number (KUNNR = 'FIO-CUST02'), before performing the join in the calculation view.

5.3.3 Example: Table Function with Multiple Value Input

In the previous example, we have understood the approach of passing values to the input parameters of table function from the input parameters of calculation views. What if the calculation view input parameter is multi-value input enabled? Earlier, we discussed about the limitation of table variables that they do not support input parameters which represents multiple values. Let us go through the following example to understand the work around solution to address this limitation.

Step #1: Create a Table function that will accept a string with concatenated set of Material numbers and returns the list of sales order items for those materials. Previously we have created a stored procedure (GET_MAT_NUMBERS) that accepts a string with comma separated material numbers and returns the list of material numbers in a table variable form. We will be calling the same stored procedure inside the Table Function.

Note:
→ In the above table function, we are calling the stored procedure GET_MAT_NUMBERS, which has been explained in in this unit under the String Functions section.
→ The stored procedure can be called by the table function, only when there are necessary privileges. Hence, we may need to run the below statement to address this.
   `GRANT SELECT, EXECUTE on SCHEMA <SCHEMA> TO _SYS_REPO with GRANT OPTION;`

Create the Table function with the logic, as shown below.

```
FUNCTION "NVARMA"."democode::TF_MAT_SALES" ( I_MATNR NVARCHAR(200))
       RETURNS TABLE (VBELN NVARCHAR(10),
                      POSNR NVARCHAR(4),
                      MATNR NVARCHAR(18),
                      ORDER_QTY DECIMAL(18,2),
                      SALES_UNIT NVARCHAR(5))
       LANGUAGE SQLSCRIPT
       AS
BEGIN

--Call the procedure to split the material numbers
 CALL NVARMA.GET_MAT_NUMBERS (:I_MATNR  , :TAB_MATNR);

 RETURN SELECT VBELN, POSNR, MATNR, KWMENG as ORDER_QTY,
               VRKME as SALES_UNIT
         from <SCHEMA_NAME>.VBAP as A
         WHERE EXISTS (     SELECT MATNR from :TAB_MATNR as B
                                 WHERE A.MATNR = B.MATNR) ;

END;
```

Let us call the Table function using the SELECT statement as shown below and observe the results. We are passing multiple value input via comma separated string to the Table function, which in turn decodes the material numbers into a table variable and uses it further in the processing.

```
SELECT * from "NVARMA"."democode::TF_MAT_SALES" ( 'M-01,M-02,DPC1010')
```

	VBELN	POSNR	MATNR	ORDER_QTY	SALES_UNIT
1	0000005351	000010	M-01	23	ST
2	0000005356	000010	DPC1010	280	ST
3	0000009521	000010	DPC1010	420	ST
4	0000009522	000020	DPC1010	480	ST
5	0000009631	000010	DPC1010	360	ST

Step #2: Consuming the Table Function in Calculation View

We need to consume the above table function (TF_MAT_SALES) in a calculation view that accepts multiple value input parameter for Material Numbers. Here the challenge is to map the same input parameter to the Table Function. Let us go through the following steps to address this requirement.

Create the following Calculation view where we will be joining the table function TF_MAT_SALES with the VBAK table to get the relevant details of Sales orders.

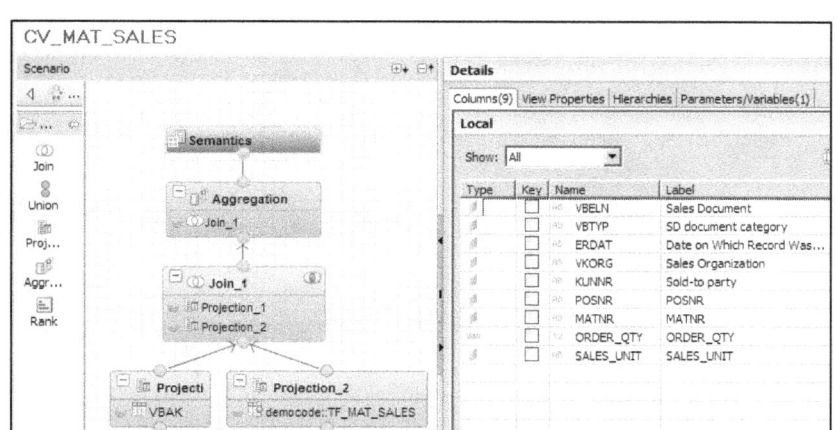

Join type: Inner join

Join columns: VBELN

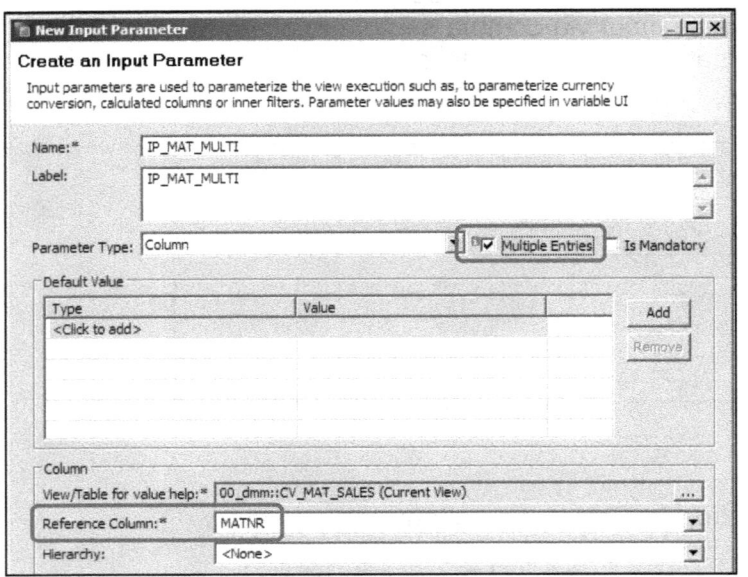

Create the Input Parameter as
shown here

Reference column: MATNR

Enable Multiple Entries

Map the input parameter of Calculation view to the Table function input parameter as
shown below:

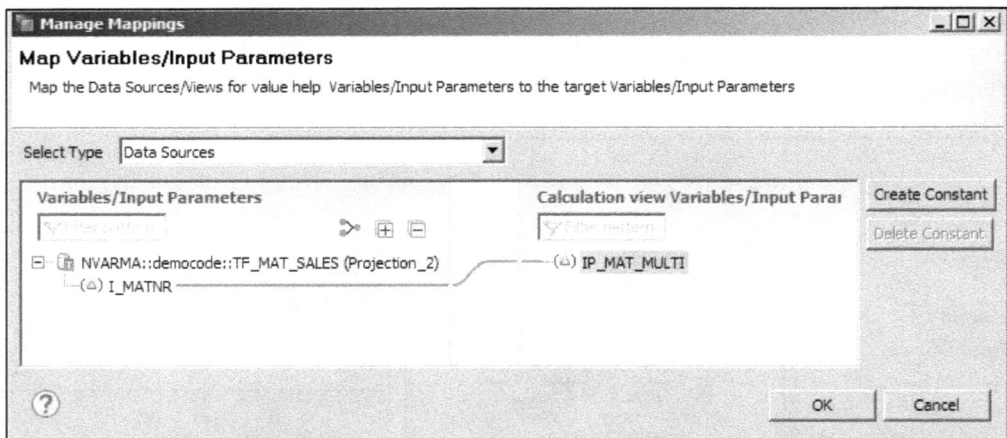

Save and Activate the Calculation View.

Perform the data preview of Calculation view.

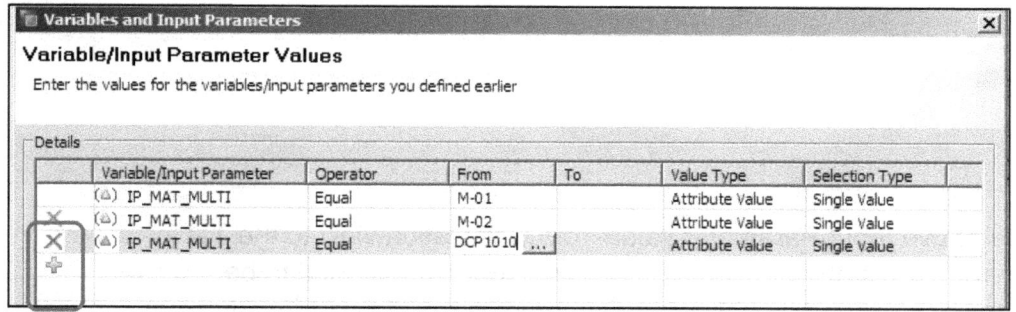

We can Add or Remove material numbers to the input value list, by using the options shown above. Display the Raw Data Tab in the Data Preview and observe the results.

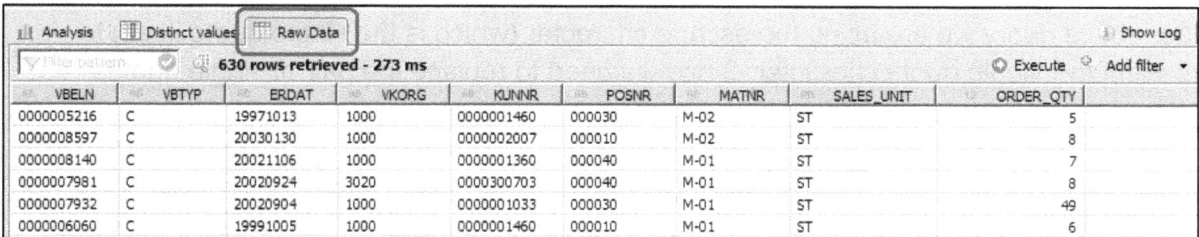

Let us check the SQL Statement which is generated during the data preview: Open the Data Preview drop down box in the Calculation view and choose "Open in SQL Editor

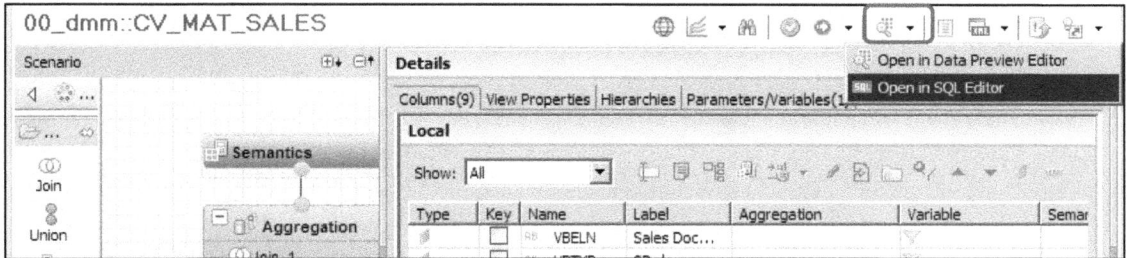

Enter the same values for the Input Parameter of Material number as shown above. We will find the following query generated, where we need to pay attention to the values of Input Parameter.

```
SELECT
        "VBELN","VBTYP","ERDAT","VKORG","KUNNR","POSNR","MATNR",
        "SALES_UNIT",sum("ORDER_QTY") AS "ORDER_QTY"
FROM "_SYS_BIC"."00_dmm/CV_MAT_SALES"
('PLACEHOLDER' = ('$$IP_MAT_MULTI$$',
        '''M-01'',''M-02'',''DCP1010'''))
GROUP BY "VBELN","VBTYP","ERDAT","VKORG","KUNNR","POSNR","MATNR",
        "SALES_UNIT"
```

When we pass the above Input Parameter value from Calculation view to the Table function input parameter, we need to ensure that additional quotes need to be removed. To handle these, we have added the following statement in the stored procedure GET_MAT_NUMBERS.

```
SELECT REPLACE (:V_MATSTR, '''' ,'') into V_MATSTR from DUMMY;
```

In the above query we are using the escape character (which is the single quote itself) to represent the single quote character. Since we need to replace the pair of single quotes, we are using the sequence of four single quotes.

`''M-01''`   →   This will be converted to M-01

6 Advanced Concepts in SQL Script

In this unit, we will explore some of the advanced programming techniques in SQL Script which are used to address various complex requirements. The list of topics includes, complex queries in SQL, processing data using *Temporary Tables*, *Cursors* and *Arrays*, using advanced functions for specific requirements, leveraging *Dynamic SQL* programming and implementing exception handling techniques to achieve error free logic. Also, we will go through some of the best practices to be adopted while implementing solutions using SQL script.

6.1 Complex Queries

Let us understand some of the techniques in SQL programming to implement queries, which are essential to address the requirements such as: complex calculations and aggregations, look up on multiple tables based on complex criteria.

Calculated columns: We can derive new columns in the SELECT statement using various built in functions and conditional expressions such as CASE.

Example: To derive a new column called "Change_Flag" based on the values in the existing columns of Creation date" (ERDAT) and Changed on date (AEDAT). Whenever the "Changed on date" is later than the Creation date, we need to stamp the value as "Changed", otherwise we will derive it as "Not Changed"

```
SELECT vbeln , netwr , erdat, aedat,
    CASE
    WHEN days_between(erdat, aedat)> 0 and aedat != '00000000' then 'Changed'
    ELSE 'Not Changed'
    END as "Change_Flag"
from VBAK
```

	VBELN	NETWR	ERDAT	AEDAT	Change_Flag
1	0000005027	275,000	19970214	19970220	Changed
2	0000005037	5,500	19970218	19970218	Not Changed
3	0000005056	47,48...	19970306	20020117	Changed
4	0000005121	382,440	19970626	19970627	Changed
5	0000005300	12,200	19971217	19980910	Changed

Sub Queries: These are quite commonly used to perform look up on another table or view, while executing a query against a table or view. Sub queries are used in the scenarios where the results of an inner query are to be validated by the outer query.

For instance, we need to get the list of sales orders where the order value is more than the average order value for the given period. Let us first check the result of the inner query that returns a single value i.e. Average Sales order Net Value.

```
SQL | Result
    SELECT AVG(NETWR) from VBAK WHERE ERDAT BETWEEN '20150101' and '20151231'
```

	AVG(NETWR)
1	15,003.93

Further we shall implement a complex query using the sub-query technique to achieve the above stated requirement, as shown below.

```
SQL | Result
    SELECT VBELN, NETWR
    from VBAK
    WHERE NETWR > (SELECT AVG(NETWR) from VBAK WHERE ERDAT BETWEEN '20150101' and '20151231' )
    AND ERDAT BETWEEN '20150101' and '20151231'
```

	VBELN	NETWR
1	0000016598	168,269.44
2	0000016632	17,727
3	0000016637	129,604.23
4	0000016652	24,472.18
5	0000016653	26,107.25

Note: We can compare the results of a sub-query using variety of operations such as =, >, IN, EXISTS. The sub-query should only return either single value or multiple values, depending on the operator in use. If a sub-query returns more than one value, it cannot be compared with the operators such as = or >.

Self joins: To address the requirements where we need to recursively fetch the records from a table or view by comparing the records of the same table or view, we need to implement self joins (join relationship where the table or view is same on both the left and right side of join condition). Typically, we need use self joins where there is parent child relationship in the dataset.

Consider the employee master data as show below:

	EMP_ID	EMP_NAME	MANAGER_ID
1	1000	John	1009
2	1001	Alex	1000
3	1002	Chris	1000
4	1003	Steve	1001

SELECT * from EMP_MASTER

We need to build a query using Self-Join, that would fetch the Employee name and his/her manager's name together in the same record.

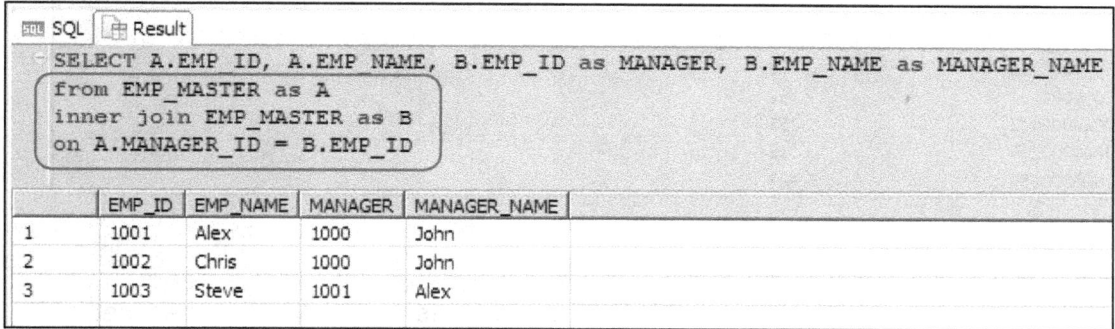

```
SELECT A.EMP_ID, A.EMP_NAME, B.EMP_ID as MANAGER, B.EMP_NAME as MANAGER_NAME
from EMP_MASTER as A
inner join EMP_MASTER as B
on A.MANAGER_ID = B.EMP_ID
```

	EMP_ID	EMP_NAME	MANAGER	MANAGER_NAME
1	1001	Alex	1000	John
2	1002	Chris	1000	John
3	1003	Steve	1001	Alex

Grouping and aggregations: The columnar storage of HANA database makes it efficient to summarize the results at the required level of granularity. We can leverage the Aggregate functions (Sum, Max, Min, Avg..) and Grouping operations (GROUP BY and HAVING) of SQL to address various requirements.

Scenario 1: Get the list of customers and the number of sales orders for each of the customers, who has placed more than 10 orders.

```
SELECT KUNNR, COUNT(VBELN) from VBAK
WHERE VBTYP = 'C' and ERDAT between '20150101' and '20151231'
GROUP BY KUNNR
HAVING COUNT(VBELN) > 10
```

	KUNNR	COUNT(VBELN)
1	FIO-CUST01	1,199
2	FIO-CUST02	616
3	FIO-CUST04	671
4	FIO-CUST03	847
5	0000003000	20

Scenario 2: Get the list of customers who has not placed any orders for the past 500 days. Here we can utilize the MAX function on Sales Order Date (ERDAT) to get the latest sales order date for each customer. Further we can use the DAYS_BETWEEN function to get the number of days between the Latest Order Date and Current Date.

```
SQL | Result
SELECT KUNNR, Days_between( MAX(ERDAT), NOW()) as DAYS_SINCE_LASTORDER from VBAK
WHERE VBTYP = 'C'
GROUP BY KUNNR
HAVING Days_between( MAX(ERDAT), NOW())   > 500
```

	KUNNR	DAYS_SINCE_LASTORDER
1	0000000001	2,495
2	0000000011	1,562
3	0000000012	1,758
4	0000000255	6,318
5	0000000257	6,407

Inline Views:

With this technique, we can implement SELECT statements to get the required set of fields from another named SELECT query (inline view) that is defined within the same SQL statement. If you observe the below query, where we have implemented an inline view called CUST_QUETY to generate the aggregated results and this inline view is further used by the actual SELECT query to produce the final result. Hence, we can use the inline views to construct complex SELECT statements using more modular approach.

```
SQL | Result
with CUST_QUERY as (
SELECT KUNNR as Customer, Days_between( MAX(ERDAT), NOW()) as DAYS_SINCE_LASTORDER from VBAK
WHERE VBTYP = 'C'
GROUP BY KUNNR
HAVING Days_between( MAX(ERDAT), NOW())   > 500
)
select
 customer, DAYS_SINCE_LASTORDER
from CUST_QUERY
```

	CUSTOMER	DAYS_SINCE_LASTORDER
1	0000000001	2,495
2	0000000011	1,562
3	0000000012	1,758
4	0000000255	6,318
5	0000000257	6,407

6.2 Cursors - operations for looping on data records

Cursors are used to fetch the records sequentially from a table or view and process these records in a loop. Cursors are ideally used in the scenarios where we need to perform record level (row by row) operations.

Note: Avoid using cursors to process larger data sets, since they are usually inefficient as they perform row by row access on the database tables.

Declare Cursor Variable:

DECLARE C_VBAK FOR

SELECT VBELN, KUNNR, NETWR FROM VBAK WHERE VBTYP = 'C'

Steps to process the records using Cursors:

- Open the cursor (Declaring cursor variable which is always linked to the respective SELECT query)
- Fetch records using cursor variable
- Close the cursor variable

We can perform the record by record processing of cursors in two different ways.

1) Explicit looping: Using OPEN cursor, FETCH records using a WHILE loop and CLOSE the cursor
2) Implicit loop on cursor variable: Using the FOR loop on cursor variable
   This is commonly used since it performs the Open / Fetch and Close operations implicitly

Explicit looping of cursor variable:

Open the Cursor:

- OPEN CURSOR C_VBAK;

Fetch data records sequentially using the Cursor:

- FETCH C_VBAK into :V_VBELN, :V_KUNNR, :V_NETWR;

Closing Cursor:

- CLOSE CURSOR C_VBAK;

Implicit processing of cursor variable:

To open a cursor variable that has been defined in the program and to iterate over the result set of the query we can use the FOR loop as shown below.

```
FOR <ROW_VARIABLE>  as <CURSOR> (<optional arguments>) DO
--Processing logic for row wise operations
END FOR ;
```

Example:

```
FOR REC_VBAK as C_VBAK   DO
--Processing logic for row wise operations
END FOR ;
```

Deriving properties of cursor variables:

Each cursor variable will have the following built-in attributes which can be accessed as per our need.

<Cursor_variable>::IS_CLOSED → To check if a cursor variable is closed

This can be used to ensure that the cursor variable is currently closed, before trying to perform OPEN Cursor or FOR Loop on this. This will help us to avoid this exception

<Cursor_variable>::ROW_COUNT→ To check the number of rows in the result set of the query attached to the cursor variable

<Cursor_variable>::NOTFOUND → To check if the previous FETCH operation is successful either explicitly or implicitly during the processing in FOR loop

➡ *Example for Practice:*
   7.2 Business Case: Sales Employee Hierarchy Flattening

6.3 Arrays and their application for complex calculations

An array is a special type of variable, which can store a group of elements of same data type. In that sense an array represents a single column. By defining multiple arrays that represents a group of columns we can achieve tabular data processing, where we can process a group of data records sequentially.

In SQL Script, we normally prefer table variables to process group of records. However, table variables do not support record by record processing. Especially in the scenarios where we need to refer to the values from another record in the same dataset, it will not be possible with table variables while accessing them in SELECT statement. This is where we can leverage the Arrays.

Possible operations on arrays
- Prepare set of elements of array variable
- Fetch the values of specific elements
- Merge data of two arrays
- Transferring data from arrays into a table variable
- Moving data from table variable into arrays
- Looping through the array elements
- Clear the memory of array variable

Declare Array Variables for storing data
- We can declare an array variable using the key word ARRAY as the data type
- We can declare an array type variable using any of the elementary data types of SQL script. (Such as DATE, NVARCHAR, INTEGER etc.)
- There is no need to specify the size of the array variable (i.e. the number of elements which are expected to be stored in an array)
- If we use DECIMAL type in array and try to read its value will lead to a compile error. In such cases we need to use DOUBLE data type and convert it back to decimal if needed.

Example:

```
DECLARE A_KUNNR TYPE NVARCHAR(10) ARRAY;
DECLARE A_NETWR DOUBLE ARRAY;
```

Fill arrays with values

We can assign the values to the elements using an index notation, which starts from 1.
Example: A_KUNNR[1] = '1001';

Fill arrays with values from a table variable

We can use the ARRAY_AGG command to fill the values of specific column of a table variable into the array

- Sort data by primary key to ensure each array have the same order, then we could use one index to access fields of same record
- Data types of array element and table column must be same

Example:

```
TAB_SALES = SELECT KUNNR, SUM(NETWR) from VBAK where VBTYP = 'C' GROUP BY KUNNR;

A_KUNNR := ARRAY_AGG(:TAB_SALES.KUNNR ORDER BY "KUNNR");
A_NETWR := ARRAY_AGG(:TAB_SALES.NETWR ORDER BY "KUNNR");
```

Loop over data from or set value to the array

- We can use FOR Loop to process the array elements in a sequence
- Use the CARDINALITY function to get the number of elements in an array

```
FOR V_INDEX IN 1 .. CARDINALITY(:A_KUNNR) DO
        IF ( :A_NETWR[:V_INDEX] = 0 );
                ELSE
        END IF;
END FOR;
```

Combine Arrays to a Table variable:

Using UNNEST command to combine (merge) the data of multiple array variables (columns) into a table variable, which has the suitable structure.
Example: He the two array variables are copied to the respective columns of table variable
TAB_SALES = UNNEST(:A_KUNNR, :A_NETWR);

Removing the elements from array variable

We can use the TRIM_ARRAY function to remove the given number of elements at the end of the array. If we want to remove all the elements in an array (i.e. to clean up the array) we can use the CARDINALITY function that will return the total number of elements in an array.

Examples:

TRIM_ARRAY(:A_KUNNR, 1);

TRIM_ARRAY(:A_KUNNR, CARDINALITY(:A_KUNNR));

➜ **Example for Practice:**

6.10.3 Requirement: Derive Validity Dates for Routing Task Lists

6.4 Exception Handling Techniques

Due to multiple reasons, statements in SQL Script programs can be terminated since the system cannot handle those situations. For example: unique constraint or primary key violation in a table, arithmetic overflow while storing value in a variable, divide by zero error. These are considered as system defined exceptions.

We can also define user defined exceptions, that will allow us to implement the actions (such as generating error messages) to handle specific scenarios in the business logic. For example, if we want to generate an exception when the user entry for date range is incorrect (Start Date is later than End Date).

HANA has few implicit variables which provides the details of the exception being raised:

::SQL_ERROR_CODE → Stores the error code (for Built-in exceptions these codes will be ranging from 1 to 9999 and for user defined exceptions we can specify between 10000 and 19999)

::SQL_ERROR_MESSAGE → Captures the related error message of the caught exception

It is quite important to add the exception handling logic to build robust programs. SQL Script provides the following statement to handle the exceptions.

- The DECLARE EXIT HANDLER statement allows you to define exception handlers to process exception conditions in your procedures.

- You use the DECLARE CONDITION parameter to name exception conditions, and optionally, their associated SQL state values.

- You can use SIGNAL or RESIGNAL with specified error code in user-defined error code range. A user-defined exception can be handled by the handler declared in the procedure. Also, it can be handled by the caller which can be another procedure or client.

Let us try to understand the exception handling approach by implementing a stored procedure shown below.

```
CREATE PROCEDURE NVARMA.PR_GET_SALES_YEAR
 (IN P_SALESORG NVARCHAR(4),
  OUT SALES_TAB TABLE(KUNNR NVARCHAR(10),
                           TOTAL_VALUE DECIMAL(18,2)))
LANGUAGE SQLSCRIPT
DEFAULT SCHEMA <SCHEMA NAME>
READS SQL DATA AS
BEGIN

DECLARE EX_MISSING_INPUT CONDITION FOR SQL_ERROR_CODE 10001;
    DECLARE EXIT HANDLER FOR EX_MISSING_INPUT
         SELECT ::SQL_ERROR_CODE, ::SQL_ERROR_MESSAGE FROM DUMMY;

 IF P_SALESORG = '' THEN

 SIGNAL EX_MISSING_INPUT SET MESSAGE_TEXT = 'Input Missing for SalesOrg';

 END IF;

      SALES_TAB = Select KUNNR,
                      SUM(NETWR) as TOTAL_VALUE
                      from VBAK
                      WHERE VKORG = :P_SALESORG
                      GROUP BY KUNNR;

END;
```

Since we are calling the stored procedure without passing appropriate value for the input parameter (SalesOrg), it will generate relevant error message via exception handling.

	SQL	Result	Result

```
CALL NVARMA.PR_GET_SALES_YEAR('',?)
```

	:::SQL_ERROR_CODE	:::SQL_ERROR_MESSAGE
1	10,001	Input Value Missing for SalesOrg

➡ *Example for Practice:*
   7.4 Business Case: Implementing Sales Order Delivery Status Snapshots

6.5 Data Manipulations (DML) using SQL Script

Let us go through the various data manipulation statements supported by SQL script and their usage and recommendations.

INSERT → To insert new records into the database table. We can insert a single record or multiple records in a table.

> INSERT into <DB Table> Values (<Col1>, <Col2>...)

> INSERT into <DB Table> (SELECT <fields> from <Table Variable / DB Table>)

UPDATE → To update the existing records in the database table

> UPDATE <DB Table> SET <Col1> = <Value> WHERE <Condition>

> Example: UPDATE EMPLOYEE SET SALARY = SALARY + (SALARY * 10 / 100) WHERE DEPT_ID = 10;

DELETE → To remove the records from a database table based on a given condition

UPSERT → This statement will behave like UPDATE or INSERT. Which means, when there is a record exists with the given primary key values, it will perform UPDATE. Otherwise it will perform INSERT.

COMMIT → To perform COMMIT on the database (Note: The COMMIT is implicitly executed at the end of the processing block. Hence, we don't need to use it often)

ROLLBACK → To revert the data manipulations in the database and bring it to the previous COMMIT state

Note: We can execute the data manipulation statements either in the SQL console or inside the stored procedures which are not defined as Read-Only (READS SQL DATA option). Most commonly we need to use the data manipulation statements while implementing persistence-based solutions using Stored Procedures in HANA.

→ *Example for Practice:*
→ 7.4 Business Case: Implementing Sales Order Delivery Status Snapshots

6.6 Data Manipulations on Table Variables – HANA 2.0

Starting from HANA 2.0 SPS 01, we can use Insert/Update/Delete operators on table variables. This allows us to perform execute DML-like operations on intermediate table variables. These are usually more optimal than using the index based cell access or processing using Arrays.

Syntax: <Table Variable>.< Operator>(Parameters)

Example: In the following example we are using INSERT, UPDATE and DELETE operators on table variable called PRODUCTS

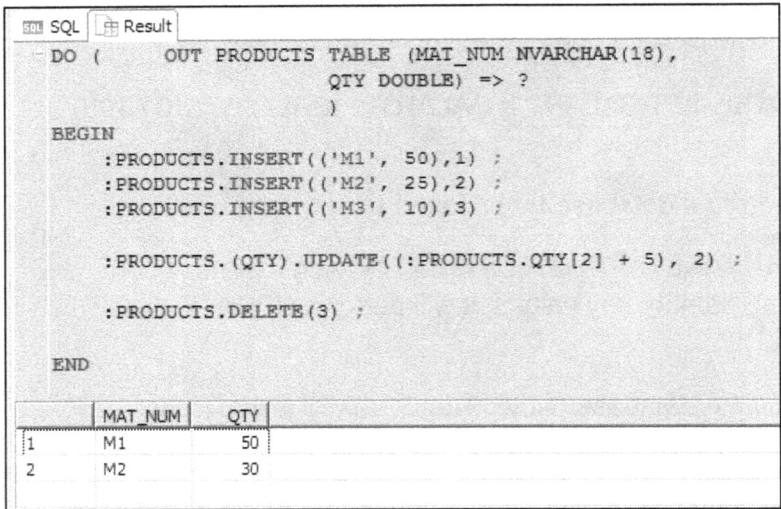

```
SQL    Result
DO (      OUT PRODUCTS TABLE (MAT_NUM NVARCHAR(18),
                             QTY DOUBLE) => ?
                )
BEGIN
    :PRODUCTS.INSERT(('M1', 50),1) ;
    :PRODUCTS.INSERT(('M2', 25),2) ;
    :PRODUCTS.INSERT(('M3', 10),3) ;

    :PRODUCTS.(QTY).UPDATE((:PRODUCTS.QTY[2] + 5), 2) ;

    :PRODUCTS.DELETE(3) ;

END
```

	MAT_NUM	QTY
1	M1	50
2	M2	30

We can also use the INSERT operation to insert the records from another table variable:

Examples:

TAB_TARGET.INSERT (TAB_SOURCE); → Insert all records into target table variable

TAB_TARGET.INSERT (TAB_SOURCE, 10); → Insert first 10 records into target table variable

TAB_TARGET.(A,B).INSERT (TAB_SOURCE); → Insert into specific columns of target table variable

6.7 Dynamic SQL for Flexible Solutions

We have gone through the capabilities of SQL Script programming to provide the answers to the known questions. For example, "Get the sales revenue for specific year and customer" or "Calculate the raw material inventory projections for the next 12 months".

However, there may be specific situations where we need to build the solutions, that can answer the questions which will be known only during runtime of the program. We shall leverage dynamic SQL to implement such solutions. Essentially dynamic SQL helps us to implement logic that needs to provide flexibility and generic behavior in the solution.

Dynamic SQL allows us to construct a SQL statement during the execution time of a procedure. Through dynamic SQL approach, SQL statements are prepared as strings of characters that are generated when the program runs. They can be entered by the programmer or generated by the program itself. But unlike static SQL statements, they are not embedded in the source program. Also, in contrast to static SQL statements, dynamic SQL statements can change from one execution to the next.

Few scenarios for dynamic solutions:

- Building utility applications such as a table browser, which takes any table name and field list as input and the output should show the records by executing the query on that table.

- Implement a custom solution such as Pricing Analytics, which calculates various type of discounts and prices based on the formulas which are dynamic in nature. To derive these formulas, the program must query respective tables and prepare the formula using specific fields from those tables.

- Generating the SQL code automatically for certain applications based on SAP HANA platform such as AMDP based planning function framework in BW-Integrated Planning

In the following sections, let us understand the syntax and implementation process of the solutions based on dynamic SQL.

6.7.1 Approach to implement Dynamic SQL

Implementing dynamic SQL operations in the code involves the following steps:

- Prepare the desired SQL statement in a string variable
- Execute the SQL statement using commands like EXEC or EXECUTE IMMEDIATE

EXEC executes the SQL statement which is passed through a string argument.

EXEC '<sql-statement>' [INTO <var_name_list>] [USING <expression_list>]

EXECUTE IMMEDIATE executes the SQL statement passed in a string argument. The results of queries executed with EXECUTE IMMEDIATE are appended to the procedure's result iterator. This behavior is illustrated in the example below.

Example for Dynamic SQL operation: In this solution, we are trying to get the number of records from any given database table

```
SET SCHEMA <SCHEMA NAME>;

DO (IN V_TABLE VARCHAR(100) => 'MARA',
    OUT V_SQL VARCHAR(1000) => ?,
    OUT V_CNT INT => ?)
BEGIN

    V_SQL := 'SELECT COUNT(*) ' ||   ' from ' || :V_TABLE ;

    EXECUTE IMMEDIATE :V_SQL into V_CNT;

END
```

```
SQL    Result
  DO (IN V_TABLE VARCHAR(100) => 'MARA',
      OUT V_SQL VARCHAR(1000) => ?,
      OUT V_CNT INT => ?)
  BEGIN

      V_SQL := 'SELECT COUNT(*) ' ||   ' from ' || :V_TABLE ;

      EXECUTE IMMEDIATE :V_SQL into V_CNT;

  END
```

	Out(1)	Out(2)
1	SELECT COUNT(*) from MARA	1,356

6.7.2   Challenges and limitations with Dynamic SQL

There are certian limitations when we implement the logic using Dynamic SQL Script. Especially we cannot leverage some of the opportunities for optimizations which are available in the static SQL.

- Dynamic SQL statements are recompiled every time the statement is executed, since the actual generated statement is not known to the SQL optimizer until the runtime of program. Due to this it cannot leverage the pre-compiled version of the program logic for dynamic SQL code. This will cause additional runtime during the program execution.

- You cannot use SQLScript variables in the SQL statements constructed using the dynamic SQL.

- You cannot bind the result of a dynamic SQL statement to a SQLScript variable.

   Note: From SAP HANA 2.0 SPS 03, this limitation has been addressed.

How to use Table Variables in Dynamic SQL?

In the earlier example, we have stored the dynamic SQL results into scalar variables, wherein we could do a SELECT <Fields> INTO scalar variables within the EXEC or EXECUTE IMMEDIATE statements. Similarly we can explore the capability to pass the result set of Dynamic SQL based SELECT query into table variables as well. Starting from HANA 2.0 SPS3 we can use Table Variabes to store the results of queries executed dynamically.

Syntax: EXEC <SQL Statement String> INTO <Table Variable>

6.7.3   Example: Table browser utility

Let us explore the practical requirement to build a table browser application, where the user inputs the name of a database table and program should output the records from the same time. We need to build this solution using dynamic SQL, since we won't know the actual table name to be used by the SELECT statement, until the runtime.

1. Declare the necessary variables and maintain initial values in the variables: such as the source table name, schema name, temporary table and SQL Query string.

2. Build the SQL string for the temporary table definition and store it in respective variable.

3. Execute the dynamic SQL statement that creates the temporary table at runtime. This temporary table is needed to store the list of fields which are be fetched from the respective database table.

4. Build the "Final" SQL String by concatenation of "Select" , "Input parameter" "From" , Where",   and save it in variable – LV_QUERY

5. Run the dynamic SQL statement using EXECUTE IMMEDAITE, to produce the results

```
do
begin

declare LV_QUERY varchar(8000);
declare LV_TEMPTABLE nvarchar(256) := '#tmp_tab_result';
declare LV_SOURCETABLE nvarchar(256) :=  'MARA';
declare LV_SCHEMA nvarchar(256) := '<SCHEMA for DB Tables>';

with columns as (
 select
  column_name, data_type_name, length, scale, position,
  '"' || column_name || '" ' || data_type_name ||
  '(' || length || (case when scale is null then '' else ',' || scale
end) || ')'
  as col_String
 from sys.table_columns
 where table_name = :LV_SOURCETABLE and schema_name = :LV_SCHEMA
 order by position
)

select
 'create local temporary table ' || LV_TEMPTABLE ||
 ' ( ' || String_Agg(col_String, ', ' order by position) || ');'
 into "LV_QUERY"
from columns;

EXECUTE IMMEDIATE :LV_QUERY;

select 'INSERT INTO ' || LV_TEMPTABLE ||
 ' SELECT * FROM ' || :LV_SCHEMA  || '.' || :LV_SOURCETABLE || ';'
into "LV_QUERY" from dummy;
EXECUTE IMMEDIATE :LV_QUERY;

select 'SELECT * FROM ' || LV_TEMPTABLE into "LV_QUERY" from dummy;
EXECUTE IMMEDIATE :LV_QUERY;

select 'DROP TABLE ' || LV_TEMPTABLE into "LV_QUERY" from dummy;
EXECUTE IMMEDIATE :LV_QUERY;

end;
```

Execute the anonymous block and observe the results by changing the table name

```
do
begin

declare LV_QUERY varchar(8000);
declare LV_TEMPTABLE nvarchar(256) := '#tmp_tab_result';
declare LV_SOURCETABLE nvarchar(256) :=  'MAKT';
```

	MANDT	MATNR	SPRAS	MAKTX	MAKTG
833	800	T-B228	E	Fly wheel	FLY WHEEL
834	800	T-B229	E	Fly wheel	FLY WHEEL
835	800	T-B230	E	Fly wheel	FLY WHEEL
836	800	T-B299	E	Fly wheel	FLY WHEEL
837	800	T-B300	E	Hollow shaft	HOLLOW SHAFT
838	800	T-B301	E	Hollow shaft	HOLLOW SHAFT

Note: We can rerun the same code by assigning multiple other database table names (KNA1, MARA..) in the variable LV_SOURCETABLE and observe dynamic table browser functionality.

Summary:

Dynamic SQL is used whenever the SQL statements are to be constructed during the application execution

6.8   Declarative and Imperative Logic in SQL Script

After going through the various programming concepts of SQL script, it is essential to understand the inner mechanics of the programs and what kind of best practices we need to adopt to implement optimized solutions.

Let us raise some the key questions and understand the important aspects related to SQL script runtime:

- How are the stored procedures and functions executed behind the scene?
- Analyzing the execution plans and identifying performance optimization areas

What are the different kinds of programming constructs and how are these constructs optimized and processed during run time?

Broadly SQL Script programming consists of two types of constructs:

Declarative language constructs: These are the kind of operations that are translated into a calculation model and allows parallel processing. When we implement a procedure or a Function which consists of only declarative constructs, then can be completely translated into an acyclic dataflow graph where each node represents a data transformation. This will lead to signification optimization of the code.

- Table Variable operations
- SELECT Queries

Imperative language constructs: It is typically used to splits the logic between several data flows. These operations does not support parallel processing.

- Assigning values to variables
- Flow control such as IF..ELSE
- Looping statements (FOR, WHILE..)
- Cursor operations
- Arrays
- Dynamic SQL
- Exception Handling
- Transaction Control (Commit, rollback etc.)

Keeping these aspects in mind, we should try to build SQL Script code with declarative constructs as much as possible to ensure optimal execution.

6.9   Best Practices in SQL Script

In SQL Script programming we need to adopt several best practices and recommended approaches to deliver reusable and optimal solutions. Let us understand these techniques in the following sections.

Adopt proper naming standards and maintain appropriate comments in the code:

- To achieve better readability and maintenance of code, it is essential to follow appropriate naming standards for the various elements such as:

  - Table Variables, Local variables, Arrays, Cursors etc.

  - Database tables, Stored procedures, Scalar functions and Table functions

- Maintaining proper comments in the code will help to simplify the readability and future maintenance of code

Implement code using modularization techniques:

- Try to decompose the complex logic into multiple reusable blocks of code by leveraging stored procedures, scalar function and table functions

- We can also leverage the calculation views as part of modularizing the complex logic. Implement the desired logic in a calculation view and use it to fetch the data inside procedures or functions

Minimizing data volumes:

- Try to minimize the amount of data fetched and processed in the memory by using appropriate filtering methods such as:

  - Enforce the necessary Joins and WHERE conditions to restrict the records as much as possible
  - Specify the desired set of fields in the SELECT statements to avoid unwanted fields
  - Perform necessary aggregations to bring only distinct set of records

- Avoid using SELECT *, since it will fetch all the columns from the table. Column store operations should be restricted to only necessary columns to achieve better performance

Use right methods while processing group of records:

- Suggested methods while performing operations on group of records:

    - To process a group of records from set of tables, where there is no need of addressing specific record – use Table Variables
    - To process the records sequentially inside a loop – Use Cursors. However, Cursors will affect the performance when large number of records are processed
    - To access a different record in the same dataset while processing a group of records – use Arrays.

- Try to insert / update or delete a set of data records into the database because a single unit is much more efficient than inserting the records one by one.

Try to achieve Parallel Processing:

- If you split a complex query into logical sub queries it can help the optimizer to identify common sub expressions and to derive more efficient execution plans.

- Following statements will cause the execution to be sequential

Implement error handling for all relevant scenarios:

- Implement exception handling to ensure there won't be any run time errors such as "Numeric Overflow" during the execution

Avoid time consuming operations

- Window functions such as RANK are executed by the Row Engine. Hence try to avoid these statements as much as possible, particularly on larger set of records

- Cursors will process the records one by one in a loop, which can be inefficient on larger data sets

- Executing dynamic SQL is slow because compile time checks and query optimization must be done for every invocation of the procedure

6.10 Practical Solutions and Examples Using SQL script

Let us go through few examples and scenarios where we can build solutions using SQL Script programming. These examples will help you to understand the application of different features of SQL script programming.

6.10.1 Requirement: Derive Previous Fiscal Period for given date

Often, we will come across the requirement to derive the previous fiscal period, or next fiscal period while building the calculation views, procedures or functions. Implement the following reporting logic to build a reusable scalar function which returns the "Previous Fiscal Period" for a given date.

Key Learnings:

- Utilizing standard functions – Character string and date functions
- Implementing Scalar Functions

```
FUNCTION "NVARMA"."democode::SF_GET_PREVIOUS_FISCPER"
    (IP_FISCPER NVARCHAR(7),
     IP_NUM_PER INTEGER )
     RETURNS PREV_FISCPER NVARCHAR(7)
     LANGUAGE SQLSCRIPT
     SQL SECURITY INVOKER AS
BEGIN
/* * * * * * * * * * * * * * * * * * * * * * * * * *
      Write your function logic
 * * * * * * * * * * * * * * * * * * * * * * * * * */

 DECLARE V_YEAR NVARCHAR(4);
 DECLARE V_MONTH NVARCHAR(3);

 DECLARE V_PREV_YEAR NVARCHAR(4);
 DECLARE V_PREV_MONTH NVARCHAR(3);

 SELECT SUBSTRING(IP_FISCPER,1,4) into V_YEAR from dummy;
 SELECT SUBSTRING(IP_FISCPER,5,3) into V_MONTH from dummy;

IF to_int(:V_MONTH) <= :IP_NUM_PER  then
    V_PREV_MONTH := :V_MONTH - :IP_NUM_PER + 12;
    V_PREV_YEAR := :V_YEAR - 1;
ELSE
     V_PREV_MONTH := to_int(:V_MONTH) - :IP_NUM_PER;
```

```
      V_PREV_YEAR := V_YEAR;
END IF;

   SELECT CONCAT(V_PREV_YEAR, lpad(V_PREV_MONTH,3,'0')) into PREV_FISCPER
from dummy;

END;
```

Test #1:

```
SQL  Result
   SELECT   "NVARMA"."democode::SF_GET_PREVIOUS_FISCPER" ('2018002', 1) from DUMMY

      NVARMA.democode::SF_GET_PREVIOUS_FISCPER('2018002',1)
   1  2018001
```

Test #2:

```
SQL  Result
   SELECT   "NVARMA"."democode::SF_GET_PREVIOUS_FISCPER" ('2018002', 2) from DUMMY

      NVARMA.democode::SF_GET_PREVIOUS_FISCPER('2018002',2)
   1  2017012
```

Note: The above scalar function logic can be used for deriving the past or future calendar months. In case of deriving the fiscal periods, we need to also consider the fiscal year variant in the logic.

6.10.2 Requirement: Flexible Input to choose between Fiscal vs Calendar Month

In some scenarios the reporting users would like to have the flexibility to choose between Fiscal period and Calendar month while running the reports. To address this, we need to build our calculation view which allows the user to choose either fiscal period or calendar month at runtime and filter the records accordingly.

In this example we will build a reusable Table Function which returns the details of the given periods. We can use this Table Function in Calculation views to apply the selection criteria on either Fiscal Periods or Calendar Months as per the user input.

This function module takes the following inputs:

1) PERIOD_CHOICE → Either CALENDAR_PER or FISCAL_PER
2) PERIOD_FROM → The value for "From Period" (Example: 2018001)
3) PERIOD_TO → The value for "To Period" (Example: 2018003)

```
FUNCTION "NVARMA"."democode::TF_PERIOD_TYPE_SELECTION"
                  (       PERIOD_CHOICE VARCHAR(15),
                          PERIOD_FROM NVARCHAR(7),
                PERIOD_TO NVARCHAR(7)  )
        RETURNS TABLE
                  ( TIME_SELECTED varchar(15),
                    CALMONTH VARCHAR(6),
                    DATE_SAP varchar(8),
                    CALYEAR varchar(4),
                    MONTH_NBR varchar(2)  )

        LANGUAGE SQLSCRIPT
        SQL SECURITY INVOKER AS
BEGIN
/****************************
        Write your function logic
****************************/
 DECLARE from_period_cal varchar(6)  :=
CONCAT(LEFT(PERIOD_FROM,4),right(PERIOD_FROM,2));

 DECLARE to_period_cal varchar(6)  :=
CONCAT(LEFT(PERIOD_TO,4),right(PERIOD_TO,2));

 If PERIOD_CHOICE = 'CALENDAR_PER' then
```

```
    RETURN
        SELECT period_choice as TIME_SELECTED,
                CALMONTH,
                DATE_SAP,
                YEAR as CALYEAR,
                MONTH as MONTH_NBR
        from "_SYS_BI"."M_TIME_DIMENSION"
        WHERE CALMONTH between from_period_cal and to_period_cal;

Elseif  PERIOD_CHOICE = 'FISCAL_PER' then

    RETURN
        SELECT period_choice as TIME_SELECTED,
                concat(FISCAL_YEAR, lpad(FISCAL_PERIOD,2,'0')) as CALMONTH,
                DATE as DATE_SAP,
                FISCAL_YEAR as CALYEAR,
                FISCAL_PERIOD as MONTH_NBR
        from "_SYS_BI"."M_FISCAL_CALENDAR"
        WHERE CALENDAR_VARIANT = 'K4'      --Specify the Fiscal year variant
          AND concat(FISCAL_YEAR, lpad(FISCAL_PERIOD,2,'0'))
          between from_period_cal and to_period_cal;

end if;

END;
```

Verify the results of Table function by executing the below query:

亘 SQL	Result				
SELECT * FROM "NVARMA"."democode::TF_PERIOD_TYPE_SELECTION"('FISCAL_PER', '201801','201803')					

	TIME_SELECTED	CALMONTH	DATE_SAP	CALYEAR	MONTH_NBR
1	FISCAL_PER	201801	20180101	2018	1
2	FISCAL_PER	201801	20180102	2018	1
3	FISCAL_PER	201801	20180103	2018	1
4	FISCAL_PER	201801	20180104	2018	1
5	FISCAL_PER	201801	20180105	2018	1
6	FISCAL_PER	201801	20180106	2018	1
7	FISCAL_PER	201801	20180107	2018	1
8	FISCAL_PER	201801	20180108	2018	1
9	FISCAL_PER	201801	20180109	2018	1
10	FISCAL_PER	201801	20180110	2018	1

We can consume this Table function in a calculation view and provide the flexibility to the user in choosing between Fiscal or Calendar periods

6.10.3 Requirement: Derive Validity Dates for Routing Task Lists

Implement a Table function with the following logic based on SAP Routing Task List (PLKO table). In this example we have created a similar table named as TASKLIST_HDR.

This table has the header details from task lists. It has a Valid-From date from each task list. However, it does not have the Valid-To date. As part of this requirement we need to derive the Valid-To date based on the Valid-From date of the previous entry in the task list.

Key Learnings:

- Processing data using Table variables
- Usage of Arrays
- Implementing Scalar Functions
- Building Table functions

Solution Details:

Calculation logic for the VALID_TO date for each of the Task List header entries.

- If the next record belongs to the same Task List group set the VALID_TO of current record
  as the VALID_FROM Minus 1, of the next record
- ELSE set the VALID_TO as '9999-12-31'

Let us see how we can achieve this requirement by using the Arrays.

Step 1: Create the following table like the task list table above: TASKLIST_HDR

Note: This table is similar to SAP Standard Table: PLKO (Task List Header)

```
select * from nvarma.TASKLIST_HDR
```

	TASKLIST_TYPE	TASKLIST_GROUP	GROUP_COUNTER	INTERNAL_COUNTER	VALID_FROM
1	R	GRP001	C1	001	Jan 1, 2017
2	R	GRP001	C1	002	Mar 1, 2017
3	R	GRP001	C1	003	May 10, 2017
4	R	GRP002	X1	001	Jan 1, 2018
5	R	GRP002	X1	002	Feb 1, 2018
6	R	GRP002	X1	003	Apr 15, 2018

Step 2: Implement the following Table Function to build the logic to derive "Valid To Date"
for each of the Task List entries.

```
FUNCTION "NVARMA"."00_dmm::TASK_LIST_VALIDITY" ( )
      RETURNS TABLE (
                          TASKLIST_TYPE NVARCHAR(1),
                          TASKLIST_GROUP  NVARCHAR(8),
                          GROUP_COUNTER NVARCHAR(2),
                          INTERNAL_COUNTER NVARCHAR(3),
                          VALID_FROM DATE,
                          VALID_TO DATE)

      LANGUAGE SQLSCRIPT
      SQL SECURITY INVOKER AS
BEGIN

DECLARE A_TASKLIST_TYPE NVARCHAR(1) ARRAY;
DECLARE A_TASKLIST_GROUP NVARCHAR(8) ARRAY;
DECLARE A_GROUP_COUNTER NVARCHAR(2) ARRAY;
DECLARE A_INTERNAL_COUNTER NVARCHAR(3) ARRAY;
DECLARE A_VALID_FROM DATE ARRAY;
DECLARE A_VALID_TO DATE ARRAY;

DECLARE V_INDEX INTEGER;
DECLARE V_NEXT INTEGER;

--Fetch the Task list entries from database into table variable

TAB_TASKLIST =    SELECT
                          "TASKLIST_TYPE",
                          "TASKLIST_GROUP",
                          "GROUP_COUNTER",
                          "INTERNAL_COUNTER" ,
                          "VALID_FROM"
               from nvarma.TASKLIST_HDR        ;

--Fill the arrays from the respective columns of table variable

A_TASKLIST_TYPE := ARRAY_AGG(:TAB_TASKLIST.TASKLIST_TYPE
                    ORDER BY "TASKLIST_TYPE","TASKLIST_GROUP","GROUP_COUNTER",
                    "INTERNAL_COUNTER");
A_TASKLIST_GROUP := ARRAY_AGG(:TAB_TASKLIST.TASKLIST_GROUP
```

```
                     ORDER BY "TASKLIST_TYPE","TASKLIST_GROUP","GROUP_COUNTER",
                     "INTERNAL_COUNTER");
A_GROUP_COUNTER := ARRAY_AGG(:TAB_TASKLIST.GROUP_COUNTER
                     ORDER BY "TASKLIST_TYPE","TASKLIST_GROUP","GROUP_COUNTER",
                     "INTERNAL_COUNTER");
A_INTERNAL_COUNTER := ARRAY_AGG(:TAB_TASKLIST.INTERNAL_COUNTER
                     ORDER BY "TASKLIST_TYPE","TASKLIST_GROUP","GROUP_COUNTER",
                     "INTERNAL_COUNTER");
A_VALID_FROM := ARRAY_AGG(:TAB_TASKLIST.VALID_FROM
                     ORDER BY "TASKLIST_TYPE","TASKLIST_GROUP","GROUP_COUNTER",
                     "INTERNAL_COUNTER");

--Loop through the Arrays to determine the VALID_TO date based on
--the VALID_FROM date of the next record

FOR V_INDEX IN 1 .. CARDINALITY(:A_TASKLIST_GROUP) DO

        V_NEXT := V_INDEX + 1;
-- If the next record belongs to the same Task List group set the
-- VALID_TO of current record as the VALID_FROM minus 1 of the
-- next record ELSE set it as '9999-12-31'

if ( :A_TASKLIST_TYPE[:V_NEXT] = :A_TASKLIST_TYPE[:V_INDEX] AND
      :A_TASKLIST_GROUP[:V_NEXT] = :A_TASKLIST_GROUP[:V_INDEX] AND
      :A_GROUP_COUNTER[:V_NEXT] = :A_GROUP_COUNTER[:V_INDEX]) THEN

A_VALID_TO[:V_INDEX] := ADD_DAYS(:A_VALID_FROM[:V_NEXT], -1);

        ELSE
A_VALID_TO[:V_INDEX] := TO_DATE ('9999-12-31', 'YYYY-MM-DD');
        END IF;

END FOR;

--Transfer the results from Arrays into another table variable
TAB_RESULT = UNNEST( :A_TASKLIST_TYPE,   :A_TASKLIST_GROUP,
:A_GROUP_COUNTER, :A_INTERNAL_COUNTER, :A_VALID_FROM, :A_VALID_TO)
              AS (TASKLIST_TYPE, TASKLIST_GROUP, GROUP_COUNTER,
INTERNAL_COUNTER , VALID_FROM, VALID_TO);

--Return the results from table function
      RETURN SELECT * from :TAB_RESULT;

END;
```

Results of Table Function:

Execute the following query on the table function and validate the results. We shall observe that the VALID_TO has been derived correctly based on the VALID_FROM of the subsequent record that belongs to the same TASKLIST_GROUP

SQL | Result

```
select * from "NVARMA"."00_dmm::TASK_LIST_VALIDITY"()
```

	TASKLIST_TYPE	TASKLIST_GROUP	GROUP_COUNTER	INTERNAL_COUNTER	VALID_FROM	VALID_TO
1	R	GRP001	C1	001	Jan 1, 2017	Feb 28, 2017
2	R	GRP001	C1	002	Mar 1, 2017	May 9, 2017
3	R	GRP001	C1	003	May 10, 2017	Dec 31, 9999
4	R	GRP002	X1	001	Jan 1, 2018	Jan 31, 2018
5	R	GRP002	X1	002	Feb 1, 2018	Apr 14, 2018
6	R	GRP002	X1	003	Apr 15, 2018	Dec 31, 9999

7 SQL Script - Practical Case studies

In this unit, we will explore some of the typical business cases, which are ideal for implementing solutions using SQL script artifacts such as Stored Procedures, Scalar Function and Table Functions. Most importantly, these case studies will provide a good understanding about the practical application of various SQL Script programming features which are explained in this book.

7.1 Business Case: Calculating Cumulative Sales Revenues

Requirement description: Cumulative measures are used to generate the running totals for various KPIs. These are needed in some of the reporting scenarios. In this scenario, we need to produce the Cumulative Sales Revenue for each of the Calendar Months in the given selection criteria.

Key Concepts:

- Table Types Definition
- Table Functions
- Consuming Table Functions in Graphical Calculation Views

Step #1: Create Table Type and Table Function with the following logic – This table function will return the set of calendar months which are supposed to be considered for cumulative calculations of each of the calendar months.

Note: In SQL Script we can define table types or structures as global data types to reuse them across multiple functions or procedures. The extension to be used for defining the structure is .hdbstructure.

As part of this solution we need to build the following Table Type / Structure:

Table Type: 00_dmm:ZTT_CUMM_MONTHS.hdbstructure
```
table.schemaName = "NVARMA" ;
table.tableType = COLUMNSTORE;
table.columns = [
{name = "CALMONTH" ; sqlType = NVARCHAR ; length = 6;} ,
{name = "CUMM_MONTH" ; sqlType = NVARCHAR;  length = 6 ;}
];
```

Implement the following table function and use the above Table Type in the signature to represent the returning Table Variable.

Table Function: 00_dmm::TF_SALES_CUMM_MONTHS.hdbtablefunction

```
FUNCTION "NVARMA"."00_dmm::TF_SALES_CUMM_MONTHS" ( )
      RETURNS "NVARMA"."00_dmm::ZTT_CUMM_MONTHS"
      LANGUAGE SQLSCRIPT
      SQL SECURITY INVOKER AS
BEGIN
```

--For every CALMONTH Return the set of Cumulative CALMONTHs

```
RETURN SELECT DISTINCT A.CALMONTH , B.CALMONTH as "CUMM_MONTH"
          from "_SYS_BI"."M_TIME_DIMENSION" as A
      INNER JOIN "_SYS_BI"."M_TIME_DIMENSION" as B
          ON B.CALMONTH <= A.CALMONTH and B.YEAR = A.YEAR
      WHERE A.YEAR between '2010' and '2024' ;
END;
```

> **Concept check:** We have implemented the *self-join* in the above table function to get all previous months of each month. Self-join is the operation where both the tables involved in the join are same.

Testing the Table Function:

Note: Table Functions are like the virtual data models (information views). Hence, we can query them in the similar way as the Calculation Views.

```
select * from "NVARMA"."00_dmm::TF_SALES_CUMM_MONTHS"() where CALMONTH = '201110'
```

	CALMONTH	CUMM_MONTH
1	201110	201110
2	201110	201101
3	201110	201102
4	201110	201103
5	201110	201104
6	201110	201105
7	201110	201106
8	201110	201107
9	201110	201108
10	201110	201109

Step #2: Build Calculation view with the following layout and properties, as shown in the following steps

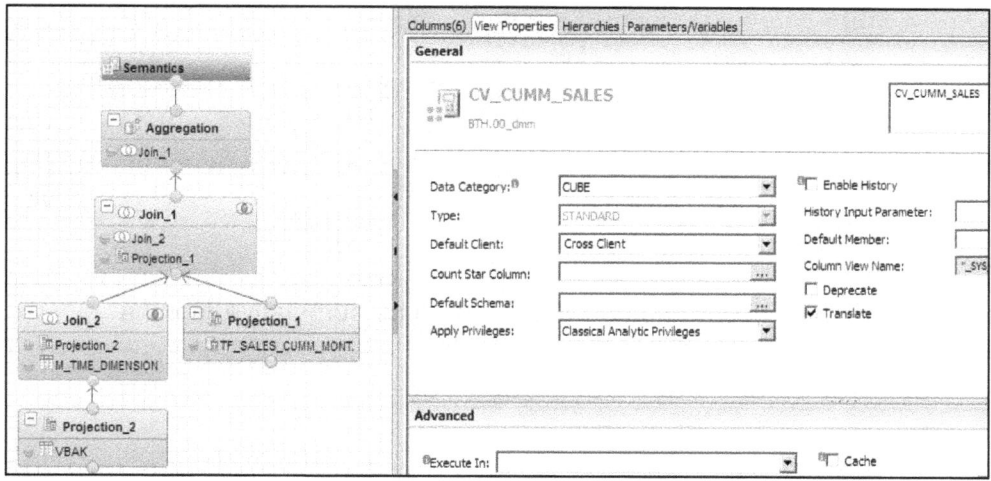

Projection on VBAK table

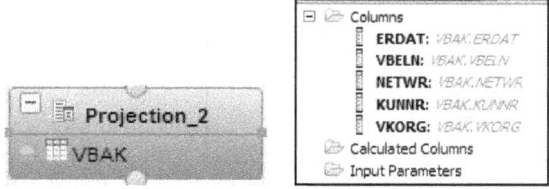

Join node with TIME dimension table: (Join type: Left Outer)

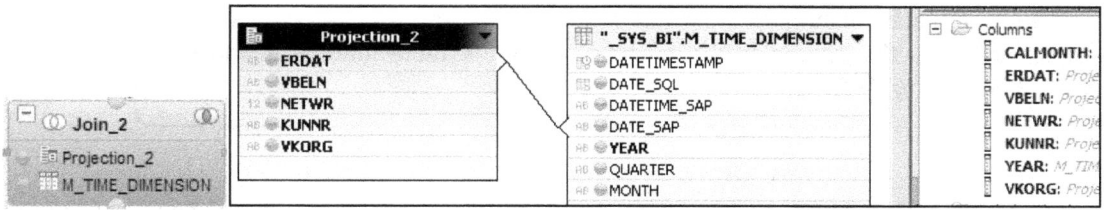

Note: Add YEAR and CALMONTH fields from M_TIME_DIMENSION to output

Projection node for Table Function to get Cumulative months

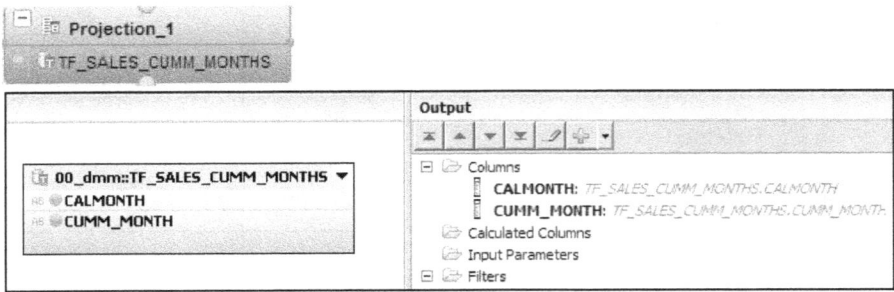

Join node to map the Sales Orders flow with the Table function for cumulative months (Join type: Inner join)

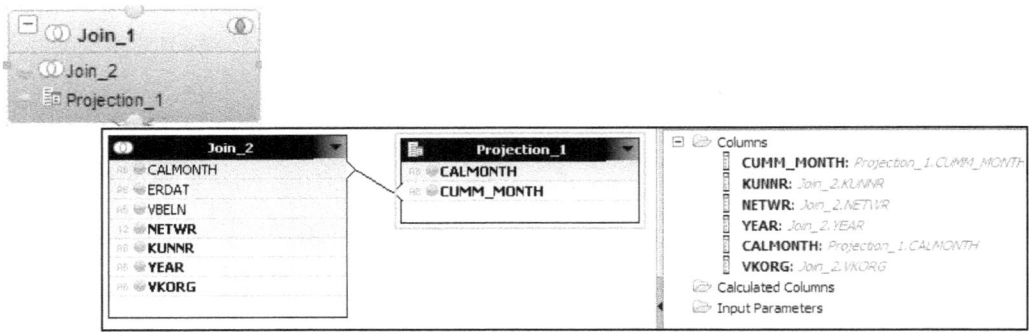

Concept check: We are consuming the Table function in a graphical calculation view here. We can also pass the values to the parameters of the table function using the "Input Parameter Mapping" feature

Final Aggregation node:

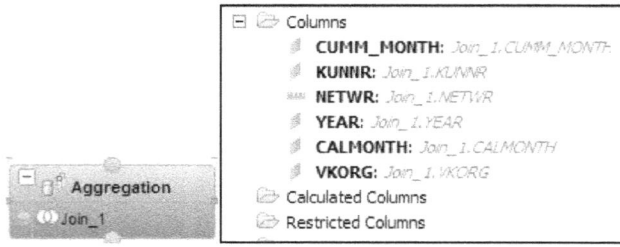

Data preview: Query the view results and observe the Cumulative values:

Case #1: Detailed results of Cumulative Months for each of the Calendar Month

```
SQL    Result
SELECT
      "CALMONTH","YEAR","CUMM_MONTH",
      sum("NETWR") AS "NETWR"
FROM "_SYS_BIC"."00_dmm/CV_CUMM_SALES"
where   ("CALMONTH" between '201301' and '201304')
      and VKORG = '1000'
GROUP BY "CUMM_MONTH", "YEAR", "CALMONTH", "VKORG"
Order by   CALMONTH, CUMM_MONTH
```

	CALMONTH	YEAR	CUMM_MONTH	NETWR
1	201301	2013	201301	266,495.5
2	201302	2013	201301	266,495.5
3	201302	2013	201302	294,310
4	201303	2013	201301	266,495.5
5	201303	2013	201302	294,310
6	201303	2013	201303	286,824.9
7	201304	2013	201301	266,495.5
8	201304	2013	201302	294,310
9	201304	2013	201303	286,824.9
10	201304	2013	201304	277,161.6

Case #2: Cumulative Sales revenue for each of the Calendar Months in the given range

```
SQL    Result
SELECT
      "CALMONTH",
      sum("NETWR") AS "CUMMULATIVE_NETWR"
FROM "_SYS_BIC"."00_dmm/CV_CUMM_SALES"
where   ("CALMONTH" between '201301' and '201304')
      and VKORG = '1000'
GROUP BY "CALMONTH", "VKORG"
Order by   CALMONTH
```

	CALMONTH	CUMMULATIVE_NETWR
1	201301	266,495.5
2	201302	560,805.5
3	201303	847,630.4
4	201304	1,124,792

We can use similar approach to implement the KPIs that needs cumulative results.

7.2 Business Case: Sales Employee Hierarchy Flattening

Requirement Description: Sales employees in an organization are set up as a hierarchy with a parent and child relationship, with the positions from top (CEO / Vice President - Sales) to the bottom (Filed Sales Executive). This will result in multiple levels of hierarchy depending on the organizational structure. To address specific reporting scenarios, it would be ideal to have the flattened hierarchy details of Sales employees, which shows the list of all employees working under a given employee across various levels in one record.

To address this requirement, following solution can be implemented to generate the flattened Sales Employee hierarchy. Since this requirement needs a recursive logic to identify the Subordinate (Child) employees at each level until the last level, it cannot be implemented using a Graphical Calculation view. However, we can achieve this using the SQL Script table functions or stored procedures. In this example we are building the solution using Table Function.

Key Concepts:

- Implementing Recursive Logic
- Operations on Table Variables
- Cursors definition and usage
- Conditional and Looping statements

Logic to implemented for Flattening Sales Employee Hierarchy

---

1. Loop through each employee record of the calculation view CV_PERNR_DIM.

1.1. Derive the list of subordinate employees by fetching all the employees where this employee is maintained as Supervisor (SUPERVISOR_PERNR) and store these employees as next level employees.

1.2. Continue with the same approach for next level employees until there are no more subordinate employees.

1.3. At each level append the records into the result table variable

Continue to perform the same for each employee record in the CV_PERNR_DIM view

---

Build the calculation view CV_PERNR_DIM: Create Dimension type calculation view for the employee details along with supervisor number and name. Implement Parent Child hierarchy to show the relationship of each employee and the supervisor. This view can be reused in various reporting views to show the employee hierarchy details.

Source Tables: Please find the sample data in the next page

Note: These tables may vary in your ECC or S/4HANA source system. Please find the corresponding tables or build custom tables to implement this solution

PA0000 Table: Employee master and status

```
SELECT PERNR, BEGDA, ENDDA, STAT2, STAT3 from PA0000
WHERE PERNR between '00001000' and '00001020'
```

	PERNR	BEGDA	ENDDA	STAT2	STAT3	
1	00001000	19950101	19950630	3	1	
2	00001000	19950701	99991231	3	1	
3	00001001	19940101	19980331	3	1	
4	00001001	19980401	99991231	3	1	
5	00001002	19940101	99991231	3	1	
6	00001003	19940101	19980331	3	1	
7	00001003	19980401	99991231	3	1	
8	00001004	19940101	19980331	3	1	
9	00001004	19980401	19980430	3	1	
10	00001004	19980501	99991231	3	1	
11	00001005	19940101	19980331	3	1	
12	00001005	19980401	99991231	3	1	

PA0001 Table: Employee name and address

SQL | Result
```
SELECT PERNR, ENAME, BEGDA, ENDDA, BUKRS from PA0001
WHERE BUKRS = '1000' ORDER BY PERNR
```

	PERNR	ENAME	BEGDA	ENDDA	BUKRS	
1	00000567	IIPP IIPP	20120101	99991231	1000	
2	00000791	Mr. I070791 I070791	20130903	99991231	1000	
3	00001000	Anja Müller	19950101	19950630	1000	
4	00001000	Anja Müller	19950701	99991231	1000	
5	00001001	Michaela Maier	19940101	19941231	1000	
6	00001001	Michaela Maier	19950101	99991231	1000	
7	00001002	Dipl.Kfm. Ulrike Za...	19940101	99991231	1000	
8	00001003	Stefan Pfändili	19940101	19941231	1000	
9	00001003	Stefan Pfändili	19950101	99991231	1000	
10	00001004	Olaf Paulsen	19940101	19941231	1000	

151

PA9001 Table: Employee and Supervisor relationship

```
SELECT * from PA9001
WHERE PERNR between '00001000' and '00001020'
```

	MANDT	PERNR	SPERNR	VALIDFROM	VALIDTO
1	800	00001000	00000000	20120101	99991231
2	800	00001001	00001000	20120101	99991231
3	800	00001002	00001000	20120101	99991231
4	800	00001003	00001001	20120101	99991231
5	800	00001004	00001001	20120101	99991231
6	800	00001005	00001001	20120101	99991231
7	800	00001006	00001001	20120101	99991231
8	800	00001007	00001001	20120101	99991231
9	800	00001008	00001010	20120101	99991231
10	800	00001009	00001010	20120101	99991231
11	800	00001010	00001005	20120101	99991231
12	800	00001011	00001005	20120101	99991231
13	800	00001012	00001010	20130101	99991231
14	800	00001013	00001010	20130101	99991231
15	800	00001014	00001011	20130101	99991231
16	800	00001015	00001011	20130101	99991231
17	800	00001016	00001011	20130101	99991231
18	800	00001017	00001011	20130101	99991231
19	800	00001018	00001011	20130101	99991231
20	800	00001019	00001011	20130101	99991231
21	800	00001020	00001011	20130101	20170101
22	800	00001020	00001011	20170102	99991231

PA0105 Table: Employee and SAP User ID mapping table

```
SELECT PERNR, USRID_LONG, BEGDA, ENDDA, SUBTY from PA0105
WHERE PERNR between '00001000' and '00001020'
```

	PERNR	USRID_LONG	BEGDA	ENDDA	SUBTY
1	00001000		19960101	99991231	0001
2	00001000	ANJA.MUELLER@MA...	20000101	99991231	0010
3	00001000		19960101	99991231	0011
4	00001001		19960101	99991231	0001
5	00001001	MICHAELA.MAIER@...	20000101	99991231	0010
6	00001001		19980101	99991231	0011
7	00001002		19960101	99991231	0001
8	00001002	ULRIKE.ZAUCKER@...	20000101	99991231	0010
9	00001003	STEFAN.PFANDILI@...	20000101	99991231	0010
10	00001004		19940101	99991231	0001
11	00001004	OLAF.PAULSEN@MA...	20000101	99991231	0010
12	00001005	HANNO.GUTJAHR@...	20000101	99991231	0010

Build the calculation view using following steps:

Preview: Calculation view layout for Employee Master data: (Name CV_PERNR_DIM)

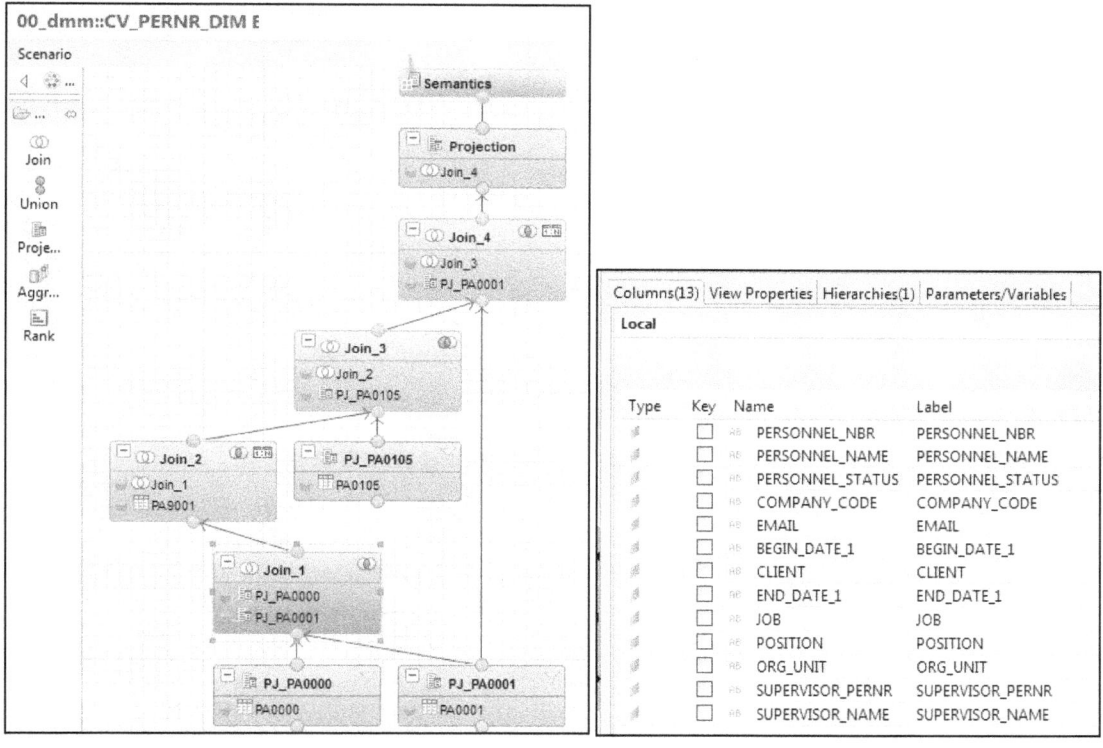

Implement the nodes and data flow within the calculation view as shown below.

Projection on PA0000 table:

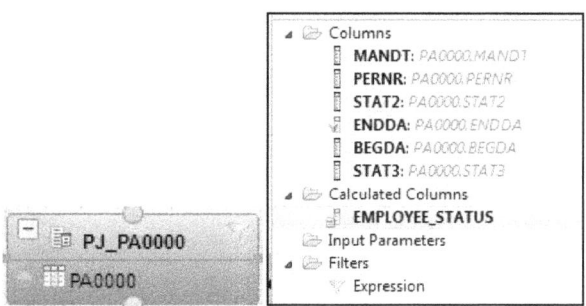

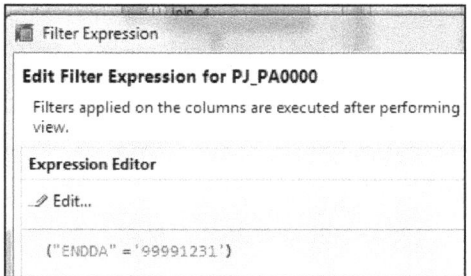

Calculated column for Employee Status:

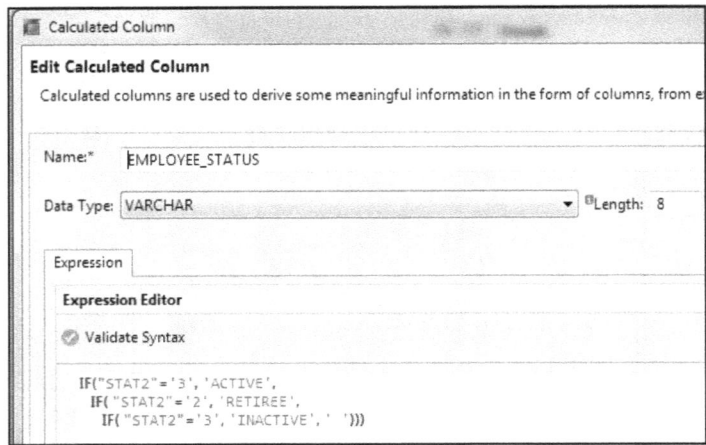

Projection on PA0001 table: To derive Employee details along with the name

Join on PA0000 and PA0001: To derive employee name (Inner join)

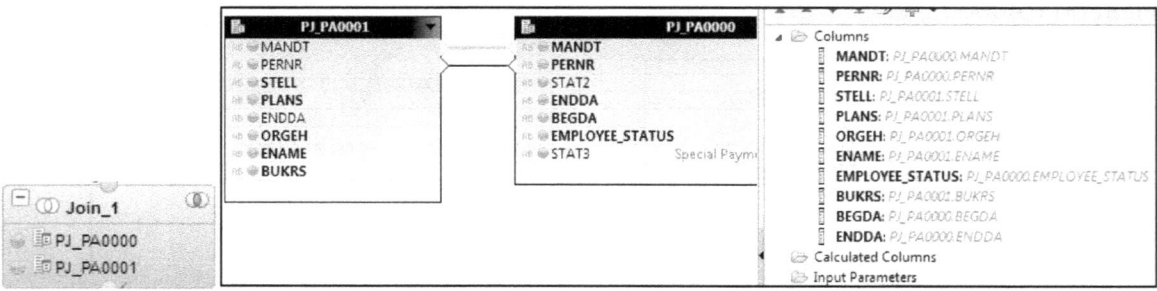

Join with PA9001 table: To derive Supervisor Number – SPERNR (Inner Join)

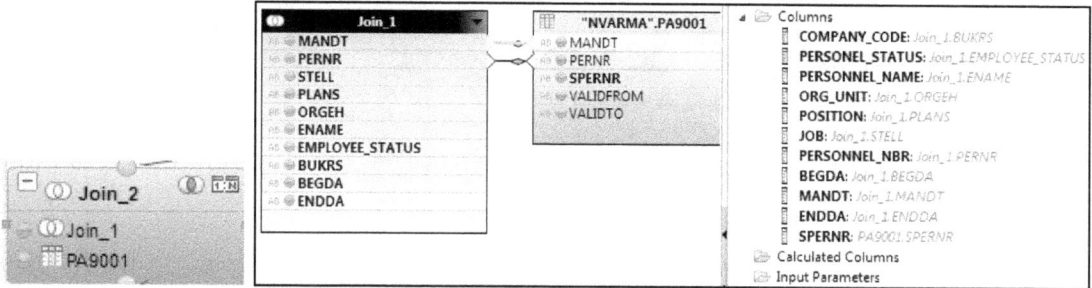

Projection on PA0105 table: To derive SAP User ID for the employee numbers

Join with PA0105 table: To derive SAP User ID (Left Outer Join)

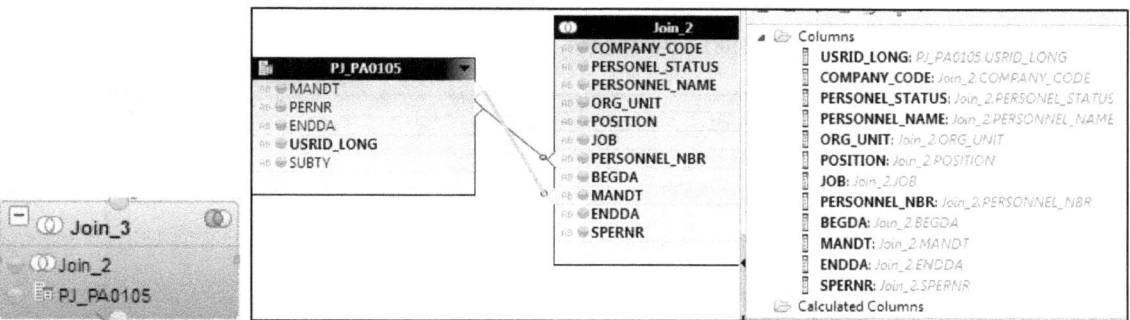

Join with PA0001 table: To derive Supervisor Employee Name (Left Outer Join)

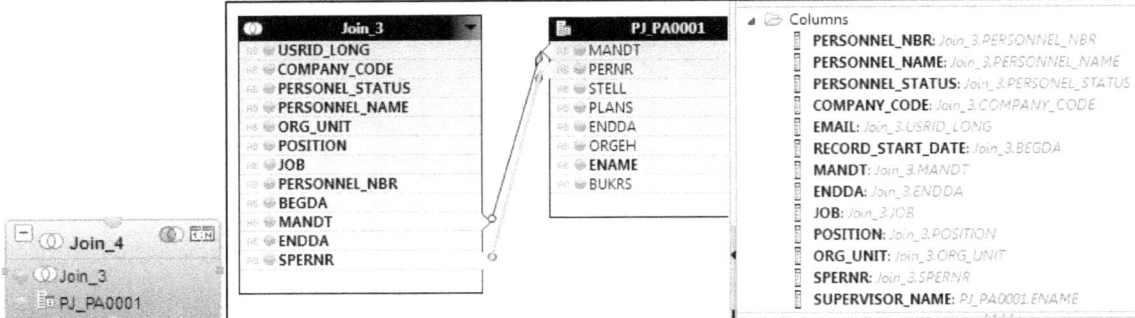

Final Projection node:

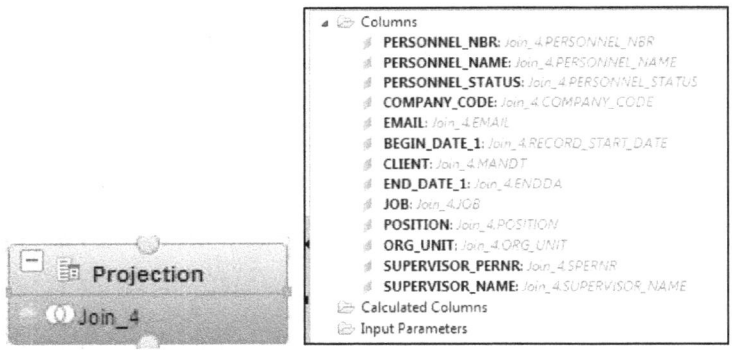

Implemment the following Parent / Child hierarchy:

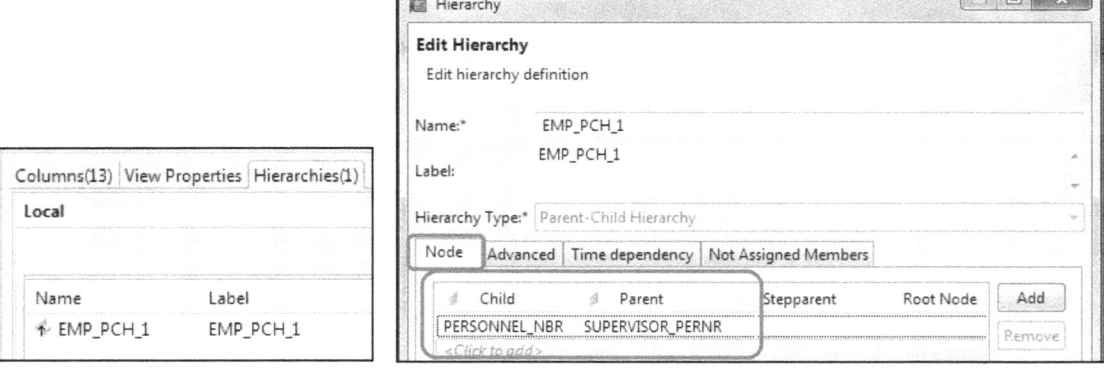

Maintain Time Dependency settings:

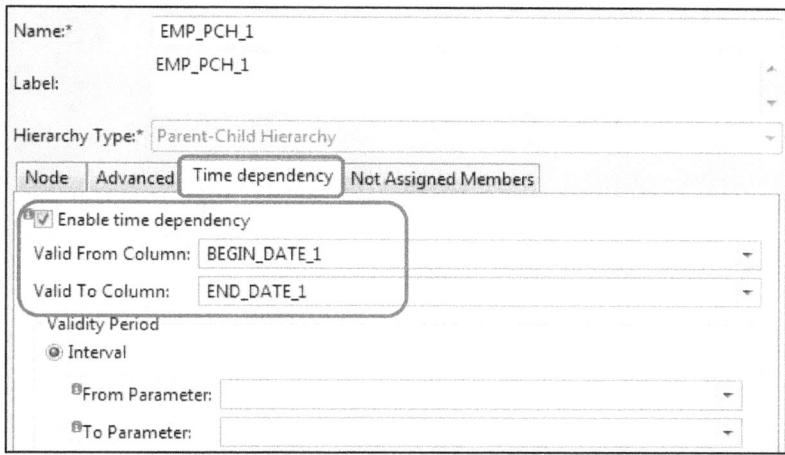

Data preview:

PERSONNEL_NBR	PERSONNEL_NAME	PERSONNEL_STATUS	COMPANY_C...	EMAIL	BEGIN_DATE_1	CLIENT	END_DATE_1
00000567	IIPP IIPP	ACTIVE	1000	?	20120101	800	99991231
00000791	Mr. I070791 I070791	ACTIVE	1000	?	20130903	800	99991231
00001000	Anja Müller	ACTIVE	1000	ANJA.MUELL...	19950701	800	99991231
00001001	Michaela Maier	ACTIVE	1000	MICHAELA....	19980401	800	99991231
00001002	Dipl.Kfm. Ulrike Zaucker	ACTIVE	1000	ULRIKE.ZAUC...	19940101	800	99991231
00001003	Stefan Pfändili	ACTIVE	1000	STEFAN.PFA...	19980401	800	99991231
00001004	Olaf Paulsen	ACTIVE	1000	OLAF.PAULS...	19980501	800	99991231
00001005	Hanno Gutjahr	ACTIVE	1000	HANNO.GUT...	19980401	800	99991231
00001006	Jasmin Awad	ACTIVE	1000	YASMIN.AW...	19980401	800	99991231
00001007	Hanna Ulrich	ACTIVE	1000	HANNA.ULRI...	19940101	800	99991231
00001008	Hilde Müller	ACTIVE	1000	HILDE.MULL...	19940101	800	99991231
00001009	Dr. Herbert Braunstein	ACTIVE	1000	HERBERT.BR...	19940101	800	99991231

Flattening of employee hierarchy- Implement a Table function with following logic:

```
FUNCTION "NVARMA"."00_dmm::TF_EMP_HIERARCHY_FLAT" ( )
 RETURNS Table (CLIENT NVARCHAR(3),
                       PERNR_MAIN NVARCHAR(8),
                       LEVEL_SUPERVISOR NVARCHAR(8),
                       HIER_LEVEL INTEGER,
                       SUB_PERNR NVARCHAR(8),
                       START_DATE DATE,
                       END_DATE DATE)
     LANGUAGE SQLSCRIPT
     SQL SECURITY INVOKER AS
BEGIN

--CURSOR to get the details of Employee Dimension view
DECLARE CURSOR C_PERNR for
     SELECT DISTINCT CLIENT, PERSONNEL_NBR  as PERNR_MAIN
     from  "_SYS_BIC"."00_dmm/CV_PERNR_DIM"
     where PERSONNEL_STATUS = 'ACTIVE' ;

/*Variable Delcaration*/
declare v_hierlevel INTEGER := 1;
declare v_rcount INTEGER := 0;
declare v_pcount INTEGER := 0;


/*Logic for flattening PERNR Hierarchy*/

--Get all the PERNRs who does not have any reporting employee (Not
--maintained as SUPERVISOR_PERNR)

out_tab = SELECT A.client,  A.PERSONNEL_NBR as
PERNR_MAIN,A.PERSONNEL_NBR as LEVEL_SUPERVISOR,  1 as HIER_LEVEL ,
' ' as SUB_PERNR, b.BEGIN_DATE_1 as START_DATE , b.END_DATE_1 as
END_DATE
FROM "_SYS_BIC"."00_dmm/CV_PERNR_DIM" as A
  left outer join "_SYS_BIC"."00_dmm/CV_PERNR_DIM" as B
  ON A.CLIENT = B.CLIENT and A.PERSONNEL_NBR = B.SUPERVISOR_PERNR
where  B.SUPERVISOR_PERNR IS NULL and A.PERSONNEL_STATUS =
'ACTIVE';

tab_pernr_nosub = select * from :out_tab;
```

```
--For each Employee(PERNR) from CV_PERNR_DIM
FOR R1 as C_PERNR DO

v_hierlevel := 1;

select count(*) into v_pcount from :tab_pernr_nosub where client =
R1.CLIENT AND PERNR_MAIN = R1.PERNR_MAIN;

if v_pcount = 0 then

--Prepare the data set for first level of employees
--which is used to build the data for next levels in hierarchy

first_pass =   SELECT CLIENT, SUPERVISOR_PERNR as PERNR,
:v_hierlevel as HIER_LEVEL ,
              PERSONNEL_NBR  as SUB_PERNR, BEGIN_DATE_1 as
              START_DATE , END_DATE_1 as END_DATE
              from "_SYS_BIC"."00_dmm/CV_PERNR_DIM"
          WHERE CLIENT = R1.CLIENT AND SUPERVISOR_PERNR =
          R1.PERNR_MAIN AND  PERSONNEL_STATUS = 'ACTIVE';

     final_result = SELECT CLIENT, R1.PERNR_MAIN, PERNR as
     LEVEL_SUPERVISOR,  HIER_LEVEL , SUB_PERNR, START_DATE,
     END_DATE from :first_pass ;

  SELECT count(*) INTO v_rcount FROM :first_pass;

--Perform the looping operation to derive the employees in the
--next levels in hierarchy until the last level

WHILE (v_rcount > 0 AND v_hierlevel < 10) DO

     v_hierlevel := v_hierlevel + 1;

next_PERNR = SELECT DISTINCT CLIENT, SUB_PERNR AS PERNR FROM
:first_pass;

first_pass = SELECT A.CLIENT, SUPERVISOR_PERNR as PERNR,
:v_hierlevel as HIER_LEVEL , PERSONNEL_NBR  as SUB_PERNR ,
BEGIN_DATE_1 as START_DATE , END_DATE_1 as END_DATE
     from  "_SYS_BIC"."00_dmm/CV_PERNR_DIM" AS A
          INNER JOIN :NEXT_PERNR AS B
```

```
              ON a.client = b.client and A.SUPERVISOR_PERNR = b.pernr
              and   A.PERSONNEL_STATUS = 'ACTIVE';

--Prepare Flat hierarchy by merging results of each level into
--Final Result Table

      final_result = SELECT CLIENT, R1.PERNR_MAIN,
      LEVEL_SUPERVISOR,  HIER_LEVEL , SUB_PERNR, START_DATE,
      END_DATE from :final_result
      UNION ALL
      SELECT CLIENT, R1.PERNR_MAIN, PERNR as LEVEL_SUPERVISOR,
      HIER_LEVEL, SUB_PERNR , START_DATE, END_DATE from :first_pass
      ;
      SELECT count(*) INTO v_rcount FROM :first_pass;

 END WHILE;

--Prepare final Flattened Hierarchy by combining results of each -
--Employ (PERNR)
      OUT_TAB = SELECT * from :OUT_TAB
                  UNION ALL
              SELECT * from :final_result;
 end if;

 END FOR;

--Returning the table variable with Flattened hierarchy details
RETURN SELECT client, PERNR_MAIN, LEVEL_SUPERVISOR,  HIER_LEVEL
,SUB_PERNR , START_DATE, END_DATE from :out_tab;

END;
```

> **Concept check:** We have used the following features to implement the solution:
> - ✓ Cursors – To process the records for employees sequentially in a loop
> - ✓ While loop and Self-join: To implement the recursive operation of deriving the next level employees until the last level

Validate the results of Table Function by executing the following query:

Under the employee (PERNR_MAIN = '00001001') there are subordinate employees at three different levels as shown (HIER_LEVEL column)

SQL   Result

```
Select * from "NVARMA"."OO_dmm::TF_EMP_HIERARCHY_FLAT" ( )
```

	CLIENT	PERNR_MAIN	LEVEL_SUPERVISOR	HIER_LEVEL	SUB_PERNR	START_DATE	END_DATE
24	800	00001001	00001001	1	00001005	Apr 1, 1998	Dec 31, 9999
25	800	00001001	00001001	1	00001006	Apr 1, 1998	Dec 31, 9999
26	800	00001001	00001001	1	00001007	Jan 1, 1994	Dec 31, 9999
27	800	00001001	00001005	2	00000567	Jan 1, 2012	Dec 31, 9999
28	800	00001001	00001005	2	00000791	Sep 3, 2013	Dec 31, 9999
29	800	00001001	00001005	2	00001010	Jan 1, 1994	Dec 31, 9999
30	800	00001001	00001005	2	00001011	Apr 1, 1998	Dec 31, 9999
31	800	00001001	00001010	3	00001008	Jan 1, 1994	Dec 31, 9999
32	800	00001001	00001010	3	00001009	Jan 1, 1994	Dec 31, 9999
33	800	00001001	00001010	3	00001012	Apr 1, 1998	Dec 31, 9999
34	800	00001001	00001010	3	00001013	Apr 1, 1998	Dec 31, 9999
35	800	00001001	00001011	3	00001014	Apr 1, 1998	Dec 31, 9999
36	800	00001001	00001011	3	00001015	Jan 1, 1994	Dec 31, 9999
37	800	00001001	00001011	3	00001016	Apr 1, 1998	Dec 31, 9999
38	800	00001001	00001011	3	00001017	Jan 1, 1994	Dec 31, 9999
39	800	00001001	00001011	3	00001018	Jan 1, 1994	Dec 31, 9999
40	800	00001001	00001011	3	00001019	Jan 1, 1994	Dec 31, 9999
41	800	00001001	00001011	3	00001020	Jan 1, 1994	Dec 31, 9999
42	800	00001005	00001005	1	00000567	Jan 1, 2012	Dec 31, 9999
43	800	00001005	00001005	1	00000791	Sep 3, 2013	Dec 31, 9999
44	800	00001005	00001005	1	00001010	Jan 1, 1994	Dec 31, 9999
45	800	00001005	00001005	1	00001011	Apr 1, 1998	Dec 31, 9999
46	800	00001005	00001010	2	00001008	Jan 1, 1994	Dec 31, 9999
47	800	00001005	00001010	2	00001009	Jan 1, 1994	Dec 31, 9999
48	800	00001005	00001010	2	00001012	Apr 1, 1998	Dec 31, 9999

7.3 Business Case: Complex Logic for Customer Greeting Name

Requirement: An organization need to send survey to each of their customers for the recently placed orders. In that regard, they need to have the correct Greeting Name to address each of the customers. We need to use the following logic to derive the Greeting Name for each customer.

Key Learnings:

- Scalar Functions and Table Functions usage
- Cursors and Looping (While loop)
- Built-in String Functions

Logic: Values of Customer First Name need to be validated for invalid values. If the First name is found to be invalid, then the value of GREET_NAME should be "Valued Customer". If the is found to be valid, then the value of GREET_NAME should be the same as the First Name.

Following table contains the rules with the list of Invalid values for the customer GREET_NAME. We need to refer to these rules and derive the valid GREET_NAME for each customer.

Note:

- If the Frist Name contains any characters other than a letter (a-z), period (.), comma (,), hyphen (-), or apostrophe ('), then it is considered as Invalid.
- If the Frist Name is only one Character long, then it is Invalid
- If the First name matches with any of the rules in the below table, then also it is Invalid.

In all these cases the Customer-GREET_NAME has to be <u>Valued Customer</u>

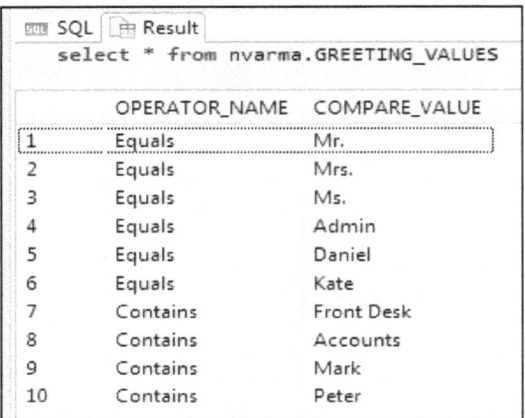

	OPERATOR_NAME	COMPARE_VALUE
1	Equals	Mr.
2	Equals	Mrs.
3	Equals	Ms.
4	Equals	Admin
5	Equals	Daniel
6	Equals	Kate
7	Contains	Front Desk
8	Contains	Accounts
9	Contains	Mark
10	Contains	Peter

select * from nvarma.GREETING_VALUES

Implement a Scalar Function:

```
FUNCTION "NVARMA"."00_dmm::SF_GET_CUST_GREETING_NAME"(IP_CUSTOMER_NAME
NVARCHAR(50) )
        RETURNS MOD_CUSTOMER_NAME NVARCHAR(50)
        LANGUAGE SQLSCRIPT
        SQL SECURITY INVOKER AS
BEGIN

-- Declare local variables
DECLARE UPPER_CUSTOMER_NAME NVARCHAR(50);
DECLARE TEMP_CUSTOMER_NAME NVARCHAR(50);
DECLARE V_COUNTER INTEGER := 1;
DECLARE V_LENGTH INTEGER := length(:IP_CUSTOMER_NAME);
DECLARE V_VALID_CHAR NVARCHAR(50) := ' abcdefghijklmnopqrstuvwxyz.,-`';
DECLARE LOWER_CUSTOMER_NAME NVARCHAR(50) := lower(:IP_CUSTOMER_NAME);

-- Declare Cursor variable to loop through the records from
--GREETING_VALUES table

 DECLARE CURSOR CUST_NAME_EQ(OPERATOR_NAME VARCHAR(20)) FOR
 SELECT UPPER(COMPARE_VALUE)
 FROM "NVARMA"."GREETING_VALUES" where OPERATOR_NAME = 'Equals';

 DECLARE CURSOR CUST_NAME_CT(OPERATOR_NAME VARCHAR(20)) FOR
 SELECT UPPER(COMPARE_VALUE)
 FROM "NVARMA"."GREETING_VALUES" where OPERATOR_NAME = 'Contains';

-- Validation logic for Customer Name which is passed as input to this
--function

 SELECT UPPER(IP_CUSTOMER_NAME) into UPPER_CUSTOMER_NAME FROM DUMMY;
 MOD_CUSTOMER_NAME := IP_CUSTOMER_NAME;

if v_length = 1 then
   MOD_CUSTOMER_NAME := 'Valued Customer';
end if;

if MOD_CUSTOMER_NAME != 'Valued Customer' THEN

--Validation logic to check if Customer Name contains only valid
--characters
```

```
WHILE v_counter <= v_length DO

if instr(:V_VALID_CHAR, substr(:LOWER_CUSTOMER_NAME,:v_counter,1)) = 0 then
   MOD_CUSTOMER_NAME := 'Valued Customer';
       break;
end if;

v_counter := v_counter  + 1;

END WHILE ;

end if;

 if MOD_CUSTOMER_NAME != 'Valued Customer' THEN

-- Validation logic to check if Customer Name matches with the given set
-- of values in GREETING_VALUES table that are based on Equals operator

 OPEN CUST_NAME_EQ('Equals');

 WHILE(1=1) DO

 FETCH CUST_NAME_EQ into TEMP_CUSTOMER_NAME;

 IF CUST_NAME_EQ::NOTFOUND THEN
 BREAK;
 END IF;
      if ((UPPER_CUSTOMER_NAME = TEMP_CUSTOMER_NAME)) THEN
      MOD_CUSTOMER_NAME := 'Valued Customer';
      BREAK;
      end if;
  END WHILE;

 CLOSE CUST_NAME_EQ;

 if MOD_CUSTOMER_NAME != 'Valued Customer' THEN

--Validation logic to check if Customer Name matches with the given set
--of values in GREETING_VALUES table that are based on Contains operator

 OPEN CUST_NAME_CT('Contains');

 WHILE(1=1) DO

 FETCH CUST_NAME_CT into TEMP_CUSTOMER_NAME;
```

```
IF CUST_NAME_CT::NOTFOUND THEN
     BREAK;
END IF;


if ((UPPER_CUSTOMER_NAME = TEMP_CUSTOMER_NAME)
  OR (LENGTH(SUBSTR_AFTER (UPPER_CUSTOMER_NAME, TEMP_CUSTOMER_NAME)) > 0)
  OR (LENGTH(SUBSTR_BEFORE (UPPER_CUSTOMER_NAME, TEMP_CUSTOMER_NAME)) > 0))
Then

  MOD_CUSTOMER_NAME := 'Valued Customer';
  BREAK;

End if;
END WHILE;

CLOSE CUST_NAME_CT;

  end if;
 end if;

END;
```

Validate the results of Scalar Function:

Case #1: Since customer name contains the word Mark, the result is – Valued Customer

```
SELECT "NVARMA"."00_dmm::SF_GET_CUST_GREETING_NAME"('Mark123') as GREET_NAME from DUMMY
```

	GREET_NAME
1	Valued Customer

Case #2: Since customer name contains does not match with the criterial from GREETING_VALUES table, the result is same as the orginal customer name

```
SELECT "NVARMA"."00_dmm::SF_GET_CUST_GREETING_NAME"('Chris Wood') as GREET_NAME from DUMMY
```

	GREET_NAME
1	Chris Wood

Next steps for this solution:

Scalar function is capable of returning a single value only. Since we need to derive the customer greeting name for all the customers, we have to implement a table function to achieve this. The table function will process each of the customer records and in turn calls the scalar function to derive the Greeting Name for each customer.

Table Function:

```
FUNCTION "NVARMA"."00_dmm::TF_CUSTOMER_GREETING_NAMES" ( )
        RETURNS  table (CUSTOMER_NUM NVARCHAR(10),
                         CUSTOMER_NAME NVARCHAR(50),
                         GREETING_NAME NVARCHAR(50))
        LANGUAGE SQLSCRIPT
        SQL SECURITY INVOKER AS
BEGIN

 RETURN SELECT KUNNR as CUSTOMER_NUM, NAME1 as CUSTOMER_NAME,
             "NVARMA"."00_dmm::SF_GET_CUST_GREETING_NAME"(NAME1)  as
             GREETING_NAME
              from KNA1;

END;
```

Validate the results of table function:

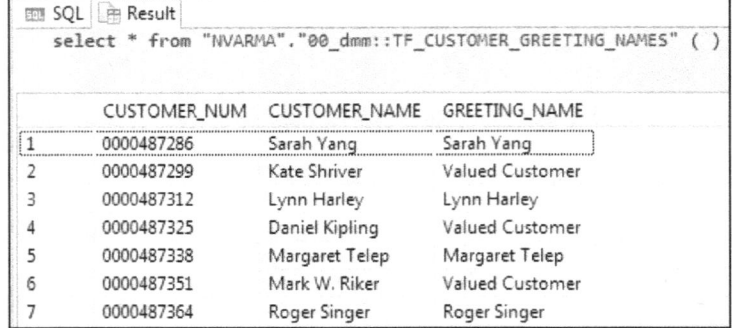

Concept check: We have used following features to implement the solution:
- ✓ Using Built-in function: Character string functions – To format and verify the string values
- ✓ Cursor and While loops: To implement the logic of validating each of the Customer names and check each of the characters in the string
- ✓ Calling scalar function inside table function to process each customer name

7.4 Business Case: Implementing Sales Order Delivery Status Snapshots

Requirement Description:

An organization would like to maintain the snapshots of sales order delivery performance (count of open sales orders and closed sales orders) for the past one year in monthly buckets. Since we need to retain the historical status of the sales orders, we need to implement a solution to persist the results in a custom table in HANA.

Criteria for open and closed sales orders:

An order is considered as "open", when the creation date <= snapshot date and actual delivery date is either blank or a later date for that specific week.

Key Learnings:

- Stored Procedures
- DML operations – Persisting results in HANA
- Table variable operations and persistence of results in database
- Exception hanlding techniques

Solution Diagram:

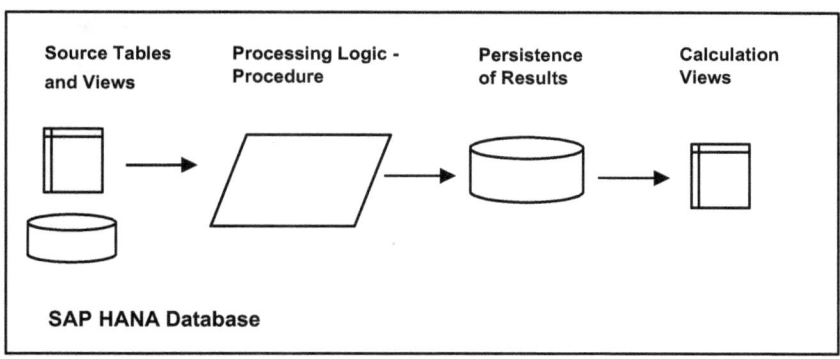

Snapshot table:

Create the database table "NVARMA"."00_dmm::SALESORDER_STATUS_HISTORY" with the following definition.

```
table.schemaName = "NVARMA";
table.tableType = COLUMNSTORE;

table.columns =
  [
    {name = "VKORG";  sqlType = NVARCHAR;  length = 4; },
    {name = "CREATION_MONTH";  sqlType = NVARCHAR;  length = 6;  },
    {name = "ORDER_COUNT"; sqlType = INTEGER;},
    {name = "ORDER_TYPE";  sqlType = NVARCHAR;  length = 10; },
    {name = "ORDER_AMOUNT"; sqlType = DOUBLE;}
  ];
```

Stored Procedure:

Create a stored procedure in HANA studio development perspective with the following properties.

File Name:	SP_SALES_ORDER_STATUS_SNAPSHOT.hdbprocedure
File Format:	Text (.hdbprocedure)
Target Schema:	NVARMA

```
PROCEDURE "NVARMA"."00_dmm::SP_SALES_ORDER_STATUS_SNAPSHOT" ( IN
SNAP_DATE DATE )
      LANGUAGE SQLSCRIPT
      SQL SECURITY INVOKER
      DEFAULT SCHEMA <SCHEMA NAME>
      AS
BEGIN

  DECLARE MONTH_NOW INTEGER;
  DECLARE YEAR_NOW INTEGER;
  DECLARE ISNULL INTEGER;

  -- User defined Exception handling code.
  DECLARE NODATA CONDITION FOR SQL_ERROR_CODE 10001;
  DECLARE EXIT HANDLER FOR NODATA
```

```
BEGIN
        SELECT ::SQL_ERROR_CODE, ::SQL_ERROR_MESSAGE FROM DUMMY;
END;

  SELECT MONTH(SNAP_DATE) INTO MONTH_NOW FROM DUMMY;
  SELECT YEAR(SNAP_DATE) INTO YEAR_NOW FROM DUMMY;

--Delete the previous snapshot results from the table
TRUNCATE TABLE "NVARMA"."00_dmm::SALESORDER_STATUS_HISTORY";

-- Join VBAP & VBAK tables.
SALES_TAB = SELECT VBAP.MANDT, VBAP.VBELN, VBAP.POSNR,VBAP.VGBEL,
VBAP.VGPOS, VBAK.ERDAT, VBAK.NETWR
              FROM VBAP INNER JOIN VBAK
              ON VBAP.VBELN = VBAK.VBELN;

--Join sales table with LIPS.
 DEL_TAB =
  SELECT S.*,LIPS.VBELN AS LIPSVBELN FROM :SALES_TAB AS S
  INNER JOIN LIPS
  ON S.VBELN = LIPS.VGBEL AND S.POSNR = LIPS.VGPOS;

--Join above table with LIKP to get actual delivery date
REQ_TABLE =
SELECT D.MANDT,D.VBELN,D.POSNR,D.ERDAT,D.NETWR,LIKP.VKORG,
LIKP.WADAT_IST,CONCAT(YEAR(D.ERDAT),MONTH(D.ERDAT)) AS
"CREATION_MONTH"
    FROM :DEL_TAB AS D INNER JOIN LIKP
       ON D.LIPSVBELN = LIKP.VBELN;

--SELECT MIN(ERDAT) FROM :REQ_TABLE;
 REQ_TABLE_YEAR =
  SELECT * FROM :REQ_TABLE WHERE
  MONTHS_BETWEEN( ERDAT,:SNAP_DATE) <= 12 AND ERDAT<= :SNAP_DATE;

-- Raise exception if snap shot data not maintained.
 SELECT COUNT(*) INTO ISNULL FROM :REQ_TABLE_YEAR;
  IF :ISNULL=0
THEN
SIGNAL NODATA SET MESSAGE_TEXT = 'Data Unavailable';
END IF;

SELECT * FROM :REQ_TABLE_YEAR;
```

```
-- Find number of closed orders. An order is closed if creation
-- date <= snapshot date and
-- actual delivery date is either blank or a later date.

Closed_order_tab =
SELECT VKORG,CREATION_MONTH, count(*) as "ORDER_COUNT",'CLOSED' AS
"ORDER_TYPE",SUM(NETWR) AS "ORDER_AMOUNT"
   FROM :REQ_TABLE_YEAR
   WHERE
      TO_INT(CONCAT(Year(WADAT_IST),month(WADAT_IST))) <=
      TO_INT(CONCAT(:YEAR_NOW,:MONTH_NOW))
   GROUP BY VKORG,CREATION_MONTH;

-- Find number of open orders. An order is open if creation date -
-- <= snapshot date and
-- actual delivery date is either blank or a later date.

Open_order_tab= SELECT VKORG AS "VKORG_O",CREATION_MONTH, count(*)
as "ORDER_COUNT",'OPEN'  AS "ORDER_TYPE", SUM(NETWR) AS
"ORDER_AMOUNT"
   FROM :REQ_TABLE_YEAR
   WHERE
      TO_INT(CONCAT(Year(ERDAT),month(ERDAT))) <=
      TO_INT(CONCAT(:YEAR_NOW,:MONTH_NOW))
   AND
      TO_INT(CONCAT(Year(WADAT_IST),month(WADAT_IST))) >
      TO_INT(CONCAT(:YEAR_NOW,:MONTH_NOW))
   OR
   WADAT_IST = 0
   GROUP BY VKORG,CREATION_MONTH;

-- Open & Closed order information is merged.
 TAB_RESULT = SELECT * FROM :OPEN_ORDER_TAB UNION SELECT * FROM
:CLOSED_ORDER_TAB;

--Result obtained is stored in a table.
 INSERT INTO "NVARMA"."00_dmm::SALESORDER_STATUS_HISTORY"
      SELECT * FROM :TAB_RESULT ;
END;
```

Execute the stored procedure using the below statement:

```
CALL "NVARMA"."00_dmm::SP_SALES_ORDER_STATUS_SNAPSHOT"
('2014-12-31')
```

Verify the results in the custom table:

```
SQL   Result
SELECT * from "NVARMA"."00_dmm::SALESORDER_STATUS_HISTORY"
    where VKORG = '3020'
    Order by CREATION_MONTH
```

	VKORG	CREATION_MONTH	ORDER_COUNT	ORDER_TYPE	ORDER_AMOUNT
1	3020	201410	2	OPEN	200
2	3020	201410	28	CLOSED	7,115.62
3	3020	201411	1	CLOSED	91.51
4	3020	201412	6	CLOSED	1,717.25
5	3020	20142	18	OPEN	1,123,918.89
6	3020	20142	46	CLOSED	1,298,896.08
7	3020	20143	1	OPEN	10,016.5
8	3020	20143	36	CLOSED	234,838.5
9	3020	20144	1	OPEN	475,000
10	3020	20144	2	CLOSED	660,000

Concept check: Following features have been leveraged to implement the solution:
- ✓ Persisting the results in HANA database using the DML operations like INSERT
- ✓ Implementing various table variable operations for achieving the complex logic
- ✓ Definition and calling of stored procedures
- ✓ Handling the errors using exception handling techniques

7.5 Business Case: Persistence of Marketing Promotion Status

Requirement: Trade promotions are the marketing objects, which are executed to increase the sales volumes and brand awareness of various products. Promotions will go trhough different changes in the status. We need to generate the concatenated promotion status for each of the trade promoitions based on the chronological events and persist the same in a custom table. This custom table can be joined in any calculation view to derive the promotion status.

Example below:

Input Dataset:

PROMO_ID	STATUS	CHANGED_ON
TP001	Draft	2018-01-01
TP001	Released	2018-01-10
TP001	Closed	2018-03-31
TP002	Draft	2018-01-01
TP002	Cancelled	2018-01-05

Expected result:

PROMO_ID	STATUS_SEQUENCE
TP001	Draft–Released-Closed
TP002	Draft-Cancelled

Proposed solution:

1. Create a database table (PROMO_STATUS_TEXT) to store the Concatenated Status for each Trade Promotion
2. Implement a stored procedure (PR_UPDATE_PROMO_STATUS) to derive the store the PROMO_ID, STATUS_SEQUENCE into the table
   a. This procedure can be scheduled to run from BODS (for every 5 minutes)
   b. Logic to only update the delta records in the table PROMO_STATUS_TEXT (Task_Guid created newly OR where the status has got changed). If the table TASK_STATUS_TEXT PROMO_STATUS_TEXT is empty then insert all records.
3. Join the table PROMO_STATUS_TEXT in any of the calculation views to fetch the Promo Status (Concatenated value)

Create the following stored procedure:

```
CREATE PROCEDURE NVARMA.PROMO_STATUS_SEQUENCE (
                OUT ov_status NVARCHAR(1),
                OUT ov_error_code INTEGER,
                OUT ov_error_message NVARCHAR(256)   )
        LANGUAGE SQLSCRIPT
        SQL SECURITY INVOKER
        DEFAULT SCHEMA NVARMA
AS
BEGIN

Declare V_count INTEGER;
-- Create handler for SQL exceptions
        DECLARE EXIT HANDLER FOR SQLEXCEPTION
        BEGIN
-- Set status as E(Error)in case of any SQL exceptions and return message
                ov_status := 'E';
                ov_error_code := ::SQL_ERROR_CODE;
                ov_error_message := ::SQL_ERROR_MESSAGE;
        END;

--Fetch the Promo details in the Chronological order of status changes
TAB_PROMO = SELECT PROMO_ID, STATUS, CHANGED_ON
                from PROMO_DETAILS
                Order By PROMO_ID, CHANGED_ON ASC;

--Concatenate the status values for each PROMO_ID
TAB_STATUS = SELECT PROMO_ID,
                    STRING_AGG(STATUS,'-') as STATUS_SEQUENCE
                    FROM :TAB_PROMO
                GROUP BY PROMO_ID;

--Fetch the existing (old) System and user status values for all PROMOS
TAB_OLD = select PROMO_ID, STATUS_SEQUENCE from PROMO_STATUS_TEXT;

select count(PROMO_ID) into v_count from :TAB_OLD ;
if :v_count > 0 then
--Delta logic
--Determine the PROMOS which are DELETED
TAB_DELETE = SELECT PROMO_ID,  STATUS_SEQUENCE from :TAB_OLD
                MINUS
                select PROMO_ID,  STATUS_SEQUENCE from :TAB_STATUS;

DELETE from PROMO_STATUS_TEXT
        WHERE PROMO_ID IN (select PROMO_ID from :TAB_DELETE);
```

```
--Determine the PROMOS which are either NEW or the status is UPDATED
TAB_DELTA = SELECT PROMO_ID,  STATUS_SEQUENCE  from :TAB_STATUS
            MINUS
            SELECT PROMO_ID,  STATUS_SEQUENCE  from :TAB_OLD;

--Perform INSERT or UPDATE to store records in PROMO_STATUS_TEXT table
UPSERT PROMO_STATUS_TEXT (PROMO_ID,  STATUS_SEQUENCE)
        select PROMO_ID, STATUS_SEQUENCE  from :TAB_DELTA;
ELSE
-- Perform FULL Insert when the PROMO_STATUS_TEXT table is empty
INSERT into PROMO_STATUS_TEXT select * from :TAB_STATUS;
end if;
-- Set status successful
ov_status := 'S';

END;
```

Execute the stored procedure using the below statement:

SQL	Result			
CALL NVARMA.PROMO_STATUS_SEQUENCE(?,?,?)				
	Out(1)	Out(2)	Out(3)	
1	S	?	?	

Verify the results stored in the custom table:

SQL	Result		
SELECT * from NVARMA.PROMO_STATUS_TEXT			
	PROMO_ID	STATUS_SEQUENCE	
1	TP001	Draft-Released-Closed	
2	TP002	Draft-Cancelled	

Concept check: We will be using the following features to implement the solution:
- ✓ Persisting the results in HANA database using the DML operations like INSERT and data manipulations using UPSERT and DELETE statements
- ✓ Implementing string aggregation using STRING_AGG function
- ✓ Identifying the delta records using the MINUS operator

7.6 Material Inventory Projections using Table Function

Business Case: For any organization, it would be essential to project the inventory levels of various materials for a certain number of future periods. This would help them to manage the supply and optimize the resources overall. We need to build a HANA model for reporting Material Inventory Projection (Rolling 18 months of Inventory balance, Requirement qty and Scheduled qty for all the contracts of the respective materials.

Solution Details:

Key datasets related to this report are 1) Contract 2) Purchase order schedule lines, 3) Material requirements, 4) Material inventory valuation etc. This information can then be leveraged for reporting the material stock position with a forecast of 18 months. The data for this report is extracted from the SAP ERP tables EKKO/ EKPO/ EKET/ MBEW/ RESB etc. The logic for this report can be implemented using a Table function.

Report Layout Sample:

Input: Material Number & Date From

Output: Inventory projection values for <N> number of months.

Month	Year	Receipt Quantity (GR)	Requirement Qty (Reservations)	Inventory Balance (Projection)	Unit of Measure
1	2019	25	20	5	Cases
2	2019	30	15	20	Cases

Let us implement the following Table function to address this requirement:

```
FUNCTION "NVARMA"."democode::TF_MATERIAL_FORECAST" ( IP_MATNR
NVARCHAR(18), IP_SNAPDATE DATE )
     RETURNS TABLE (MONTH_NUM NVARCHAR(2),
                         YEAR_NUM NVARCHAR(4),
                         REC_QTY DOUBLE,
                         REQ_QTY DOUBLE,
                         INV_BAL DOUBLE,
                         BASE_UNIT NVARCHAR(3))
     LANGUAGE SQLSCRIPT
     SQL SECURITY INVOKER
     DEFAULT SCHEMA "ES7_SLT_BTH"
     AS
```

```
BEGIN
 declare v_index integer;
 declare v_curr_balance decimal(15,2);
 declare v_Rec_total decimal(20,2);
 declare v_Req_total decimal(20,2);
 declare v_start date;
 declare v_end date;
 declare v_month_start date;
 declare v_month_end date;
 declare v_date date;
 declare v_lastdate date;
 declare v_month_year nvarchar(6);
 declare v_month nvarchar(2);
 declare v_year nvarchar(4);

 --Array declarations
 DECLARE A_MONTH NVARCHAR(2) ARRAY;
 DECLARE A_YEAR NVARCHAR(4) ARRAY;
 DECLARE A_REC_QTY DECIMAL(20,2) ARRAY;
 DECLARE A_REQ_QTY DECIMAL(20,2)  ARRAY;
 DECLARE A_INV_BAL DECIMAL(20,2) ARRAY;
 DECLARE A_BUNIT NVARCHAR(3) ARRAY;

 --select now() into v_start from dummy;
 V_START := IP_SNAPDATE;
SELECT LAST_DAY (TO_DATE(:v_start, 'YYYY-MM-DD')) into v_start FROM
DUMMY;
SELECT ADD_DAYS (TO_DATE (:v_start, 'YYYY-MM-DD'), 1) into v_start FROM
DUMMY;

SELECT ADD_MONTHS (TO_DATE (:v_start, 'YYYY-MM-DD'), 12) into v_end FROM
DUMMY;
SELECT LAST_DAY (TO_DATE(:v_end, 'YYYY-MM-DD')) into v_end FROM DUMMY;

-- Get the current stock and Moving avg price of Material from MBEW
 TAB_STOCK = SELECT A.MATNR, A.BWKEY, A.BWTAR , A.LBKUM, B.MEINS,
A.VERPR, A.PEINH
   from MBEW as A Inner Join MARA as B
   On A.MATNR = B.MATNR    and A.MANDT = B.MANDT
   where A.MANDT = 100 and A.MATNR = :ip_matnr;

--Fetch all the schedule lines for the given material
TAB_RECEIPTS = SELECT A.EBELN, A.EBELP, A.ETENR, A.EINDT, A.MENGE,
B.MEINS, B.MATNR
             from EKPO as B inner join  EKET as A
             on B.EBELN = A.EBELN and B.EBELP = A.EBELP
```

```
                 where B.MATNR = :IP_MATNR AND to_date(A.EINDT) between
:V_START and :V_END;

--Fetch all the Reservations for the given material
TAB_REQ = select RSNUM, RSPOS, RSART, BDART, RSSTA, XLOEK, MATNR, WERKS,
                 BDMNG, MEINS, BDTER
          from RESB
          where MATNR = :IP_MATNR and
                to_date(BDTER) between :V_start and :V_end;
v_date := :v_start;

SELECT sum(lbkum) into v_curr_balance from :tab_stock;
IF :v_curr_balance is null then
 v_curr_balance := 0 ;
end if;


FOR V_INDEX IN 1 .. 18 DO
--Derive the values for all the 18 months and store in the array elements

 SELECT LAST_DAY(TO_DATE(:v_date, 'YYYY-MM-DD')) into v_lastdate FROM
DUMMY;

 select Month(:v_date) into v_month from dummy;
 A_MONTH[:V_INDEX] :=  :v_month;

 if :v_month <> '10' and :v_month <> '11' and :v_month <> '12' then
    select concat('0', :v_month) into v_month from dummy;
 end if;

 select Year(:v_date) into v_Year from dummy;
 A_YEAR[:V_INDEX] :=  :v_year;

 select SUM(MENGE) into v_Rec_total from :tab_receipts
     where to_date(eindt) between :v_date and :v_lastdate ;

 IF :v_Rec_total is null then
 v_Rec_total := 0 ;
 end if;
   A_REC_QTY[:V_INDEX] := :v_Rec_total ;

select sum(BDMNG) into v_Req_total  from :tab_req
     where to_date(BDTER) between :v_date and :v_lastdate;

 IF :v_Req_total is null then
   v_Req_total := 0 ;
 end if;
```

```
A_REQ_QTY[:V_INDEX] :=  :v_REQ_TOTAL;
 v_curr_balance := :v_curr_balance + :v_REC_TOTAL -  :v_REQ_TOTAL;
 A_INV_BAL[:V_INDEX] :=  :v_curr_balance;

A_BUNIT[:V_INDEX] :=  'EA';

SELECT ADD_MONTHS (TO_DATE (:v_date, 'YYYY-MM-DD'), 1) into v_date FROM
DUMMY;

End For;

--Output: MATNR, MONTH, RECIEPT_QTY, REQ_QTY, ENDING_INVENTORY
var_out =  UNNEST(:A_MONTH, :A_YEAR, :A_REC_QTY, :A_REQ_QTY, :A_INV_BAL,
:A_BUNIT ) as ("MONTH_NUM",
 "YEAR_NUM", "REC_QTY", "REQ_QTY", "INV_BAL", "BASE_UNIT");

 RETURN select * from :VAR_OUT;
END;
```

Execute the following query on Table function and verify the results:

```
SELECT * from "NVARMA"."democode::TF_MATERIAL_FORECAST" ( 'FI1-T-IT122' , '2015-01-01' )
```

	MONTH_NUM	YEAR_NUM	REC_QTY	REQ_QTY	INV_BAL	BASE_UNIT
1	2	2015	0	0	0	EA
2	3	2015	0	0	0	EA
3	4	2015	0	0	0	EA
4	5	2015	60	0	60	EA
5	6	2015	170	0	230	EA
6	7	2015	0	0	230	EA
7	8	2015	0	0	230	EA
8	9	2015	0	0	230	EA
9	10	2015	0	0	230	EA
10	11	2015	0	0	230	EA
11	12	2015	0	0	230	EA
12	1	2016	0	0	230	EA

Concept check: We have implemented the following in this solution:
- ✓ Processing the records sequentially using Array variables and FOR Loop
- ✓ Transferring the data between table variables and Arrays
- ✓ Implementing Table functions
- ✓ Leveraging built-in functions related to Arrays and Date & Time

8 SQL Script for ABAP on HANA

Briefly about ABAP Programming:

ABAP (Advanced Business Application Programming) is the proprietary language of SAP, which has rich set of features and functionalities. ABAP programming is easy to understand and build applications and it supports both procedural and object-oriented techniques. One of the key features of ABAP is the Open SQL statements which provides unified data access to the range of database platforms.

Following are the key building blocks of ABAP Programming:

- Internal tables → To store process data during the runtime of a program
- Function Modules and Subroutines → Procedural entities to modularize the code and acts as reusable modules
- Classes and Methods → Object oriented entities to build applications

Traditional DB model -"Data to Code"

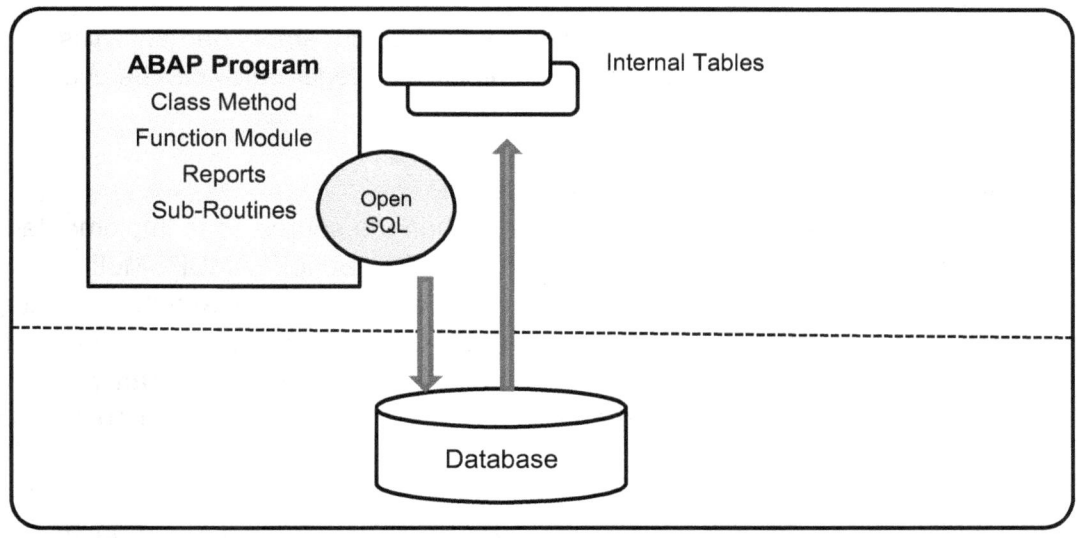

8.1 Evolution of ABAP Programming for HANA

Until the introduction of SAP HANA database platform, most of the logic in SAP applications is implemented to run based on "Data to Code" approach. In this approach, only data retrieval and update requests are processed in the database server and all the processing logic is executed in the application server. This approach was mainly adopted to avoid the data processing overhead on database and to implement the application logic which is independent of underlying database.

However, SAP HANA being a powerful in-memory database, it would be ideal to push the complex calculations and processing logic to the database server. Due to this, SAP has enhanced the ABAP programming to support the integration of SQL script programming as part of ABAP application logic. This has led to the optimization possibilities in various process and data intensive applications such as BW transformations, Integrated Planning functions etc.

Key techniques to achieve code push down in ABAP on HANA:

1) Core Data Services – ABAP CDS
   Core Data Services (CDS) framework is mainly used to implement the Virtual Data Models for analytics and operational reporting either by building CDS Views or implementing CDS Table functions.
   - CDS Views are the building blocks to implement embedded analytics.
   - CDS Table functions contains the processing logic which can be used either in reporting or other application needs.

2) ABAP Managed Database Procedures – AMDP
   It is basically an ABAP Class method, which has the source code implemented in a Database specific language like HANA SQL Script. AMDP Methods are introduced to achieve code push down in SAP applications to take the advantage of the HANA database performance. Another major benefit with the AMDP methods is related to the transport of content, since these are transported as ABAP development artifacts and does not need any additional transport of native HANA objects.

In the following sections, let us understand the framework and the approach of implementation solutions using ABAP Managed Database Procedures (AMDP). Please note that the ABAP CDS views are not in the scope of this book.

8.2 ABAP to SQL Script coding techniques

In this section, we will explore some of the essential programming techniques to re-implement or replace the ABAP code using SQL Script programming. It is very much important to understand the key differences in the programming approaches, best practices and data processing options of both ABAP and SQL script programming to be able to build effective logic which is highly optimized and easy to maintain.

8.2.1 Handling Data Retrieval operations in ABAP vs SQL Script

In ABAP Program we will use "Internal Tables" to read and process the records from database tables. In HANA SQL Script, we need to use "Table Variables" to fetch the records and process them. Let us understand the key difference in the programming approaches for data retrieval and processing in both ABAP and SQL Script.

Example: Simple query to fetch records from a database table

ABAP Statement	SQL Script statement
SELECT VBELN KUNNR NETWR from VBAK into table IT_VBAK Where VKORG = '1000'.	TAB_VBAK := SELECT VBELN, KUNNR, NETWR from VBAK Where VKORG = '1000' ;
Key Points: • Internal tables to store the data records and process them in the application server. This will help in reducing the load on database server. • Starting with Netweaver 7.40, ABAP also supports inline declaration of table variables. Prior to that, we need to explicitly declare the structure of internal tables before using them.	Key Points: • We use Table variables to store the data records and process them in the in-memory layer of database itself. • Table variables need not to be declared explicitly. They will be generated automatically with the same structure as the result of the SELECT statement

8.2.2 Implementing Look-Up operations

Quite commonly we need to derive the data from various tables to fetch the desired values as per the calculation and output requirements. In ABAP Programming we will use either FOR ALL ENTRIES option or Join Operations to derive the data records (for the specific fields) from related tables. In SQL Script we will mainly use the JOIN operation or Sub queries (using the EXISTS or IN predicates) to perform the look up operation.

Example: Query to fetch the data from a look up table

ABAP Statement	SQL Script statement
Option #1: Using FOR ALL ENTRIES SELECT KUNNR, NAME1. LAND1 from KNA1 into table IT_KNA1 for ALL ENTRIES in IT_VBAK where KUNNR = IT_VBAK-KUNNR.	Option #1: Using EXISTS and Sub query TAB_KNA1 := SELECT KUNNR, NAME1, LAND1 from KNA1 as C Where EXISTS (SELECT DISTINCT KUNNR from :TAB_VBAK as S Where S.KUNNR = C.KUNNR) ;
Option #2: Using JOIN operation SELECT C~KUNNR C~NAME1 C~LAND1 from KNA1 as C inner join IT_VBAK as S On C~KUNNR = S~KUNNR into table IT_KNA1.	Option #2: Using JOIN operation TAB_KNA1 := SELECT KUNNR, NAME1, LAND1 from KNA1 as C Where EXISTS (SELECT DISTINCT KUNNR from :TAB_VBAK as S Where S.KUNNR = C.KUNNR) ;

8.2.3 Calculations and Formulas

Processing one or more data sets to achieve the desired application logic is the essential part of any program. As part of this, we often need to implement the operations such as filtering the records, applying formulas, transforming the field values, aggregating the results and merging the results of multiple data sets etc. Let us understand the key approaches to process the data records in both ABAP and SQL Script programming.

Example #1: To derive new fields by performing some calculations and transformations on existing records

ABAP Statement	SQL Script statement
Processing records of internal tables: LOOP AT IT_SALES INTO WA_SALES. <<Process record by record>> WA_SALES-NET_AMOUNT= WA_SALES-GROSS_AMOUNT - WA_SALES-DISCOUNT. ENDLOOP. Processing single row of internal tables: READ TABLE IT_SALES into WA_SALES with KEY ORDER_NUM = <>.	Processing table variables: TAB_RESULT = SELECT ORDER_NUM, CUSTOMER, ORDER_QTY, PRICE, **GROSS_AMOUNT - DISCOUNT as NET_AMOUNT** from :TAB_SALES;
Key Points: ▪ In most of the cases we need to process the internal table records sequentially in a loop	Key Points: ▪ Processing of table variables is always on the group of records and we can derive the calculated columns using the same SELECT query

Example #2: Aggregating results in the internal tables and Table variables

ABAP Statement	SQL Script statement
Aggregating the records of internal tables: LOOP AT IT_SALES into WA_SALES. WA_SUMMARY-CUSTOMER = WA_SALES-CUSTOMER. WA_ SUMMARY -ORDER_VALUE= WA_SALES-ORDER_VALUE. COLLECT WA_ SUMMARY to IT_ SUMMARY. ENDLOOP.	Aggregating the records of table variables: TAB_SUMMARY := SELECT CUSTOMER, SUM(GROSS_AMT) from :TAB_SALES GROUP BY CUSTOMER;

8.3 Framework of ABAP Managed Database Procedure - AMDP

AMDP is implemented by using the ABAP Objects framework which provides the special interface IF_AMDP_MARKER_HDB, which has the necessary elements to implement the method. Let us understand the definition and the implementation of AMDP Class and method and the programming rules for implementing the logic in SQL Script.

Any ABAP program that uses the AMDP methods to push the processing logic to HANA database, need to implement a class that has the interface IF_AMDP_MARKER_HDB.

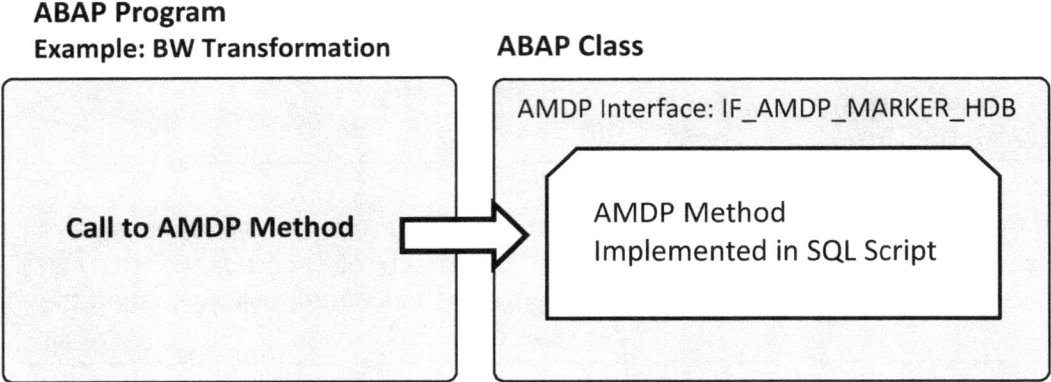

AMDP Class Definition:

For each of the AMDP implementation scenarios, an ABAP Class will be either created explicitly or it will be generated implicitly. This class need to implement the interface IF_AMDP_MARKER_HDB to be able to define and implement the methods which are based on AMDP framework.

Let us try to understand the implementation of AMDP Class in the context of SAP BW Transformation. Whenever we create a start routine, end routine or expert routine based on AMDP Script in an SAP BW transformation, the AMDP framework generates an ABAP class with a method called PROCEDURE. Let us understand the details of the AMDP class and method in the following sections.

Structure of AMDP Class: Generated for BW Transformation End Routine

```
CLASS <Generated Class Name> definition
  Public
  create public .
public section.

  interfaces IF_AMDP_MARKER_HDB.

-------------<Source structure Fields>--------
  types:
    begin of TN_S_IN1,

    begin of TN_S_ERROR1,
       ERROR_TEXT type string,
       SQL__PROCEDURE__SOURCE__RECORD type C length 56,
    end of TN_S_ERROR1 .

  types:
    begin of TN_S_ERROR.
       include type TN_S_ERROR1.
     types end of TN_S_ERROR .
  types:
    TN_T_ERROR TYPE STANDARD TABLE OF TN_S_ERROR .


  class-methods PROCEDURE
    Importing
      value(i_error_handling) type STRING
      value(inTab) type /BIC/00O2TLGXBRQY8Y9N6Q8HPRL52=>TN_T_IN
    Exporting
      value(outTab) type /BIC/00O2TLGXBRQY8Y9N6Q8HPRL52=>TN_T_OUT
      value(errorTab) type /BIC/00O2TLGXBRQY8Y9N6Q8HPRL52=>TN_T_ERROR .
protected section.
private section.
ENDCLASS.
```

AMDP Interface -
mandatory

Structures used to
define the Input &
Output data sets

AMDP Methods
definition

185

AMDP Method Implementation

This declaration specifies the method to the HANA database (HDB), the language to SQLSCRIPT and further on defines that the database procedure is READ ONLY

To access any of the ABAP Dictionary tables or any Methods of other classes in this method, we need to explicitly specify them with the key word USING in the signature.

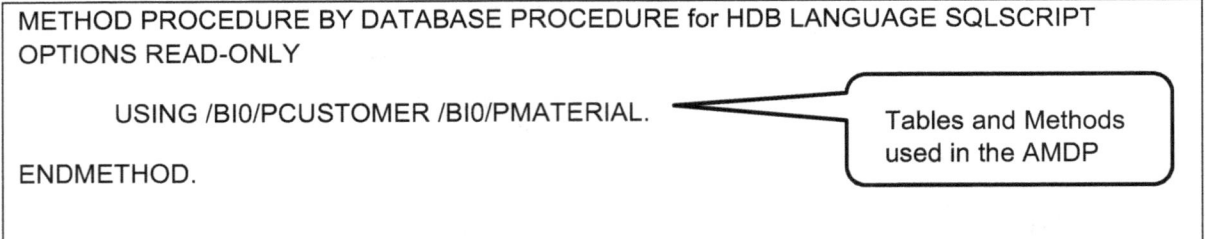

```
METHOD PROCEDURE BY DATABASE PROCEDURE for HDB LANGUAGE SQLSCRIPT
OPTIONS READ-ONLY

     USING /BI0/PCUSTOMER /BI0/PMATERIAL.

ENDMETHOD.
```

Tables and Methods used in the AMDP

8.3.1 AMDP Use Cases and Features

AMDP Methods are used in various use cases to push the data intensive calculations to the database.
- SAP BW Transformations
- SAP BW Integrated Planning – Planning Functions
- S/4HANA Embedded Analytics – Table Functions which can implement the source code based on AMDP

We need to be aware of the following features of AMDP while implementing the logic.
- We can only implement an AMDP class within the ABAP Development Tools (ADT) which is based on the Eclipse.
- AMDP can be implemented only when the underlying database is SAP HANA (as of now)
- In ABAP Open SQL, it supports automatic handling of Client (MANDT) column which ensures that the SQL statements will filter the records as per the Session Client. However, in AMDP this automatic handling of client is not supported, since it runs directly on the database layer.

8.4 HANA based Transformations in SAP BW using AMDP

Starting with BW 7.4 SP05 there is a new execution mode introduced to run BW transformations in HANA, which helps to optimize the execution using "Code Push down" approach. In the ABAP based BW transformations, we will be transferring larger volumes of data from the database and run the processing logic in the application server and again writing the results back to the database. By implementing the BW transformations using AMDP approach, we will be able to achieve the code push down (to the HANA Database layer) which leads to optimal performance during data loads.

Here the logic of the BW transformation is converted into a HANA Calculation Scenario, which is generated when we activate the Transformation. At runtime of the transformation an "INSERT AS SELECT" statement is executed on this Calculation Scenario and the INSERT writes the data directly into the tables of the target Data Provider by executing the SELECT which has all the transformation logic expressed in SQL Script.

Key benefits of implementing BW Transformations using AMDP approach:

- The data packages are entirely processed within the database server which avoids the data transfer between application server and database server

- The transformation logic can potentially make use of the full CPU power and parallelism of the HANA database.

- The degree of the performance improvement heavily depends on several factors, like the amount of data read and written, the transformation logic and the possible parallelism in there

- Expected improvements between a factor of 3 up to a factor of 10 were shown -but in some cases (e.g. very low data volumes) the performance improvement may also be negligible.

BW Transformations Data Transfer and Processing Comparison:

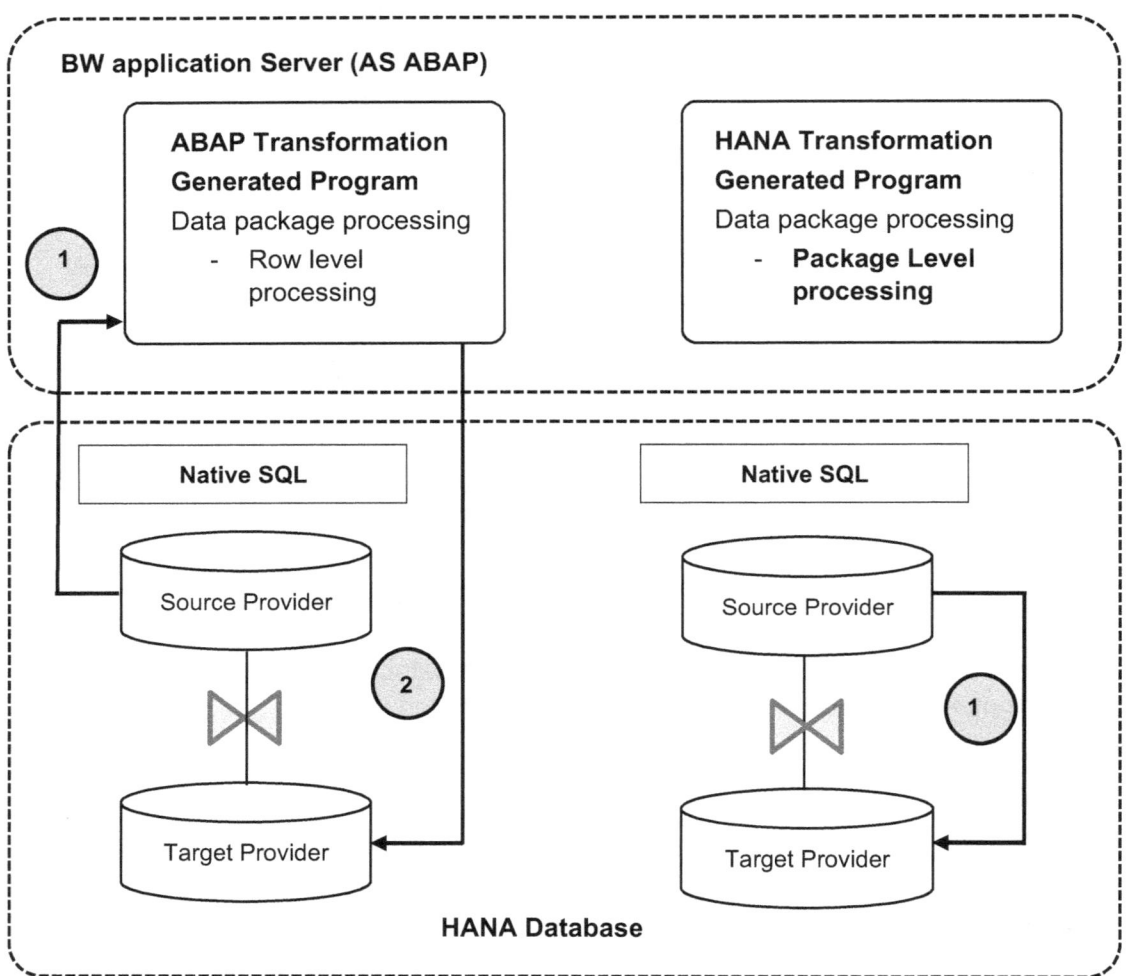

We shall notice the data transfer requirements in both the ABAP based transformation and HANA based transformations. In ABAP based transformations each of the data packages are moved to application server and the result data packages are sent to database after the processing. In HANA based transformations, the entire processing will be performed in the HANA Database (in-memory) itself, which results in significant performance benefits.

8.4.1 Example: SAP BW End Routine Logic using AMDP Script

In this section, let us go through a step-by-step example to implement the SAP BW Transformation routine using AMDP Script. We will implement a transformation with end routine between two Advanced DSO objects.

Business Case: There is an Advanced DSO ZSDITM1 which is mapped to the standard extractor 2LIS_11_VAITM to pull the sales order items. We would like to build an advanced DSO (ZSDITM2) to store the sales order items along with the delivery quantity and status details. Also, there is a need to look up the customer master data and derive the Account Group for each customer. We need to implement the logic to derive the Total Delivered Qty of each Sales Order item from another Advanced DSO ZDLITM1 (Delivery document items). We will implement a transformation based on AMDP script the achieve optimal processing of the transformation.

Source Advanced DSO: ZSDITM1

Details: ZSDITM1

Fields

Filter Pattern

Name	InfoObject	Key	Type
☐ 📂 [GROUP 1]			
[0DOC_NUMBER] Sales document	0DOC_NUMBER		CHAR
[0DOC_ITEM] BW: Document Item Number	0DOC_ITEM		NUMC
[0DOC_DATE] Document Date	0DOC_DATE		DATS
[0MATERIAL] Material	0MATERIAL		CHAR
[0SOLD_TO] Sold-to party	0SOLD_TO		CHAR
[0DOC_TYPE] Sales document type	0DOC_TYPE		CHAR
[0BILL_BLOCK] Billing block in SD document	0BILL_BLOCK		CHAR
[0COMP_CODE] Company code	0COMP_CODE		CHAR
[0SALESORG] Sales Organization	0SALESORG		CHAR
[0DISTR_CHAN] Distribution Channel	0DISTR_CHAN		CHAR
[0DIVISION] Division	0DIVISION		CHAR
[0ORDER_QTY] Order Quantity of the Customer	0ORDER_QTY		QUAN
[0SALES_UNIT] Sales unit	0SALES_UNIT		UNIT
[0NET_VALUE] Net value of the order item in doc	0NET_VALUE		CURR
[0DOC_CURRCY] Document currency	0DOC_CURRCY		CUKY

Sample data from the DSO – ZSDITM1

Data Browser: Table /BIC/AZSDITM12 Select Entries   200

Sales document	BW: Document Item	R	Document Date	Material	Sold-to party	Order quanti...	Sales unit	Net Value	Document currency
0000006391	10	N	24.07.2000	R-1140	0000001172	4	ST	2.597,36	EUR
0000006392	10	N	24.07.2000	R-1140	0000001460	25	ST	16.233,52	EUR
0000006395	10	N	28.07.2000	DPC1012	0000002007	293	ST	10.672,36	EUR
0000006399	10	N	28.07.2000	M-16	0000002007	9	ST	11.660,52	EUR
0000006400	10	N	28.07.2000	M-20	0000001360	12	ST	10.569,01	EUR
0000006403	10	N	02.08.2000	DPC1013	0000001460	254	ST	12.598,40	EUR
0000006405	10	N	03.08.2000	M-13	0000002007	12	ST	9.939,60	EUR
0000006406	10	N	03.08.2000	M-17	0000001172	13	ST	18.743,40	EUR
0000006409	10	N	04.08.2000	DPC1014	0000001360	123	ST	8.657,85	EUR
0000006411	10	N	07.08.2000	M-10	0000001460	13	ST	16.471,00	EUR
0000006421	10	N	10.08.2000	DPC1012	0000001172	315	ST	11.466,00	EUR
0000006423	10	N	11.08.2000	M-16	0000002130	9	ST	11.660.40	EUR

Target Advanced DSO: ZSDITM2

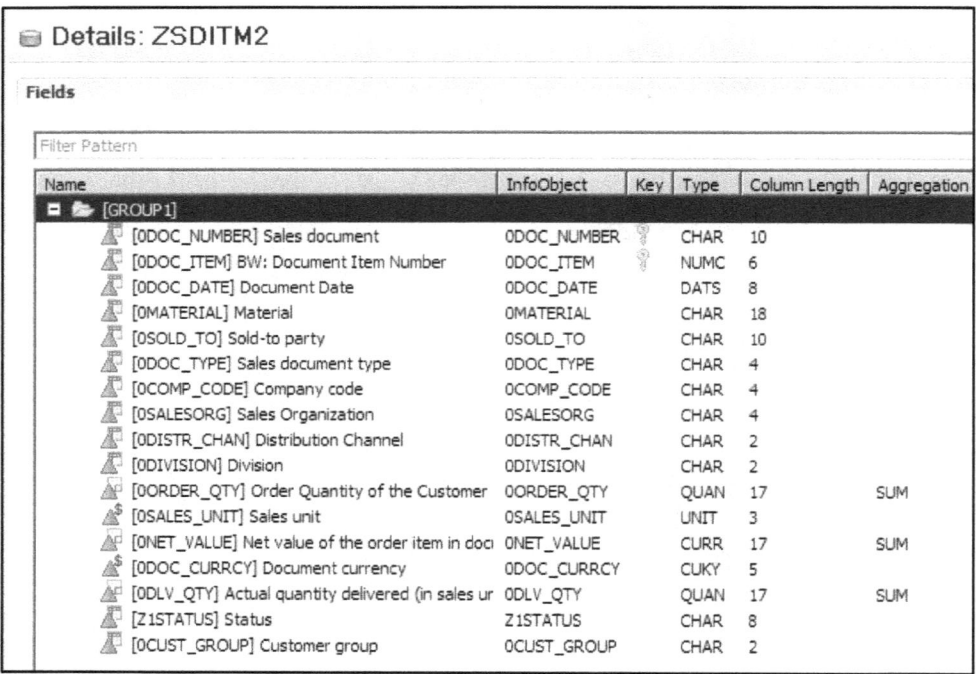

Details: ZSDITM2

Fields

Filter Pattern

Name	InfoObject	Key	Type	Column Length	Aggregation
[GROUP 1]					
[0DOC_NUMBER] Sales document	0DOC_NUMBER	✓	CHAR	10	
[0DOC_ITEM] BW: Document Item Number	0DOC_ITEM	✓	NUMC	6	
[0DOC_DATE] Document Date	0DOC_DATE		DATS	8	
[0MATERIAL] Material	0MATERIAL		CHAR	18	
[0SOLD_TO] Sold-to party	0SOLD_TO		CHAR	10	
[0DOC_TYPE] Sales document type	0DOC_TYPE		CHAR	4	
[0COMP_CODE] Company code	0COMP_CODE		CHAR	4	
[0SALESORG] Sales Organization	0SALESORG		CHAR	4	
[0DISTR_CHAN] Distribution Channel	0DISTR_CHAN		CHAR	2	
[0DIVISION] Division	0DIVISION		CHAR	2	
[0ORDER_QTY] Order Quantity of the Customer	0ORDER_QTY		QUAN	17	SUM
[0SALES_UNIT] Sales unit	0SALES_UNIT		UNIT	3	
[0NET_VALUE] Net value of the order item in doc	0NET_VALUE		CURR	17	SUM
[0DOC_CURRCY] Document currency	0DOC_CURRCY		CUKY	5	
[0DLV_QTY] Actual quantity delivered (in sales ur	0DLV_QTY		QUAN	17	SUM
[Z1STATUS] Status	Z1STATUS		CHAR	8	
[0CUST_GROUP] Customer group	0CUST_GROUP		CHAR	2	

Look up DSO:

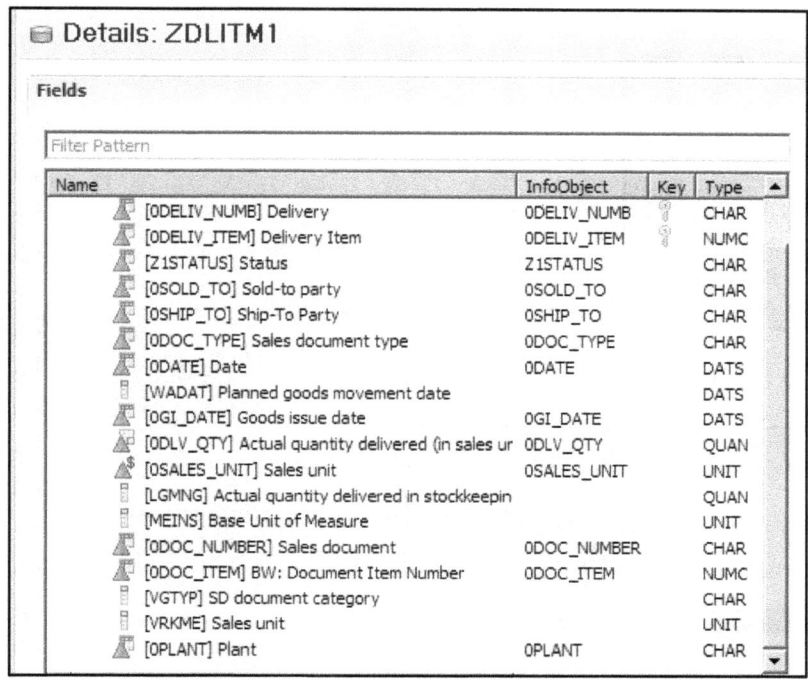

Sample data: DSO – ZDLITM1

Data Browser: Table /BIC/AZDLITM12 Select Entries   34

Delivery	Item	R	Status	Sold-to party	Ship-To Party	WADAT	Goods issue	Delivery quantity	Sales unit	LGM...	Unit of Measure	Sales docum...	BW: Document Item
0080007392	10	N	C	0000001172	0000001172	26.07.2000	26.07.2000	4	ST	4	ST	0000006391	10
0080007393	10	N	C	0000001460	0000001460	26.07.2000	26.07.2000	25	ST	25	ST	0000006392	10
0080007397	10	N	C	0000002007	0000002007	01.08.2000	01.08.2000	293	ST	293	ST	0000006395	10
0080007416	10	N	C	0000002007	0000002007	01.08.2000	01.08.2000	9	ST	9	ST	0000006399	10
0080007417	10	N	C	0000001360	0000001360	01.08.2000	01.08.2000	12	ST	12	ST	0000006400	10
0080007547	10	N	C	0000001460	0000001460	04.08.2000	04.08.2000	254	ST	254	ST	0000006403	10
0080007548	10	N	C	0000001360	0000001360	08.08.2000	08.08.2000	123	ST	123	ST	0000006409	10
0080007550	10	N	C	0000001172	0000001172	14.08.2000	14.08.2000	315	ST	315	ST	0000006421	10
0080007554	10	N	C	0000002007	0000002007	07.08.2000	07.08.2000	12	ST	12	ST	0000006405	10
0080007555	10	N	C	0000001172	0000001172	07.08.2000	07.08.2000	13	ST	13	ST	0000006406	10
0080007559	10	N	C	0000001460	0000001460	09.08.2000	09.08.2000	13	ST	13	ST	0000006411	10
0080007569	10	N	C	0000002130	0000002130	15.08.2000	15.08.2000	9	ST	9	ST	0000006423	10

Sample data: Info object 0CUSTOMER

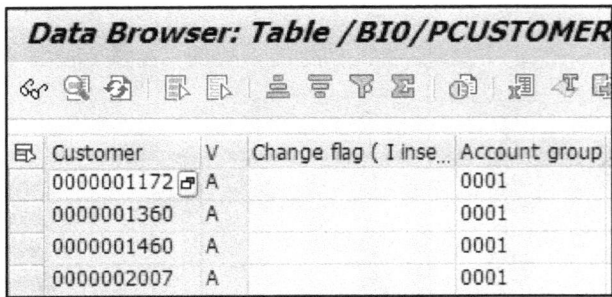

Create transformation between the two DSOs

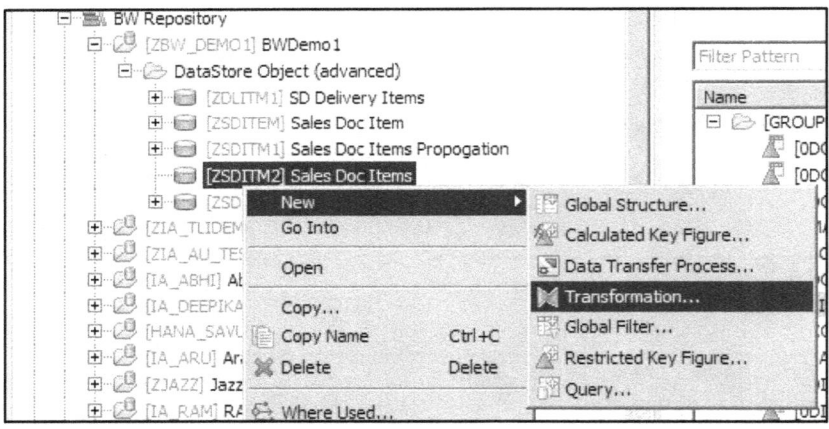

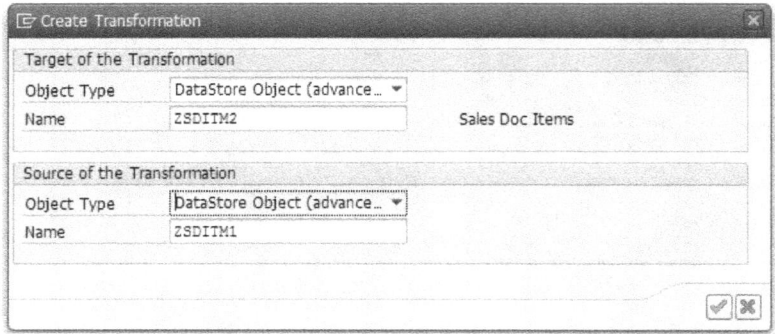

Implement the transformation mappings as shown below:

Note: We may need to map the result fields where we do not have the corresponding source fields (0DLV_QTY, Z1STATUS and 0ACCNT_GRP) to the CONSTANT values to avoid the activation errors.

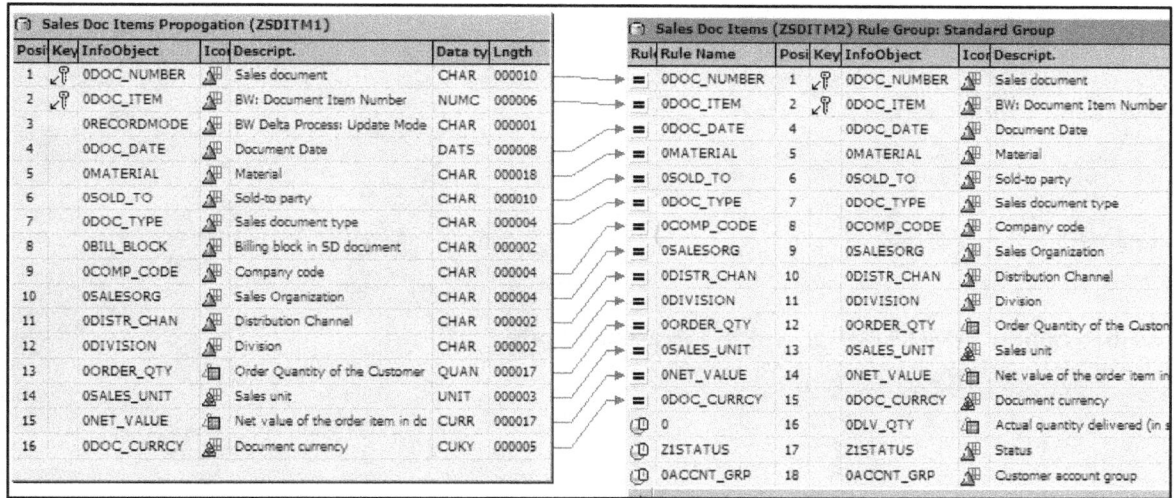

Create "End Routine" to derive the values into the following columns

1) Actual Delivery Qty (0DLV_QTY)
2) Status for delivery completion (Z1STATUS)
3) Customer Account Group (0ACCNT_GRP)

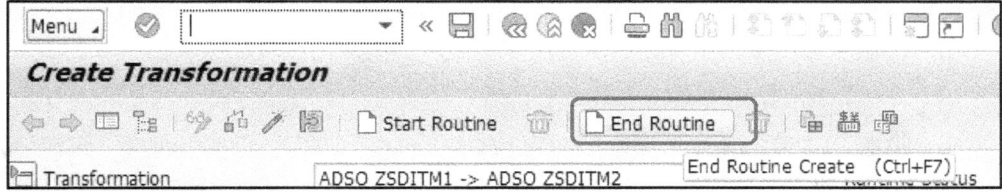

Choose all the Target fields to proceed with the implementation of end routine.

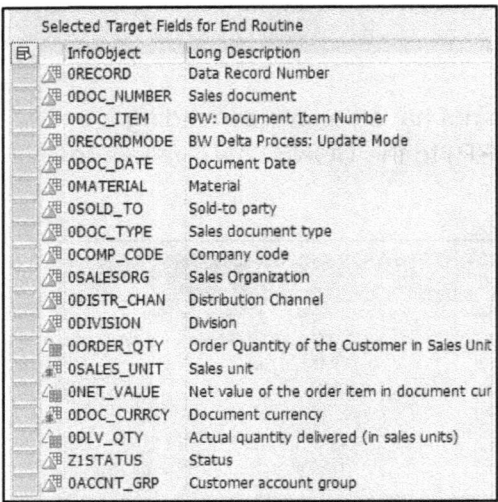

Choose the option "AMDP Script" in the following popup.

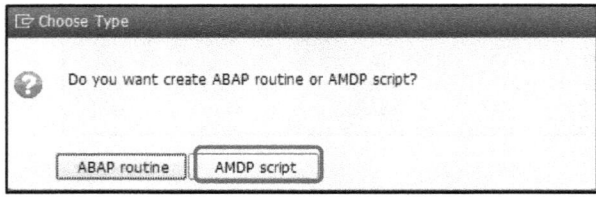

Login to the BW Project with the credentials

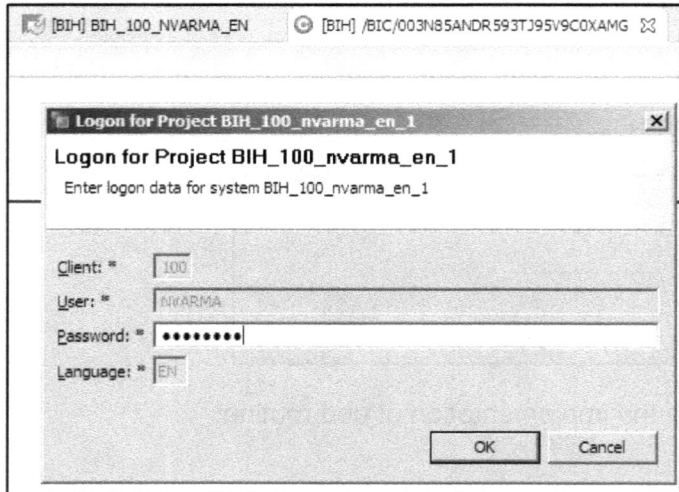

We will find the generated class for the AMDP Transformation:

```
class /BIC/003N85ANDR593TJ95V9C0XAMG definition
  public
  create public .

public section.
  interfaces IF_AMDP_MARKER_HDB .

  types:
    begin of TN_S_IN1,
      REQTSN type RSPM_REQUEST_TSN, " InfoObject: 0REQTSN
      DOC_NUMBER type /BI0/OIDOC_NUMBER, " InfoObject: 0DOC_NUMBER
      DOC_ITEM type /BI0/OIDOC_ITEM, " InfoObject: 0DOC_ITEM
      RECORDMODE type RODMUPDMOD, " InfoObject: 0RECORDMODE
      DOC_DATE type /BI0/OIDOC_DATE, " InfoObject: 0DOC_DATE
      MATERIAL type /BI0/OIMATERIAL, " InfoObject: 0MATERIAL
      SOLD_TO type /BI0/OISOLD_TO, " InfoObject: 0SOLD_TO
      DOC_TYPE type /BI0/OIDOC_TYPE, " InfoObject: 0DOC_TYPE
      COMP_CODE type /BI0/OICOMP_CODE, " InfoObject: 0COMP_CODE
      SALESORG type /BI0/OISALESORG, " InfoObject: 0SALESORG
      DISTR_CHAN type /BI0/OIDISTR_CHAN, " InfoObject: 0DISTR_CHAN
      DIVISION type /BI0/OIDIVISION, " InfoObject: 0DIVISION
      ORDER_QTY type /BI0/OIORDER_QTY, " InfoObject: 0ORDER_QTY
      SALES_UNIT type /BI0/OISALES_UNIT, " InfoObject: 0SALES_UNIT
      NET_VALUE type /BI0/OINET_VALUE, " InfoObject: 0NET_VALUE
      DOC_CURRCY type /BI0/OIDOC_CURRCY, " InfoObject: 0DOC_CURRCY
      DLV_QTY type /BI0/OIDLV_QTY, " InfoObject: 0DLV_QTY
      /BIC/Z1STATUS type /BIC/OIZ1STATUS, " InfoObject: Z1STATUS
      ACCNT_GRP type /BI0/OIACCNT_GRP, " InfoObject: 0ACCNT_GRP
      RECORD type C length 56,
      SQL__PROCEDURE__SOURCE__RECORD type C length 56,
    end of TN_S_IN1 .
  types:
    begin of TN_S_IN.
      include type TN_S_IN1.
    types end of TN_S_IN .
  types:
    TN_T_IN TYPE STANDARD TABLE OF TN_S_IN .
  types:
    begin of TN_S_OUT1,
      REQTSN type RSPM_REQUEST_TSN, " InfoObject: 0REQTSN
      DOC_NUMBER type /BI0/OIDOC_NUMBER, " InfoObject: 0DOC_NUMBER
      DOC_ITEM type /BI0/OIDOC_ITEM, " InfoObject: 0DOC_ITEM
      RECORDMODE type RODMUPDMOD, " InfoObject: 0RECORDMODE
      DOC_DATE type /BI0/OIDOC_DATE, " InfoObject: 0DOC_DATE
```

195

```
        MATERIAL type /BI0/OIMATERIAL, " InfoObject: 0MATERIAL
        SOLD_TO type /BI0/OISOLD_TO, " InfoObject: 0SOLD_TO
        DOC_TYPE type /BI0/OIDOC_TYPE, " InfoObject: 0DOC_TYPE
        COMP_CODE type /BI0/OICOMP_CODE, " InfoObject: 0COMP_CODE
        SALESORG type /BI0/OISALESORG, " InfoObject: 0SALESORG
        DISTR_CHAN type /BI0/OIDISTR_CHAN, " InfoObject: 0DISTR_CHAN
        DIVISION type /BI0/OIDIVISION, " InfoObject: 0DIVISION
        ORDER_QTY type /BI0/OIORDER_QTY, " InfoObject: 0ORDER_QTY
        SALES_UNIT type /BI0/OISALES_UNIT, " InfoObject: 0SALES_UNIT
        NET_VALUE type /BI0/OINET_VALUE, " InfoObject: 0NET_VALUE
        DOC_CURRCY type /BI0/OIDOC_CURRCY, " InfoObject: 0DOC_CURRCY
        DLV_QTY type /BI0/OIDLV_QTY, " InfoObject: 0DLV_QTY
        /BIC/Z1STATUS type /BIC/OIZ1STATUS, " InfoObject: Z1STATUS
        ACCNT_GRP type /BI0/OIACCNT_GRP, " InfoObject: 0ACCNT_GRP
        RECORD type C length 56,
        SQL__PROCEDURE__SOURCE__RECORD type C length 56,
      end of TN_S_OUT1 .
  types:
    begin of TN_S_OUT.
        include type TN_S_OUT1.
     types end of TN_S_OUT .
  types:
    TN_T_OUT TYPE STANDARD TABLE OF TN_S_OUT .
  types:
    begin of TN_S_ERROR1,
        ERROR_TEXT type string,
        SQL__PROCEDURE__SOURCE__RECORD type C length 56,
      end of TN_S_ERROR1 .
  types:
    begin of TN_S_ERROR.
        include type TN_S_ERROR1.
     types end of TN_S_ERROR .
  types:
    TN_T_ERROR TYPE STANDARD TABLE OF TN_S_ERROR .

  class-methods PROCEDURE
    importing
      value(i_error_handling) type STRING
      value(inTab) type /BIC/003N85ANDR593TJ95V9C0XAMG=>TN_T_IN
    exporting
      value(outTab) type /BIC/003N85ANDR593TJ95V9C0XAMG=>TN_T_OUT
      value(errorTab) type /BIC/003N85ANDR593TJ95V9C0XAMG=>TN_T_ERROR .
protected section.
private section.
ENDCLASS.
```

```
CLASS /BIC/003N85ANDR593TJ95V9C0XAMG IMPLEMENTATION.

METHOD PROCEDURE BY DATABASE PROCEDURE FOR HDB LANGUAGE SQLSCRIPT OPTIONS
READ-ONLY.

OUTTAB   = SELECT * FROM :INTAB;
ERRORTAB = SELECT '' AS ERROR_TEXT, '' AS SQL__PROCEDURE__SOURCE__RECORD

FROM DUMMY WHERE DUMMY <> 'X';
ENDMETHOD.
ENDCLASS.
```

Implement the following code changes in the AMDP Method called PROCEDURE:

```
METHOD PROCEDURE BY DATABASE PROCEDURE FOR HDB LANGUAGE SQLSCRIPT OPTIONS
READ-ONLY
          USING /BIO/PCUSTOMER "Customer attributes
                /BIC/AZDLITM12 "Delivery items
                .
```

TABLES used in the method code

Look up operations to derive the fields

```
TAB_CUST = SELECT customer, ACCNT_GRP from "/BIO/PCUSTOMER" as C
                WHERE EXISTS (SELECT distinct SOLD_TO from :INTAB as IT
                            WHERE IT.SOLD_TO = C.CUSTOMER);

TAB_DLV = SELECT IT.DOC_NUMBER, IT.DOC_ITEM, SUM(D.DLV_QTY) AS DLV_QTY
from "/BIC/AZDLITM12" as D
        INNER JOIN :INTAB as IT
        ON D.DOC_NUMBER = IT.DOC_NUMBER and D.DOC_ITEM = IT.DOC_ITEM
        GROUP BY IT.DOC_NUMBER, IT.DOC_ITEM;

OUTTAB    = SELECT
            IT.REQTSN ,
            IT.DOC_NUMBER ,
            IT.DOC_ITEM ,
            IT.RECORDMODE,
            IT.DOC_DATE,
            IT.MATERIAL ,
            IT.SOLD_TO ,
```

Populate the target datapackage (table)

```
               IT.DOC_TYPE ,
               IT.COMP_CODE ,
               IT.SALESORG ,
               IT.DISTR_CHAN ,
               IT.DIVISION ,
               IT.ORDER_QTY ,
               IT.SALES_UNIT ,
               IT.NET_VALUE ,
               IT.DOC_CURRCY ,
               D.DLV_QTY ,
               CASE when D.DLV_QTY = IT.ORDER_QTY then 'Y'
               else 'N'
               End as "/BIC/Z1STATUS" ,
               C.ACCNT_GRP ,
              RECORD ,
              SQL__PROCEDURE__SOURCE__RECORD
                FROM :INTAB as IT

       Left Outer Join :TAB_DLV as D
       ON IT.DOC_NUMBER = D.DOC_NUMBER and IT.DOC_ITEM = D.DOC_ITEM
       Left Outer Join :TAB_CUST as C
       on IT.SOLD_TO = C.CUSTOMER   ;

ERRORTAB = SELECT '' AS ERROR_TEXT, '' AS SQL__PROCEDURE__SOURCE__RECORD
FROM DUMMY WHERE DUMMY <> 'X';

ENDMETHOD.
```

Next steps:

- Activate the class and the BW transformation.
- Create the DTP and execute to load the data

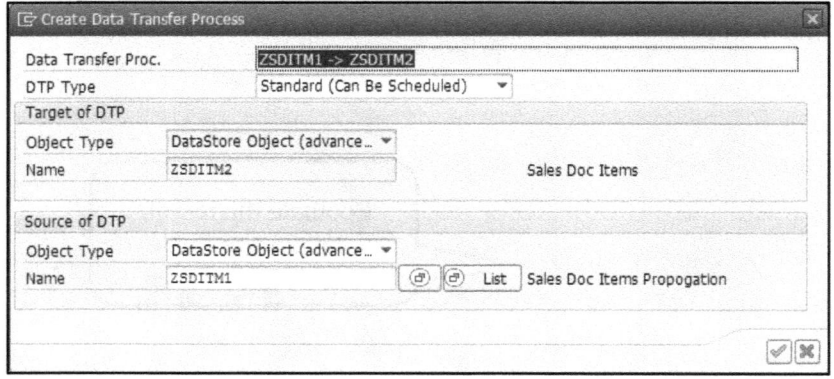

```
▼ ☐ Request {2018-07-04 06:10:48 000001 CST}
     · ☐ Generate Request
     · ☐ Set Status to 'Executable'
     · ☐ Process Request
     · ☐ Prepare for Extraction
   ▼ ☐ Data Package 1 ( 16.557 Data Records )
       · ☐ ADSO ZSDITM1 -> ADSO ZSDITM2 : 16.557 -> 16.557 Data Recor
```

Verify the records in the DSO table.

Sales document	BW: Docum..	Document Date	Material	Sold-to party	Order quantity	Sales unit	Net Value	Document ..	Delivery quantity	Status	Account group
Data Browser: Table /BIC/AZSDITM21 Select Entries 200											
0000006391	10	24.07.2000	R-1140	0000001172	4	ST	2.597,36	EUR	4	Y	0001
0000006392	10	24.07.2000	R-1140	0000001460	25	ST	16.233,52	EUR	25	Y	0001
0000006395	10	28.07.2000	DPC1012	0000002007	293	ST	10.672,36	EUR	293	Y	0001
0000006399	10	28.07.2000	M-16	0000002007	9	ST	11.660,52	EUR	9	Y	0001
0000006400	10	28.07.2000	M-20	0000001360	12	ST	10.569,01	EUR	12	Y	0001
0000006403	10	02.08.2000	DPC1013	0000001460	254	ST	12.598,40	EUR	254	Y	0001
0000006405	10	03.08.2000	M-13	0000002007	12	ST	9.939,60	EUR	12	Y	0001
0000006406	10	03.08.2000	M-17	0000001172	13	ST	18.743,40	EUR	13	Y	0001
0000006409	10	04.08.2000	DPC1014	0000001360	123	ST	8.657,85	EUR	123	Y	0001
0000006411	10	07.08.2000	M-10	0000001460	13	ST	16.471,00	EUR	13	Y	0001
0000006421	10	10.08.2000	DPC1012	0000001172	315	ST	11.466,00	EUR	315	Y	0001

We shall observe that the result fields Delivery Quantity, Status and Account Group are derived correctly in the end routine.

9 Troubleshooting Tools and Techniques

There are several tools and options available in the HANA studio, which helps us in troubleshooting the issues, maintaining the SQL Script development artifacts in a simplified manner. These tools are quite handy to analyze dependencies between the objects, maintain object versions and fix errors etc. Effective usage of these tools will lead to better productivity and minimize the errors. One of the important technique that we will understand in this unit is the debugging of stored procedures. Let us understand how to leverage these tools and features while building and maintaining HANA views.

9.1 Debugging stored procedures

One of the essential tools for the programmers to validate the logic is the debugging mechanism, which is used to execute the programs statement by statement and verify the results at various steps. SAP HANA provides the Debug perspective to perform debugging of stored procedures.

Debugging Procedures

The SAP HANA SQLScript debugger allows you to debug and analyze procedures. In a debug session, your procedures are executed in serial mode, not in parallel (not optimized). The stored procedure call stack appears in the debug view allowing us to view the nested calls. This allows us to test the logical correctness of the procedure to understand the flow of execution and if it is generating the results as per the requirement.

The following debug session types are available:

1) Design-Time – Use it to debug a design-time procedure artifact (.procedure/.hdbprocedure)
2) Catalog - Enables you to debug a runtime procedure object
3) External - Enables you to debug procedures that are executed by an external session
4) Unified - Enables you to debug targets of both XS JavaScript and SQLScript in the debug view

Following are the main steps to debug stored procedures:

1. Create a Debug configuration for specific stored procedure

    Debug configuration contains the settings that controls the debugging flow of a stored procedure, such as the procedure type (Catalog vs Repository procedure), Procedure name, Input parameters values to be used etc. This will allow us to repeat the debugging of a procedure with the same settings.

    Open the stored procedure in the development perspective and choose the Debug Configurations from the pop-up menu as shown below.

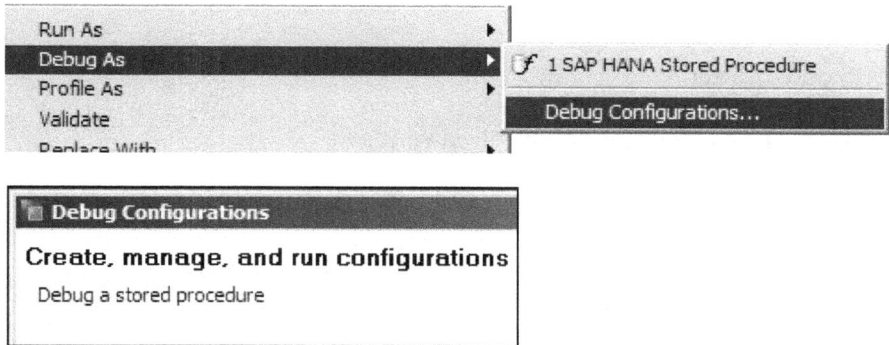

Note: To work on the below steps for debugging stored procedures, you need to first implement the following stored procedure, which is explained in the Unit: 7 (Section: 7.4 Business Case: Implementing Sales Order Delivery Status Snapshots)

`"NVARMA"."00_dmm::SP_SALES_ORDER_STATUS_SNAPSHOT"`

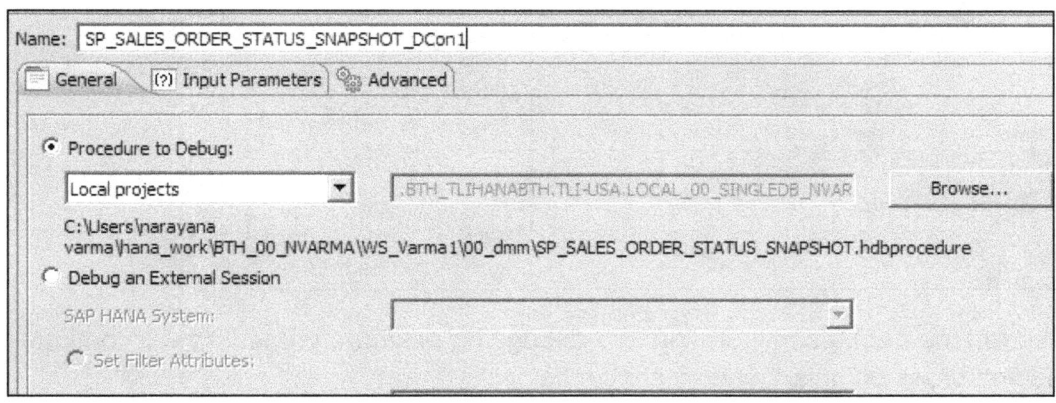

Enter values for input parameters – enter value for SNAP_DATE as shown below

Click on the "Apply" button

2. Execute the debug configuration

Click on the Debug button on the debug configuration window:

Add break points for the required statements of stored procedure.

We can use the "Toggle Breakpoint" option to set or remove the breakpoints for any of the executable statements as shown below. (Right click on the grey area and choose this option.

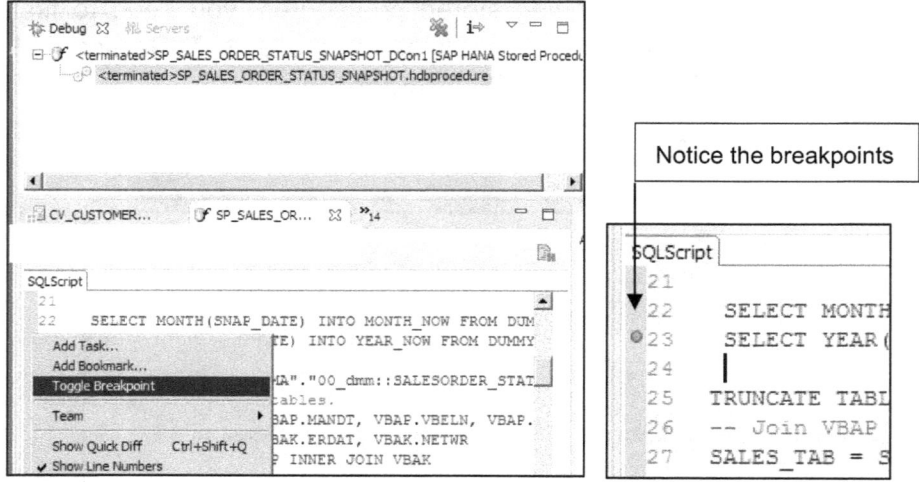

Once we run the debug configuration, the debugging of stored procedure will continue until the first break point is found as shown below:

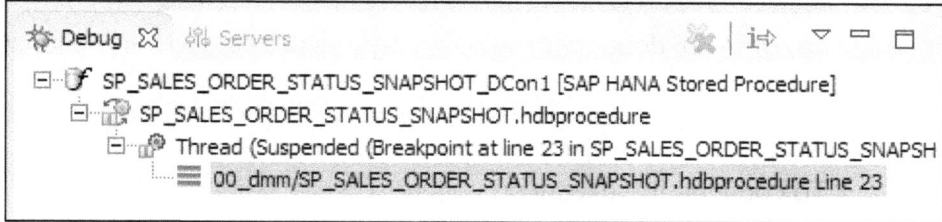

For example: in the above screen the stored procedure is currently in debugging and it is at the Line 23.

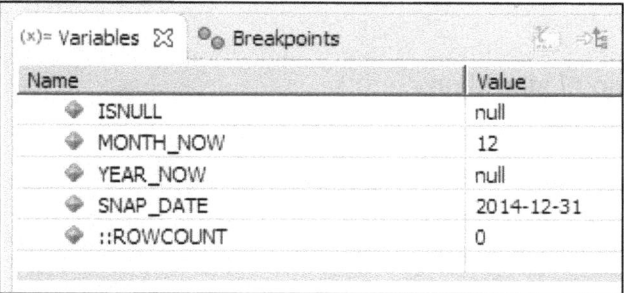

We can review the values of variables in the above section.

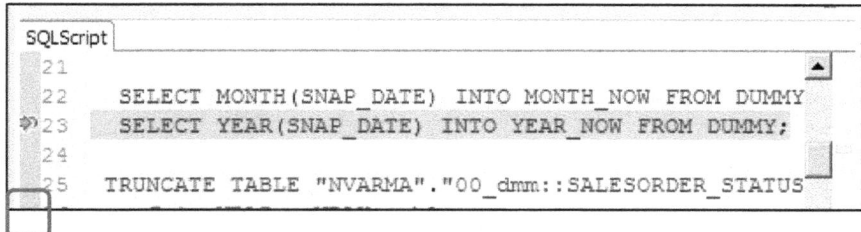

In the above section, we shall monitor the control flow of the procedure which is currently under debugging.

We can also create additional break points here during the debugging process. Use the Toggle Breakpoint option mentioned earlier.

We shall continue to navigate in debugging session by using the toolbar options shown below.

Resume (F8) → To continue the execution until next break point

Use Step filters → To continue the debugging statement wise or skip the current block etc.

Terminate → To end the debugging of stored procedure

9.1.1 Managing Table Variables during Debugging

Let us create the following debug configuration for the stored procedure "NVARMA"."democode::PR_SALES_ORDER_DELIVERY_STATUS" to explore the functionality of accessing table variables during debugging.

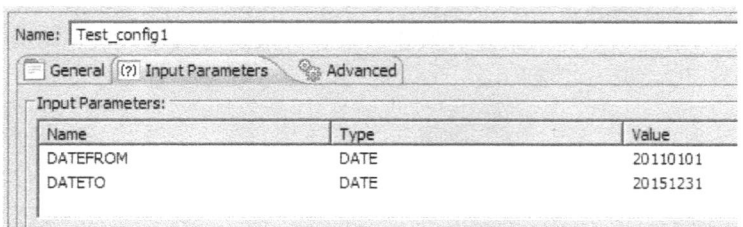

Run the debug configuration after placing the break points in the code.

Debug configuration and Variables / Breakpoints area:

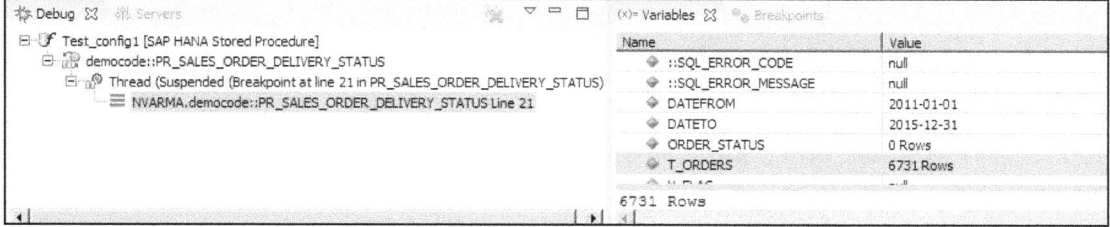

Procedure code and navigation:

```SQLScript
20  --Fetch sales order items of the corresponding orders
21  T_ORDER_ITEMS = SELECT ITEM.MANDT, ITEM.VBELN , ITEM.POSNR, MATNR, KWMENG, MEINS from VBAP as ITEM
22              INNER JOIN :T_ORDERS as HDR
23              on ITEM.MANDT = HDR.MANDT and
24                 ITEM.VBELN = HDR.VBELN;
25
26  --Fetch Delivery items for the respective Sales order Items
27  T_DEL_ITEMS = SELECT ITEM.VBELN , ITEM.POSNR, ITEM.MATNR, ITEM.KWMENG, ITEM.MEINS, DLV.LFIMG  from :T_
28              LEFT OUTER JOIN LIPS as DLV
29              on ITEM.MANDT = DLV.MANDT and
30                 ITEM.VBELN = DLV.VGBEL and
```

Drill down to the Table Variables: We can observe the Table Variables and perform data preview to view the records

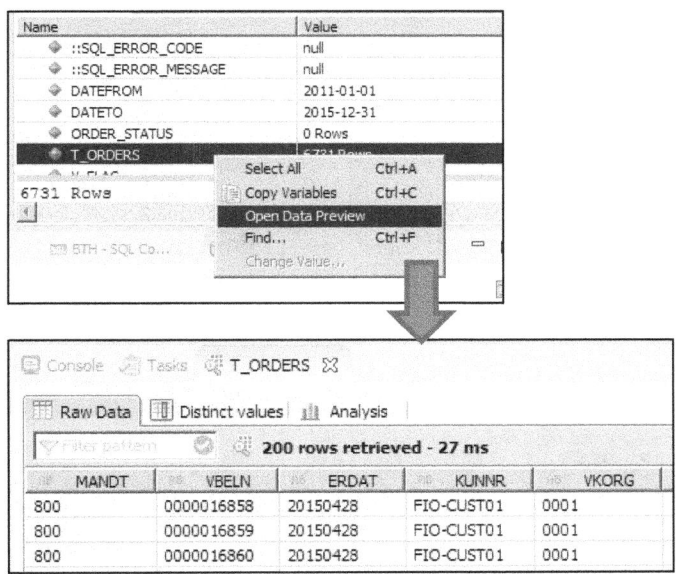

9.2   Performance Analysis of Stored Procedures

How can we analyze the performance of stored procedures and identify the logic or statements which need to be optimized further? Well, we can use the Plan visualizer tool to achieve this. This is almost similar approach like how we analyze the performance of calculation views.

We need to run the stored procedure call statement using the Plan Visualizer tool as shown below:

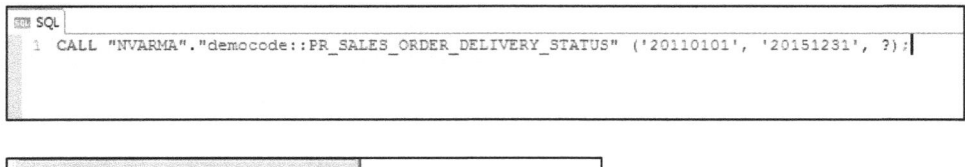

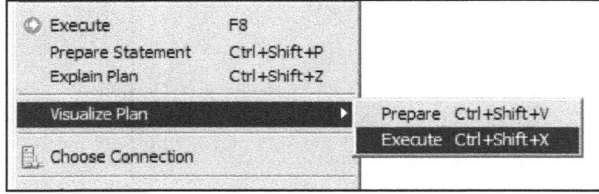

Now the control switches to the "PlanViz" perspective in HANA studio.

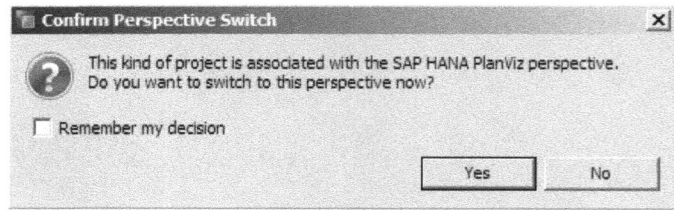

In the Statement Statistics tab as shown below, we can observe the runtime of various statements

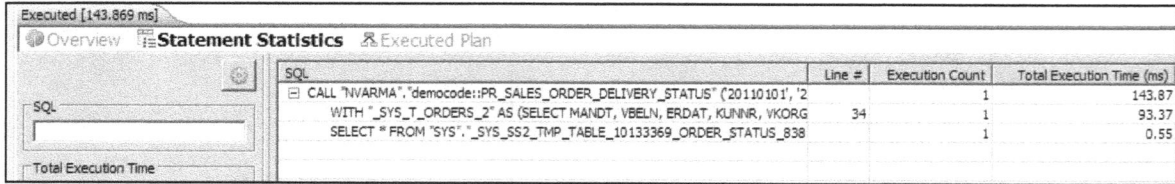

Navigate to the tab "Overview" – It providers the details of dominant operators and total number of records / memory allocated and execution time etc.

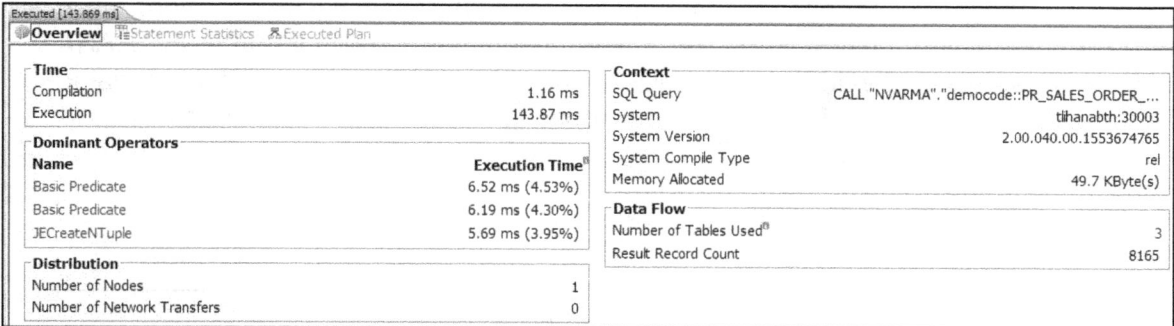

We can directly drill down to the dominant operators to verify further.

Navigate to the tab "Executed Plan" – To observe the detailed data flow and runtime of each operation etc. Click on the Arrow to branch to the details of each node.

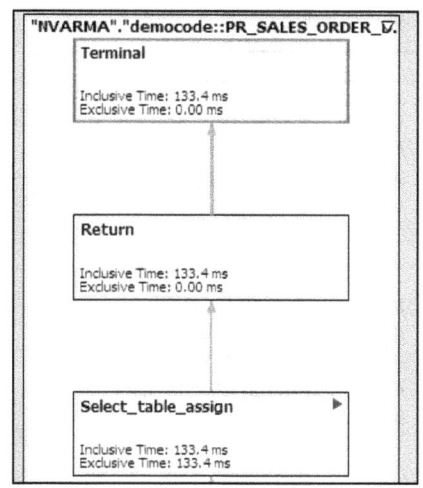

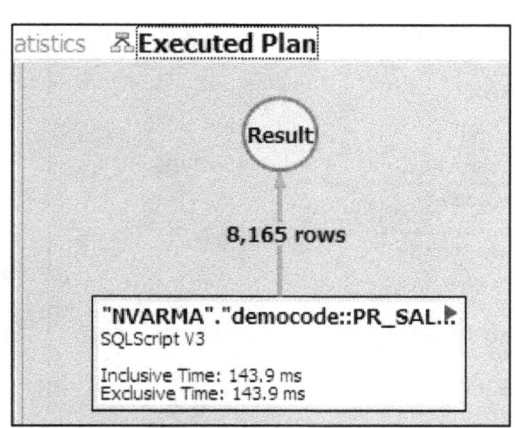

Also notice the performance details in the below tabs for detailed analysis.

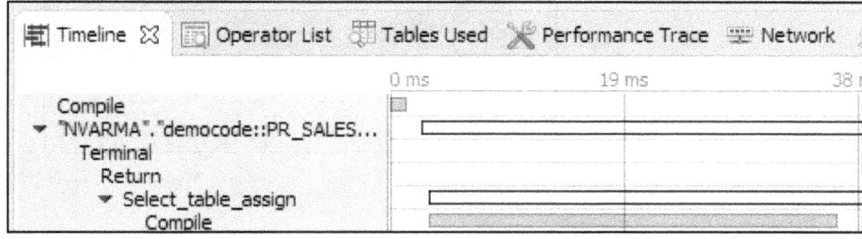

9.3 Managing Repository Objects

In this section we will understand some of the important options to be used, while managing the repository objects in HANA. These options are usually found in the HANA Development perspective, when we right click on any repository objects. It is essential to understand the importance of each of these options, to be able maintain the HANA development objects effectively.

9.3.1 Key options for Repository object maintenance

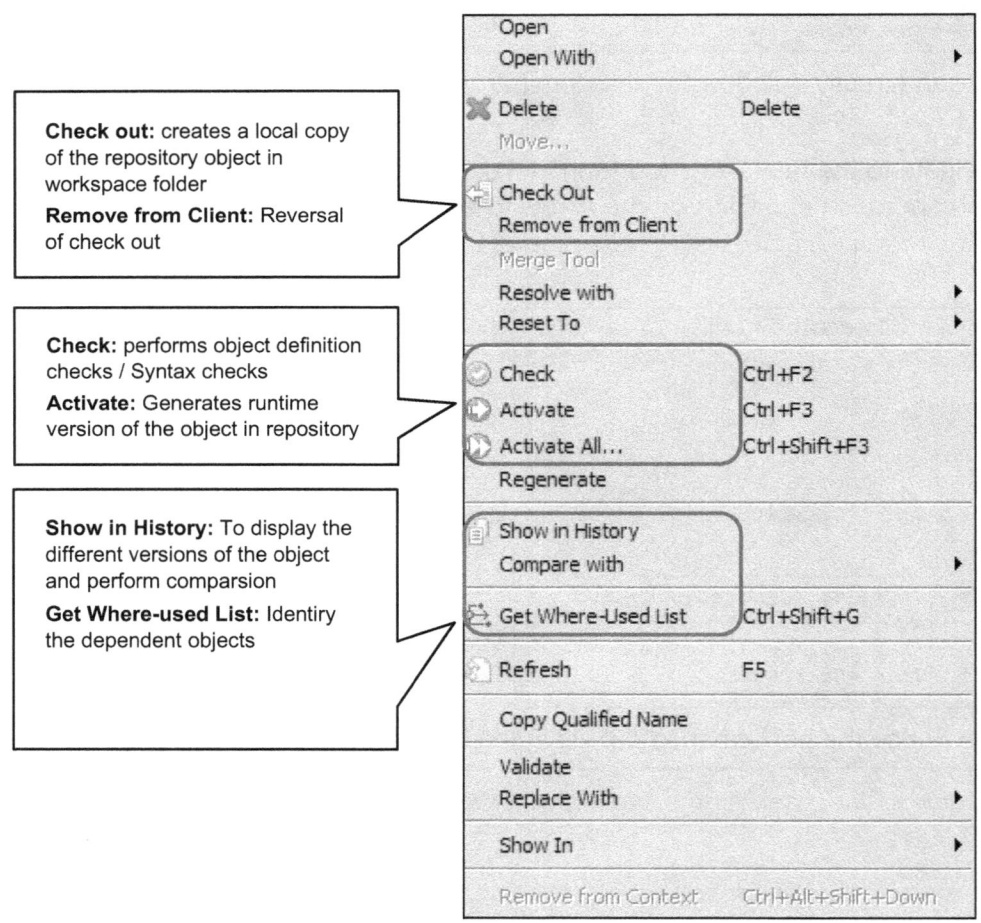

Check out: creates a local copy of the repository object in workspace folder
Remove from Client: Reversal of check out

Check: performs object definition checks / Syntax checks
Activate: Generates runtime version of the object in repository

Show in History: To display the different versions of the object and perform comparsion
Get Where-used List: Identiry the dependent objects

9.3.2 Version Management

Versioning will be an essential feature of the development objects, since it allows us to track the various changes related to the object and switch the object to specific version whenever needed. All the SAP HANA development artifacts, which are created as repository objects will have the version control feature. In this section let us understand the process of comparing different versions of an object and reverting the changes back to an earlier version.

How to view the versions of HANA development objects

From the popup menu of the calculation view: Choose "Show in History". This will show all the list of versions which are generated during the previous activations.

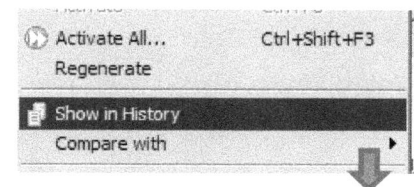

How to compare two different version of a repository object

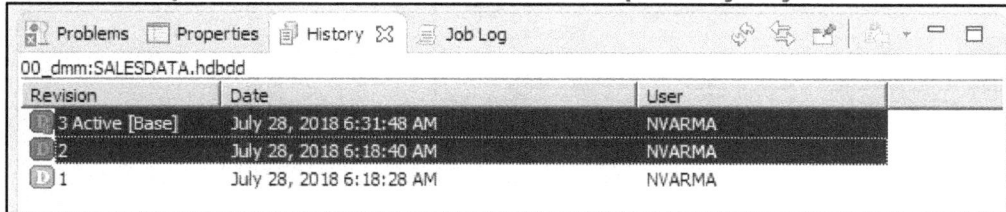

Once you choose the two versions that we need to compare, right click and choose the following option.

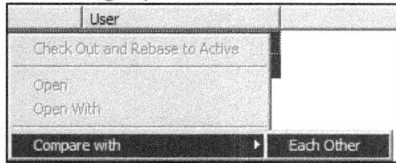

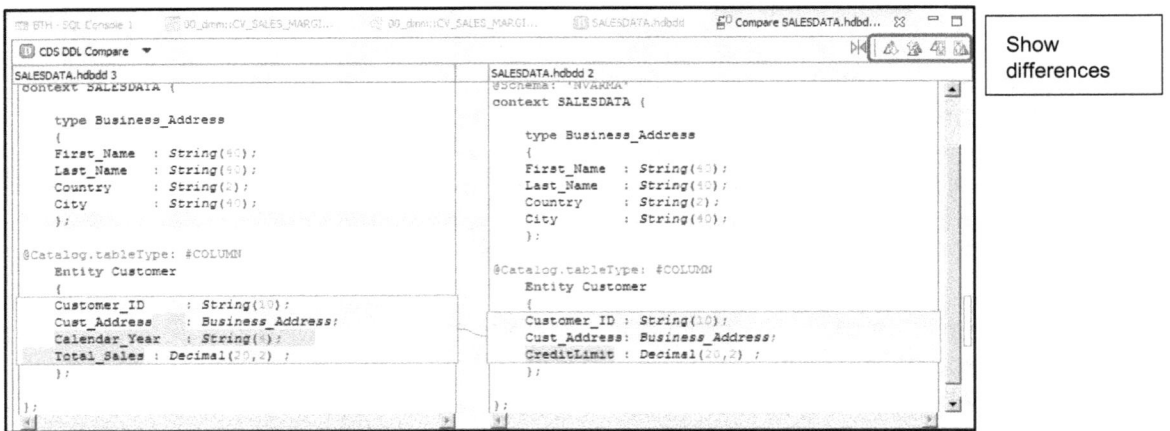

Switching the repository object to specific version

Using the "Check out and Rebase to Active" option we can switch the object to any of the previous active versions

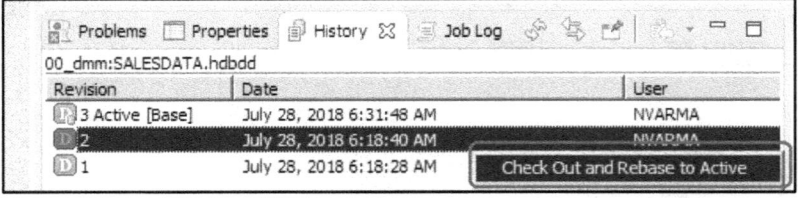

9.3.3 Analyzing Dependencies

It is quite essential to know the list of objects which are using a specific stored procedure or function. This can be achieved with the help of "Where Used List"

For example, we would like to identify the dependent objects of the following Scalar Function.

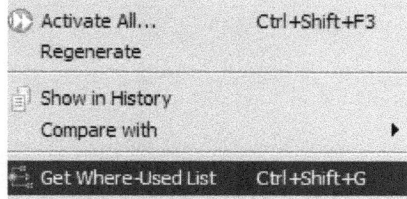

Right click on the Scalar Function and choose the option "Get Where Used List"

Activate All...	Ctrl+Shift+F3
Regenerate	
Show in History	
Compare with	▶
Get Where-Used List	Ctrl+Shift+G

It will produce a list of dependent objects, which are using this scalar function.

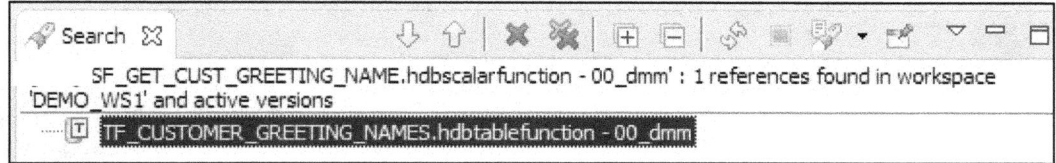

Other books from the Author

https://www.amazon.com/SAP-HANA-Modeling-Practical-World-ebook-dp-B07BYST8Z3/dp/B07BYST8Z3

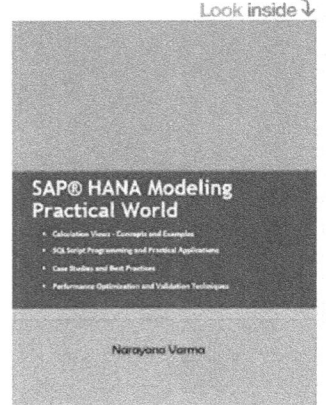

Look inside ↓

SAP HANA Modeling Practical World [Print Replica] Kindle

by Narayana Varma (Author)

☆☆☆☆☆ ˅   22 ratings

> See all 2 formats and editions

Kindle	Paperback
$7.64	$26.00
Read with Our Free App	3 Used from $24.24 5 New from $24.30 1 Collectible from $23.99

This book provides various insights on the overall HANA modeling process, which essentially involves the activities such as requirement analysis for the KPIs, solution design, creating information models (views), implementing SQL Script based solutions, performance optimization of the models, testing and validations. It will help the learners, in understanding the practical application of various SAP HANA modeling concepts to achieve complex reporting requirements.

‹ Read more

www.ingramcontent.com/pod-product-compliance
Lightning Source LLC
Chambersburg PA
CBHW080524060326
40690CB00022B/5020